NEW ORLEANS

NEW ORLEANS

Sarah Searight

STEIN AND DAY / *Publishers* / New York

First published in 1973
Copyright © 1973 by Sarah Searight
Library of Congress Catalog Card No. 72–96293
All rights reserved
Published simultaneously in Canada by Saunders of Toronto, Ltd.
Designed by Bernard Schleifer
Printed in the United States of America
Stein and Day/*Publishers*/ 7 East 48 Street, New York, N.Y. 10017
ISBN 0–8128–1548–3

Contents

Illustrations

Foreword

New Orleans mercilessly bludgeons the stranger with its much-advertised attractions. As one enters the city, hamburger stands parade their Creole cuisine and mansard-roofed apartments line the freeways. "View the Vieux Carré," shout the billboards. Crinolined ladies and endless talk about the romantic South are almost enough to drive one out before his bags are unpacked in a pseudo-Gallic motel decked out with imitation wrought iron. A dreadful whimsy assaults the stranger's intelligence, threatens everything of beauty in the city, peers out between the pages of the countless "stories of New Orleans."

So the stranger probes gingerly lest the whimsy prove indeed to be like candy floss—all sugar. The probe is rewarding, however; it gradually eats into the layers of floss in which the city has embedded itself since the Civil War and reveals a good deal of substance. This book is a stranger's attempt to appreciate New Orleans.

The city's reputation has always been highly colored—its legendary Latin culture and elegance clashing with its equally legendary corruption and turpitude. Both legends have an element of truth, and it is often difficult to separate fact from fiction. A wandering and footloose stranger is helped by the unchanging atmosphere of the city. One passes the austerely masked salons of the French Quarter, where aspiring outsiders (to whom one instantly warms) like Judah P. Benjamin, Edward Livingstone, and Samuel Peters met their elegant Creole wives; or mercantile mansions in the Garden District, anchored amid beds of sweet-smelling shrubs, built with fortunes made from similar, floating palaces on the Mississippi. Or one is led through the city's past by its street names: Poydras—Julien, the poet; Carondelet—of the canal, the governor and unexpected pronunciation; Tchoupitoulas—dim echo of Indian antecedents. Sometimes the optimism of street names recalls the fragility of the notorious Mississippi Bubble without whose inflater, John Law, New Orleans might never have been—Elysian Fields, Desire, Jasmine, for streets far less paradisal. Statues to Robert E. Lee, avenues for Napoleon, swampy suburbs (absurdly called heights) memorializing Jefferson, revive past loyalties. Water everywhere—thick gray swirl of the river, smooth blue of the lake, puddles, overflows, floods. Greenery thrusting greedy fingers into every cranny. A city of smells —frying catfish, mud at low tide, sweet olive, and azalea. A city whose inhabitants dance to the music of the past—a waltz, a tarantella, a jig, or a jive, and always in the background the sad nostalgic wail of a Buddy Bolden or Bunk Johnson.

A place of such contrasts, past and present, real and unreal.

I should like to thank the staffs of Tulane University Library and of the New Orleans Public Library for their invaluable help in elucidating the city's past, and my New Orleanian friends for their generous introduction to the city's present. I want particularly to thank Mrs. Le Bourgeois for reading and commenting on my efforts.

1. A Background of Louisiana

THE DELTA OF THE Mississippi, where the great river enters the Gulf of Mexico, still wears the bleak and inhospitable expression that made it one of the last areas to be settled on the eastern seaboard of North America. One can still appreciate the obstacles faced by prospective settlers of the eighteenth century, though the desolation has been tempered by the black snouts of oil wells and the silence broken by the roaring engines of workboats servicing oil rigs. Early in the morning the entrance to the river where the warm Gulf waters meet the icy stream of the river, is often shrouded by fog, heightening the solitude of the Delta. From the sea it appears as a lonely gray-green savanna without horizon or landmarks to help the explorer. Inland the featurelessness of the landscape is occasionally relieved by clumps of shrunken, contorted trees huddled on a bank of shells, but for the most part it is a maze of cane brakes, stagnant water and secretive waterways.

A Spaniard, Hernando de Soto, discovered the Mississippi in 1541, but further exploration was postponed for over a century. During the hiatus, Spanish energies were devoted to consolidating possessions elsewhere in America; the English were settling the

Atlantic seaboard and the French were occupied with religious and civil wars at home. In 1682 the French arrived, in the person of Robert Cavelier, Sieur de la Salle, "a man of vast intellect, brought up for literary pursuits, capable and learned in every branch especially mathematics, naturally enterprising, prudent and moral." La Salle traveled from Canada down the Mississippi to the mouth in hopes of establishing a French settlement whose inhabitants would be in a position to prey upon Spanish treasure fleets in the Gulf. He raised the French flag a few miles up the river and proclaimed "possession of that river, of all the rivers that enter it and of all the country watered by them" as belonging to France and Louis XIV —Louisiana. In 1684 he returned to the Gulf with a larger expedition to establish a colony about a hundred miles inland. But the shifting sands and horizons of the Gulf shore misled him and he never found the mouth of the river, landing instead in Texas, where he was murdered by mutinous companions.

La Salle's vision of the whole American continent as belonging to France appealed to Louis' imagination not only for *la gloire* but also to spike the ambitions of Britain, whose colonial charters generally claimed all lands beyond the Appalachians and whose fur traders were already pushing westward. In 1699 a French Canadian, Pierre le Moyne, Sieur d'Iberville, left France with instructions to found a colony in the Gulf of Mexico, taking with him two hundred prospective settlers. Accompanied by his brother, Jean Baptiste de Moyne, Sieur de Bienville, Iberville first explored the Mississippi as far as Baton Rouge but decided to place his colony, named Biloxi after the local Indians, on the north Gulf coast as being less swampy and more accessible to ships while still controlling the mouth of the Mississippi. Later the colony moved west to Dauphin Island and then to Mobile on the mainland. In 1706 Iberville died of yellow fever while raiding British possessions in the West Indies.

The colony barely survived its first few years, decimated as it was by disease and deprivation, and wholly dependent on ships from France for provisions. Louis XIV, heavily involved in expensive

European wars, eventually sold a fifteen-year charter for the whole of Louisiana and its trade to Antoine Crozat, a prominent French merchant. His first governor, Cadillac, who had founded Detroit, tried to foster trade with the Spanish colonies and to encourage agriculture but with little success; "decidedly this colony is a monster without head or tail and its government is a shapeless absurdity," he complained to Crozat, who seems to have agreed, selling his monopoly back to the French government in 1717. It was then granted to the Company of the West to make what it could of the situation.

The Company of the West was founded by John Law, a Scot remarkable not only for "his elegance of person and engaging powers," which had won him influential friends throughout Europe, but also for a vivid financial imagination. He made a fortune gambling and established himself as the favorite of the French Regent, the Duc d'Orléans, whom he persuaded to adopt his financial schemes. In 1717 he founded the Company of the West to take up Crozat's surrendered charter, Law undertaking to develop the colony's prosperity. In 1719 the company was merged with all French overseas trading companies into the Company of the Indies. Law was still at its head, devising ever grander schemes for tapping the untold resources of Louisiana.

Within the colony, Bienville was confirmed as commandant general and in 1718 was authorized to found a new settlement about a hundred miles up the Mississippi. Four years later, the colony's capital was transferred to the new settlement, known as New Orleans.

Law's schemes did little to improve conditions in the colony; the reality of the climate proved very different from the paradise depicted in the company's propaganda, and the company was obliged to meet its colonization obligations by forcible recruiting from the prisons and brothels of France. It has been said that no American colony was settled by a poorer quality of colonists than French Louisiana—"sans religion, sans justice, sans discipline, sans ordre et sans police." Law's Mississippi Bubble burst in 1720 as rumors of unfulfilled expectations filtered through to France and a discredited but unrepentant Law was forced to flee the country.* Ten years later, overcome by the ceaseless demands of the colonists and the expenses of Indian wars, the company sold its charter back to the king. Its apparent failure, however, obscures the fact that in the fourteen years since Law first acquired the proprietary rights of the colony, its inhabitants had increased from fewer than a thousand to over seven thousand, and the founding of New Orleans and the expansion of the settled limits of the colony with groups of farmers at last laid the elusive foundations of Louisiana.

Bienville's later verdict of the colonists as worthless, lazy, and dissolute seems also to have been held by the French government in 1762, when it surrendered most of Louisiana to Britain and ceded the "island" of New Orleans to Spain, thereby giving Spain vital control of the Mississippi. Effective government passed from the remote control of Versailles to the remote control of Madrid and Havana, and a rebellion in 1768 by frustrated colonists was easily suppressed. By the 1780s Spanish control of the river was being challenged ever more loudly by American pioneers, "men of the Western waters." To meet the challenge, Spain in 1800 returned the territory to France. In 1803 Napoleon betrayed his promise to Spain to keep Louisiana French when he decided (allegedly in his bath) to sell the entire province to the United States for a hard-driven price of $15 million.

An account of Louisiana in the Philadelphia archives described the territory at about the beginning of the nineteenth century as sparsely populated, the various settlements "separated from each other by immense and trackless deserts, having no communication with each other by land," though connected increasingly by river travel. American opponents of the Purchase echoed Bienville's opinion of the inhabitants, describing them as a race of "Anglo-Hispan-

---

*Law died a relative pauper in Venice in 1729; a contemporary ballad marked his death:

> "Ci gît cet écossois célèbre,
> Ce calculateur sans égal,
> Qui, par les règles de l'algèbre,
> A mis la France à l'hopital."

Gallic-Americans who bask on the sands in the mouth of the Mississippi." The southern portion of French Louisiana, which came to be Louisiana proper, soon benefited from three vital inventions: sugar granulation, the cotton gin, and steam transport. Louisiana became known as the Cotton Kingdom. Cotton plantations covered the northern part of the state, sugar the southern part, and steam made the Mississippi the main exit route for the agricultural produce of the West, with New Orleans the leading American port for a while. In Louisiana as a whole, though the traditional picture is one of gracious living in plantation mansions, the truth was that most farming was still small-scale and the rich planter of Deep South folklore was comparatively rare. Frederick Law Olmsted, a journalist from New York who traveled extensively in the South in the years immediately before the Civil War, found that even on the grandest plantations life was remarkably simple while most farmers lived on a far more primitive and impoverished scale than their equivalent in the Northern states. The famous Southern civilization was easygoing rather than luxurious, and the planter's wealth was displayed by the number of his slaves, not by stately surroundings.

The Civil War was the epilogue to a period of relative prosperity for Louisiana, the end of which was in sight at least a decade earlier. New Orleans fell to Union forces in 1862, and Louisiana was one of the most devastated areas of the South. Reconstruction was a period of chronic disorder in the state, and economic recovery only got under way in the 1880s. The state's prosperity focused as before on New Orleans, which also throve as "the focal point of graft and corruption." At the turn of the century, lumber and rice were beginning to make fortunes in the state, and in 1902 oil was found, a major source of wealth for twentieth-century Louisiana. The Populist revolt of the 1880s and 1890s attempted to wrest control from the alliance of "Bourbon" planters and the New Orleans political machine, but the impoverished majority of small farmers remained unrepresented in state politics until Huey P. Long.

Politics is to the conversation of Louisiana what horse racing is to England's, said A. J. Liebling. Louisiana politics during this century has been characterized by a system of "invisible government," and local political machines are closely linked with the vice interests of the underworld. An attempt was made early in the 1900s to reform local government, but not until Huey P. Long invaded the scene in the 1920s, representing the poor white farmers against the big plant- ers and city bosses, were the political machines defeated, only to be replaced by Long's own machine. His family and political descend- ants have kept the machine ticking ever since, and most state elec- tions have been fought over its control of Louisiana politics.

Louisiana still rates as one of the nation's poorest and most con- servative states. It is a state of many contrasts—geographically rang- ing from desolate Delta swamps to thickly wooded red hills in the north, climatically from the hot, humid tropicality of New Orleans to the dry, dusty cotton plantations of the undulating plains, socio- logically from what seems to be the epitome of gracious living to some of the most degrading poverty in the United States. It is also a most beautiful state, a land of a million bayous, of dense forests, and of wide, fast rivers. The corruption and violence that are as endemic as the poverty contribute to a frontier atmosphere, whose other aspects—an untarnished landscape, a simplicity, a friendliness —an outsider finds hard to resist; he is even hypnotized by it all, as if the heavy scent of the flowers, the rank acridity of the Delta, the heat and haze and humidity had lulled him like a lotus-eater to forget the harsher realities. The trouble is that so many Louisianians have fallen under such a trance. Louisiana, like the rest of the Deep South, has suffered more than its fair share of writers for whom the line between fact and fiction has seemed irrelevant so long as the story is romantic. The following account is an attempt to redress the imbalance.

PART ONE

THE PEOPLE

"I doubt if there is any city in the world where the resident population has been so divided in its origins, or where there is such a variety in the tastes, habits, manners and moral codes of the citizens."

(FREDERICK OLMSTED)

2. The French

THE ESTABLISHMENT OF New Orleans, more or less in the middle of a cypress swamp, is an intriguing story. The city's foundations were undermined both by nature's subversion, particularly floods and hurricanes, and by its human counterpart—dissatisfaction with government and economy, disillusion with its unparadisal character, the incompatibility of many of its early inhabitants. Looking back today, one marvels that the town survived, beset by so many obstacles; contemporaries marveled too, either applauding the New Orleanians for what graces they did display in such unfavorable circumstances or lamenting their inability to cooperate to make a success out of such a hazardous enterprise. In some ways it is easy to imagine the first few years of New Orleans by observing the New Orleans of today. Climate, politicking, emotional inhabitants—these complaints of eighteenth-century French governors might well be echoed by twentieth-century Federal officials sent from time to time to sort out the city's problems.

The advantages of a settlement upriver from the mouth of the Mississippi had been apparent ever since La Salle claimed as Louisiana all those lands bordering the great river. Iberville's expedition had confirmed the strategic necessity, and his brother Bienville had regularly argued its merits—mainly that such a settlement alone would secure French domination of vast territories, especially desirable in view of British designs on the great plains beyond the Appalachians. Bienville had already set up two small mosquito-ridden garrisons at the mouth of the river; more promising of development were reports from planters established since the beginning of the century along Bayou St. John, about a hundred miles from the mouth. These planters had made friends with the local Indians, generally considered more docile than those around the Gulf settlements, and the plantations benefited from being a few feet above sea level, well below the level of the river, and above the worst of the swamps. The bayou itself, which runs from Lake Pontchartrain to within two miles of the river, ultimately determined the site of the new town, providing relatively sheltered communications with the Gulf settlements; and a crescent bend in the river at the point nearest the end of the bayou gave ships entering the river some protection from the storms that attacked the coast with even more damaging regularity than foreign ships.

Bienville submitted his plans for the new settlement to the company in 1717 and, receiving their approval, set out in the spring of 1718 for the Mississippi, accompanied by eighty salt smugglers deported to the colony, whose task it was to clear the site of the dense entangled cane brakes. Anyone familiar with the thick undergrowth beyond the sprawling northwestern suburbs of the modern city has an idea of what they were up against. Matted canes with cutting leaves build up patches of dry, dead vegetation interspersed with pools of water, which are sometimes so thickly covered with livid green weed that they appear to be firm ground. Malarial mosquitoes have long since been eradicated, but not myriads of other species. In the evening, when the raucous cacophony of the grackle and the red-wing blackbird has died away, one's ear is assaulted by the monotonous hum, and one's body, even through clothing, by what seem to be the largest and hungriest mosquitoes ever encountered. As an eighteenth-century visitor remarked, "The little insect has caused more swearing since the French came to the Mississippi than had been done before that time in all the world." One's heart goes out to the wretched salt smugglers who were to clear the site, especially since the salt tax in France was one of the most iniquitous measures ever taken to boost the French economy.

Not surprisingly, Bienville's men failed to make much impression on the landscape, and the few huts they did build were destroyed by hurricane and flood the following year. Fortunately the company, now merged into the Company of the Indies (whose optimistic expectations of the Mississippi were advertised in its official seal of a river god leaning on a horn of plenty pouring forth gold coins), had undertaken to make the necessary moral and financial investment in the scheme, and in 1720 a group of architects and engineers reached Biloxi to prepare a more professional approach. The engineer in charge, Le Blond de la Tour, drafted plans for the town, and his deputy Adrian de Pauger, more optimistic about the site than his superior, went off to the Mississippi to see to their execution.

Little remains of French New Orleans today except for de Pauger's original layout of the town in the orderly right angles and squares of the typical colonial settlement. The town was located on the sheltered bend in the river, although the original crescent, which led to the city's nickname of the Crescent City, has long since been obscured by subsequent expansion. Unsurfaced streets were drained by ditches on either side, crossed by bridges onto the sidewalks or *banquettes* (little dikes), which were supposed to keep water out of the houses. Father Charlevoix, one of the Jesuits whose wanderings in the Mississippi valley resulted in some of the earliest descriptions of the great Western plains, visited New Orleans in 1722 and liked the plan but voiced the popular doubt that it would not be as easy to follow as it had been to put on paper. Instead of the prosperous paradise described in the company's propaganda, Charlevoix found a few log cabins, a warehouse, and a shed temporarily serving as a church. Nevertheless, with optimism worthy of Law himself, Charlevoix declared that "this wild and deserted place . . . shall one day . . . become the capital of a large and rich colony. Rome and Paris had not such considerable beginnings, were not built under such happy auspices and their founders met not with the advantages on the Seine and the Tiber which we have found on the Mississippi in comparison with which these two rivers are no more than brooks."

Few of New Orleans' early inhabitants would have been as confident, even when the company declared its faith in the settlement's future by making it the capital of Louisiana. An early watercolor shows a straggling village hemmed in on three sides by jungle and on the fourth by the Mississippi, on which Indians in glorious war apparel are prancing in improbable boats. It was a precarious-looking settlement in spite of its resounding name—Nouvelle Orléans, after Law's patron the Duc d'Orléans—and the grandiose street names— Chartres, Bourbon, Dauphine, Orléans, Royal, Conti—recalling various branches of the Bourbon family and their household saints, St. Peter, St. Anne, and St. Louis. Today these names strike one as incongruous on the narrow unassuming streets of the French Quarter.

The Indians in their boats were not wholly an example of artistic license. The possibility of Indian attack was always present in the first years of the settlement, though there is no record of one ever having been attempted. In 1729 the French colony of Fort Rosalie, upriver in Natchez Indian country, was massacred by local Indians, throwing New Orleans into a justifiable panic, in view of the ill-equipped state of its garrison. When a drunken woman came running into the town from Bayou St. John with the news that a horde of Indians had attacked and killed all the settlers in that neighborhood, everyone rushed to the Place d'Armes (Jackson Square) to defend the town, until scouts reported that the alarm was caused by hunters shooting in the vicinity. An expedition by Governor Perier captured some Indian prisoners, who were subsequently buried alive in the middle of the parade ground in the Place d'Armes. Despite such gruesome reprisals, the threat remained chronic and panic endemic; Bienville, for instance, spent most of his second governorship campaigning against the Indians along the Gulf coast and was ultimately recalled for his failure to eradicate the menace.

Local government of the colony was in the hands of the Superior Council, first formed in 1712 and moved to New Orleans in 1722. But the effective ruler was the king in France and the council's officers were generally political appointees from France, who clashed all too frequently with the earlier arrivals. The membership of the council varied but always included the commandant general or governor; the intendant, who was also president of the council; and the attorney general. Ideally the council was a check on the governor; and the intendant, for instance, as the man responsible for the colony's finances, was often more powerful. Such a clash of authority occurred between Bienville as governor, a Canadian with no friends at court, and the intendant de la Chaise, appointed from France, and led to Bienville's recall in 1725 after a royal commission had been sent to investigate the colony's administration.

From 1725 to 1732 the Superior Council was suppressed and Bienville's replacement as governor, Perier, was able to effect several reforms in the city's administration. Rather surprisingly, in view of the circumstances of his earlier recall, Bienville was reappointed governor in 1733. His second period in command, which lasted for nine years, was chiefly marked by his unsuccessful campaigns against the Gulf coast Indians, and he seems to have lacked the optimism and energy that inspired his earlier founding of the city. He died in Paris in 1767.

As one of the leading actors in the city's early history, Bienville has received unwarranted adulation on one hand—his career has been described as one of "unsullied purity and continual usefulness" —and exaggerated vilification on the other—"a man whose evil influence contributed in no small way to the bad character of the colonial administration and the population, resulting in disaster beyond repair." A more accurate appraisal would probably be that the bad character of both administration and population resulted from policies directed from France, which had their influence on Bienville—not the other way round.

As a young man Bienville had been carried away by La Salle's grand vision of a vast American empire belonging to France; by the 1730s he appears deeply disillusioned by the government's apathy and the lack of enthusiasm among the inhabitants, most of whom intensely resented their exile in a squalid riverside encampment (though by then conditions were improving) in an impossible climate, and retained a compulsive desire to copy metropolitan fashions. Years of trying to cope aged Bienville prematurely and he left New Orleans in 1742 a gloomy and dispirited man.

Bienville's replacement, the Marquis de Vaudreuil, was a very different man: a French Canadian like Bienville but, unlike Bienville, well known at Versailles, thanks to his mother's persistent efforts. Vaudreuil's administration was more corrupt than most, but the glamour of his "little Versailles" says something in favor of his economic policy and impressed visitors into writing the enthusiastic accounts the settlement needed so badly. Vaudreuil, a wiser politician than Bienville, flattered in the right places, in particular one Captain Boissu, sent to join the garrison, who later published a glowing account of Louisiana and repaid Vaudreuil's hospitality with hyperbolic praise. "The Governor does the honours of his table in so noble and generous a manner, that he acquires the esteem and friendship of all the officers who justly style him the father of the colony." When Vaudreuil left to become governor of Canada in 1753, he gave a banquet for four hundred guests, and the two fountains in the Place d'Armes flowed with wine, a vision of gracious living that clashes somewhat with the fact that most of the four hundred were still living in wooden cottages. Few of them would have agreed with Boissu that "the merchants, tradesmen and strangers who live here enjoy as it were an enchanted abode, rendered delicious by the purity of its air, the fertility of its soil and the beauty of its situation." But most would have commended Vaudreuil for bringing a ray of sequined sunshine into their otherwise cheerless lives.

Vaudreuil was succeeded by a bluff ex-naval officer named Kerlerec, who was bewildered by the problems, chiefly financial, besetting the colony, and the old rivalry between governor and intendant flared up again. Kerlerec was recalled in 1761 and imprisoned in the Bastille because of scandals connected with public building in New Orleans; he remained there for seven years and on his release was ordered to remain "30 leagues from Paris and from the chateaux and houses that His Majesty inhabits or might inhabit"—an exile perhaps preferable to life on the banks of the Mississippi.

A study of the political history of French New Orleans is a disheartening business; the social history is far more cheering, and one can sense a steady improvement in the standard of living and in the sorts of people attracted to live there. In the view of some, anything would have been an improvement. Charlevoix condemned the population in 1722 as "miserable wretches driven from France for real or supposed crimes or bad conduct"—quite different from the dedicated Puritans of New England. Everyone considered Louisiana a place of exile. "Nothing interests them in the progress of a colony of which they are only members in spite of themselves, and they are very little concerned with the advantages which it may procure to the state; the greater part are not even capable of appreciating them."

It was hoped that a priestly presence would remedy the situation. One of the conditions of the company's charter in 1717 was that the company should be responsible for providing religion in Louisiana, but there is no record of a priest resident in New Orleans until the arrival of the Capuchins in 1723. "Since they will experience great difficulty in establishing the spirit of religion in hearts so ill-disposed," wrote the Bishop of Quebec (in whose diocese Louisiana fell), the company must be prepared to support them. Accordingly, the company fitted out each monk with "one cask of Bourdeaux wine, two quarts of flour, one half quart of bacon, one half quart of beef, one and a half quarts of brandy, 25 pounds of large beans . . ., 8 pounds of Holland or Gruyère cheese, 24 pounds of candles, one and a half pounds of pepper, 20 pots of vinegar, 25 pounds of salt and 12 pounds of oil"—a list that gives an indication of New Orleans' dependence on outside supplies.

Before very long, the fathers had to remind the company of its commitment to keep them alive. "You will have the goodness to remember Sir," wrote their leader, Father Raphael, "that at Paris you promised us two cows and a bull. If you will kindly give orders that these cattle be delivered to us, we shall be deeply obliged to you, for a little milk with our bit of pork and the rice that we can find here will render our life less hard." Another of their problems was the inhabitants' refusal to attend Mass, although there was a slight improvement in attendance after the fathers moved their "church" from the kitchen of their shack to a former tavern, where pews were auctioned off to pay for its rent. But the souls of the New Orleanians left much to be desired: "Almost all the inhabitants live in the most scandalous conditions," complained Father Raphael, "and in such a profound ignorance of the truths of our holy religion that they may be said to be ignorant even of the first elements."

Much of the Capuchins' energy was absorbed in jealously guarding their monopoly of the city's souls against what they regarded as a determined assault by the Jesuits. In 1726 they had to surrender their "spiritual care of the savages" outside New Orleans and its immediate surroundings to the Jesuits, who alone had the financial and human resources to proselytize in the wilderness. That same year, the Jesuit leader Father Beaubois was given permission to live in New Orleans and bought a house where Jesuits arriving from France or returning from Indian missions could rest and recover— an ominous intrusion, thought the Capuchins, who seem to have been inspired principally by fears of Jesuit power as they had known it in France, without making allowance for the special conditions of Louisiana. The quarrel simmered over the years, but when the Jesuits were expelled from the colony in 1762 after the disbanding of the order in France, the Capuchins, magnanimous in victory, took their former rivals into their own quarters until a ship arrived to take them back to Europe.

The Capuchins themselves suffered from similar vicissitudes when Spanish members of the order arrived in 1772 to take over their parochial duties. The Spanish leader wrote to his superior in Havana that his French colleagues were hardly worthy of the name Capuchins for they had forgotten the meaning of poverty. But as the Spanish governor Unzaga remarked when called on to settle relations between them, "I know how difficult it is to come to a correct appreciation of the true merits of men of that sacred calling, when they choose to quarrel among themselves."

The raffishness of the early years gradually gave way to a more settled way of life, more in spite of than because of priestly attentions. The arrival of a group of Ursuline nuns, acting as chaperones for girls sent out at government expense as wives for settlers, marks a turning point in this respect. Under the terms of its original contract, the company had been obliged to provide settlers with female companions (who would propagate more settlers), and met its obligation by dispatching occupants of the prisons and brothels of France to the colony. Some writers later tried to glamorize the prostitutes who helped populate Louisiana in the early years. The Abbé Prèvost's tragic heroine, Manon Lescaut (heroine also of operas by Massenet and Puccini), was dragged off the streets of Paris and thrown onto a ship for New Orleans, whither she was followed despairingly by her lover, only to die a beautiful death in the neighboring swamps as they were trying to flee the lascivious clutches of the governor's son. But one reason for the failure, and discontinuance of this company policy is shown in Perier's disgusted complaint that after "these women and girls of bad life" became pregnant, "they will not give the name of the fathers of the children so that today the Company is obliged to feed five or six nursing children whose fathers are not known."

A later, more respectable, solution to the problem of underpopulation was the *filles de cassette*, girls of decent upbringing who were sent to Louisiana with modest dowries (hence the name) provided at the king's expense to their husbands, usually retired soldiers. Each couple was well set up with a piece of land, a cow, a calf, a cock and five hens, a gun, an ax, and a hoe, together with rations for the first three years and a small amount of powder, shot, and grain seed. In spite of the later fame of New Orleans' Creole beauties who claimed descent as far back as possible from these early settlers, one must assume that the *filles* were either less respectable or considerably plainer than many accounts have allowed. But they did help to solve the population problem until the discontinuance of the scheme in 1751, when the standard of living in New Orleans invited female emigration without forceful or financial inducement.

The first group of Ursulines arrived in 1726; the venture had been organized by the Jesuit Father Beaubois, much to the consternation of the Capuchins. Among them was a novice, Madeleine Hachard, whose letters to her father describing New Orleans and the voyage out provide us with one of the most graphic pictures of the early settlement—a welcome change from the accounts that were colored by an ecstatic optimism or by disappointed hopes. Some of the horror of nature the inhabitants felt when they found themselves abandoned in the midst of a subtropical swamp can be sensed in her description of the five-day journey from the river mouth to New Orleans: camping every night an hour before sunset in order to be settled before the mosquitoes descended, noting the unfamiliar creatures of the swamp like some medieval bestiary—serpents, snakes, scorpions, crocodiles, vipers. The relief of actually reaching New Orleans must have been overwhelming and accounts for the almost rosy glow of the nun's first descriptions of her new home. Echoing Charlevoix, she told her father that the settlement was growing daily, despite the shortage of skilled workmen and of population generally, and would eventually become as large and beautiful as the principal cities of France. But she disparaged the claims of a popular song comparing New Orleans favorably with Paris.

The Ursulines' first convent lasted a bare twenty years; what with the shortage of workmen and the perennial quarreling of officials, it took so long to build, and remained unroofed for so long that it was nearly in ruins before the nuns had even moved in, and was already far too small for their multiplying activities. The present convent, completed about 1752, has survived ferocious onslaughts by climate (one New Orleans historian wrote that it looked as if it had never drawn a dry breath since it was built) and more recently by neglect. Today, a bronze plaque denotes it the oldest building in the Mississippi valley. The nuns abandoned it in 1824, when soaring real estate prices convinced them to sell and move to more commodious quarters farther down the river; but when that site was wanted for the present Industrial Canal, they were moved to South Claiborne Street. There the huge forbidding buildings of their school sternly remind New Orleanians of the Ursulines' contribution to the city's history.

The nuns played a vital role in those early years, supplying an image of respectability that was just as likely to attract immigrants as glossy propaganda from the company or the central government.

They looked after the *filles de cassette* until they had been married to suitable husbands, and sheltered the unwanted offspring of Perier's much-maligned prostitutes, when necessary placing them in correction rooms in the convent, which must have been more comfortable than many New Orleans dwellings of the period. They also opened a school for girls, including slave and Indian children. They cultivated French manners and tastes in their pupils, preparing them for the Creole society that Frenchmen later found so lacking in finesse but that was a considerable improvement on earlier society and something of an achievement in the circumstances.

By the 1740s and Vaudreuil's appointment as governor, the city was beginning to attract wealthier settlers, who furnished their crude cottages with the elaborate and fashionable furniture and furnishings they were accustomed to in France. Madeleine Hachard had earlier commented on the costly and unsuitable clothes worn by the New Orleanians. The early introduction of slaves encouraged what was considered gracious idleness: a French officer wrote home in 1743 that "the rich spend their time in seeing their slaves work to improve their lands, and get money, which they spend in plays, balls and feasts; but the most common pastime of the highest as well as the lowest, and even of the slaves, is gambling." As early as 1723, the Superior Council had marked New Orleanians' predilection for gambling and had issued a decree forbidding games of chance, but the decree seems to have encouraged the pastime, as is usual with such prohibitions.

The city itself improved in appearance over the years as de Pauger's plan was gradually filled in and building materials became more easily obtainable. The climate of New Orleans is not conducive to orderly development—that is half its charm even today. With its mosses and creepers the humidity makes fake antiques of houses less than fifty years old; weeds quickly choke the gutters to form grassy verges along the sidewalks; and in the modern suburbs the greedy fingers of the swamp jungle reclaim cleared land almost as fast as developers pound in their concrete piles. It was no different in the eighteenth century. The houses of the early settlement, most of which had to be rebuilt within a few years, were single-storied, made of bark and reeds; some, more sophisticated, were built of wood or of brick, supported by wooden struts, a more lasting form of construction common in contemporary Europe and known as *briquetté entre poteaux*. Few of them had glass in the windows, Governor Perier writing to the company in 1726 to ask for crates of glass: "every six months we have to change the linen cloths that are put on the windows because they rot," he complained. Each house was separated from its neighbor by a garden or vegetable plot; de Pauger in his original plan for New Orleans insisted that every house should have a garden "which here is half of life."

Not so very different, one might say, from some of the back streets of New Orleans today; if one turns off the main roads dissecting the city's impoverished Ninth Ward, for instance, it does not require much imagination to visualize early conditions—unsurfaced roads a muddy morass after a summer storm, frame houses fighting a losing battle against damp and decay, the bleak discomfort and idleness of their occupants on crumbling front porches: these were and are the realities that the optimism of city administrations has tried to evade throughout the history of the city.

At least the flood risk, which at first annually jeopardized de Pauger's plans, diminished with the construction of the levee along the river, thanks chiefly to the efforts of Joseph Dubreuil. Dubreuil, "one of the most laborious and most intelligent of all the planters," according to one admirer, came to Louisiana from Dijon in 1717 and became the general contractor for most public works in the town, including the levee. "The establishment of New Orleans in the beginning was awful," he wrote, "the river when it was high spreading over the whole ground, and in all the houses there were two feet of water which caused general and mortal diseases." He went on, "as I was known to be enterprising and not capable of refusing a service," he agreed to build two-thirds of the levee without salary, though he forebore to mention the protection this would give his own extensive plantations above and below the town.

Food also improved over the years. Early settlers had been interested in the mining and trading prospects of Louisiana, to the detriment of agriculture and their own well-being, dependent en-

tirely on erratic supplies from France. Now agriculture was seen as
a more promising investment, due largely to Jesuit and German
enterprise. Jesuit Bend, downriver from New Orleans, is thought to
be the first site settled by the Jesuits in the early eighteenth century,
famous both then and now as a vegetable-growing area. The Jesuits
also bought some land from Bienville above the settlement, which
proved well worth the dissension it aroused; the plantation, around
what is now Gravier Street (named after a later owner of the property), became before the end of the century one of the most successful in the colony. Most of the Germans settled up-river.

The Jesuits were the first planters to experiment with seed cane,
which had been sent over by colleagues in San Domingo, producing
molasses and rather inferior sugar. Other crops they introduced
included oranges, figs, and indigo. Indigo became the principal crop
in lower Louisiana until overtaken by sugar (and disease) at the end
of the century, and oranges are still the principal crop of the river
lands below New Orleans. Dubreuil, a neighbor of the Jesuits, was
so impressed by their introduction of sugar that he built a sugar mill,
a gamble that left his family bankrupt on his death soon after,
without producing much sugar. The colder winters of Louisiana are
not as suited as the West Indies' to cane-growing, and even today
the predominance of this crop in lower Louisiana is feasible only
with careful tariff protection. It was not until the end of the century
that a satisfactory method of granulation was developed.

Living conditions improved, settlers were coming to terms with
the environment, houses were built to withstand the humidity and
heat, and the levee was better maintained because of better local
administration. With these improvements the unsatisfactory relationship between the colony and the home government became
increasingly apparent, the fiscal policies of the latter reflected in the
chronic deficits and currency fluctuations of the former. From the
settlers' point of view the commercial and financial policy of the
central government seemed hopelessly out of touch and far too
restrictive. Shortages of specie were ineffectually countered by the
overuse of bills of exchange, which were often sold in advance of the
public issue at wildly inflated values. Trade, hampered from the first

by the typical eighteenth-century policy of allowing colonies to trade only with each other and the home country, suffered still more during the Seven Years' War. The same war brought home the unpleasant truth that France was no longer able to withstand the pressure on Louisiana of Britain's expanding seaboard colonies and demonstrated how lowly the French Crown rated the interests, loyalties, and sentiments of its scattered inhabitants and those of its leading settlement, New Orleans.

3. The Spaniards

DESPITE RELATIVE IMPROVEMENTS in the standard of living, New Orleans in the 1760s had a long way to go before its dreams of grandeur took root in reality, especially by comparison with Northern colonial towns. Many people would argue that the city had to await the onslaught of the Northerners before it became a reasonable place to live. Only in relation to the surrounding wilderness was New Orleans a haven—for trappers and missionaries and the few farmers. To European governments the city's only value was strategic, its guardianship of the Mississippi Delta of considerable importance in Anglo-French rivalry for the great Northern plains. The Seven Years' War, which ended in February 1763, proved the vulnerability of French communications with Louisiana: all an impoverished France could do to thwart British hopes of controlling North America was to cede New Orleans to Spain in a secret treaty signed before the end of the war in November 1762.

The colony remained unaware though suspicious of its fate for another two years, during which, to all appearances, it continued under French rule. The French governor, Jean Jacques d'Abbadie, spoke for the French government, however, when he criticized the settlers as lazy drunkards: "The facility offered by the country to live

on its natural productions has created habits of laxness . . . hence
the spirit of insubordination and independence which has manifested itself under several administrators." D'Abbadie died soon after
news of the cession reached New Orleans in 1764, and was succeeded by a former officer of the garrison, Charles Aubry, who was
to earn opprobrium for his part in handing over the colony to Spain.
A Spanish governor, Antonio de Ulloa, finally arrived in March
1766.

Ulloa was a curious choice as governor. He was one of the most
eminent scientists and astronomers of his time (a moon crater is
named after him) but as governor he seems to have been absent-
minded, impractical, greatly concerned with minutiae, with little
feeling for human relations, and by no means the policy builder
demanded by circumstances. A verdict on his later naval career—
"Although possessing in the most eminent degree the theory of
navigation, [he] did not rise above mediocrity in its practical applica-
tion"—is all too applicable to his governorship of Louisiana. He
refused to take possession officially until he had Spanish troops and
used Aubry (rather than the Superior Council—to the rage of its
members) to administer the colony. The British governor of neighboring West Florida reported that "Mr. Ulloa has been examining
every Part of the Province as narrowly as a Jew does his Bride and
still seems in doubt. He is a man of indefatiguable Genius and
Industry, though there is something piddling in the Mechanical
Part."

Ulloa's "despotism" was considered the "more intolerant, as it
shocked the manners of the French nation"—especially when he
offended New Orleanians by vanishing to the Balise, of all places,
for the winter. "How could anybody but a prejudiced ascetic, an
iron-willed Spaniard, forgo the conveniences of a home in New
Orleans to perch, like a sea-bird, during the wintry season, on the
shaking piles driven into the mud and amidst the reeds of the mouth
of the Mississippi?" mused the historian Gayarré, who usually had
little sympathy for New Orleanians. It later turned out that Ulloa
was waiting for a bride from Peru, whom he insisted on marrying
there and then, in the middle of the marshes. He thus insulted the

settlers, who liked any excuse for display and pageantry, by depriving them of an opportunity for a ceremony.

Opposition to Spanish rule built up slowly. There was little loyalty to France, since most settlers felt that the home government had treated them badly enough over the years. What prosperity there was, however, was dependent on France and French markets, which Ulloa immediately set about replacing with Spain and Spanish markets. The leaders of the 1768 rebellion against Spanish rule, all of whom lived in and around New Orleans, were among the few who had made some success as planters and merchants and whose success had been vested in their authority as members of the Superior Council, which had also been upset by Ulloa. The rebellion was a movement of independence against the presumption of distant governments who thought they could manipulate their colonies as they wished, and as such it was a foretaste of the more successful revolt further north.

It was a remarkably pacific affair. German and Acadian support was recruited by planters with property in the area, and New Orleanians were virtually unanimous in their enthusiasm. Aubry, who was still *de facto* governor, was taken unawares—incredible as this seems in a town the size of New Orleans. He reckoned that the rebels were led astray by "some dozen factionists, whose affairs were in the greatest disorder," but the lack of bloodshed implies support by a large majority. Ulloa and his family were hustled ignominiously on board a Spanish frigate, making his escape, according to one source, when his opponents cut the mooring rope and released the ship with its unwanted cargo.

The French government neither could nor would do anything to help, but there was no hesitation behind Spanish reactions to the ejection of their governor. Alejandro O'Reilly, an Irish mercenary who is said once to have saved the life of the King of Spain, was already on his way to Havana and was diverted to New Orleans, where he arrived six months after Ulloa's departure. He took over the city with all the pomp and ceremony that Ulloa had disdained. Aubry, at his request, gave him the names of the rebel leaders, and two weeks later he arrested them unopposed. After a three-week trial, five of the leaders were shot (a sixth died in jail), and six others were jailed.

About the only favorable verdict on O'Reilly among contemporary and nineteenth-century historians was that of Charles Gayarré. Gayarré's grandfather, Estevan de Gayarré, had come to Louisiana with Ulloa. His qualms about such a miserable exile had been set at rest with reassurances that it would not upset his chances of promotion in the event he decided to stay. Charles Gayarré, who has already been quoted several times, was the author of the four-volume *History of Louisiana* (published between 1854 and 1866) and the most influential of many nineteenth-century writers on the subject. In a memorable preface to the English-language edition of his history, he stressed the importance of bringing out "the hidden sources of romance" in historical events: "When history is not disfigured by inappropriate invention, but merely embellished and made attractive by being set in a glittering frame, this artful preparation honies the cup of useful knowledge, and makes it acceptable to the lips of the multitude." Later, claiming that he had never aspired to great literary heights, he said he was satisfied with "having erected in the wilderness the modest wooden structure which, I hope, will soon give way to more stately edifices, showing the elegant proportions of a more classical architecture." Gayarré's modest wooden structure, particularly those parts devoted to the French "domination," resembles some of the more florid examples of New Orleans architecture, and it has been responsible for many a fanciful description of Louisiana history.

Gayarré alone stood out against the prevailing trend to condemn O'Reilly, who drew more than his fair share of criticism—one critic wrote that O'Reilly was unrestrained and bloodthirsty, another referred to his perfidious cruelty, and Thomas Wharton Collins wrote a verse play, *The Martyr Patriots*, about the rebels. Only Gayarré came to the "butcher's" defense. Aubry commented judiciously that he put in force "all the wise and useful provisions which the government had for several years failed to compel the community to observe."

Louisiana was now organized as a dependency of Cuba. O'Reilly replaced the Superior Council by a similar town council known from its meeting place as the Cabildo. What little independence the Superior Council had gained under French rule, the Cabildo lost under the Spanish, all effective power being in the hands of the governor (answerable to the Captain General in Havana) and the bishop as representative of the Church. There were ten members of the Cabildo, four of whom were elected each year and six life tenures which could be bought.

In general, Spanish policy was remarkable for its leniency. Spanish officials paid lip service to Spanish colonial practices while allowing the population considerable freedom to adapt practice to their particular needs. The colony's prosperity was founded on such flexibility. This included the gradual freeing of trade under O'Reilly's successor, Luis de Unzaga, who set an example by declaring an orthodox policy of trade regulations while turning a very blind eye to the flourishing trade carried on through Bayou St. John and up the Mississippi with the British. Smuggling along the Bayou was facilitated in the 1770s by Governor Carondelet's construction of the canal named after him (now covered over), bringing the waterway to the very edge of the city—the quay on Basin Street was later to be the heart of New Orleans' restricted brothel district, Storyville.

Freer trade was one way of achieving prosperity and thence security of tenure; immigration was another. "Louisiana wants working hands," wrote a New Orleanian, the Baron de Pontalba. "Give her population and she will become an inexhaustible source of wealth." Underpopulation had been a nagging problem for the French; hence the repeated efforts to describe New Orleans as the paradise it clearly was not. Spanish policy did not exactly invite immigration. But events outside Louisiana—British possession of Canada, American independence, war and revolution in the Caribbean—brought in the immigrants that Spanish officials at first welcomed and were later powerless to discourage. New Orleans gradually began to acquire that heterogeneity that today characterizes most American cities but which was then sufficiently unusual to cause visitors to the city to exclaim as they pushed their way through crowds of French, Spaniards, French Canadians, Canary Islanders,

Germans, and Africans. "No city perhaps on the globe, in an equal number of human beings, presents a greater contrast of national manners, languages and complexion, than does New Orleans," wrote the traveler William Darby at the beginning of the nineteenth century.

The French Canadians, known as Acadians (since corrupted to Cajuns), first began reaching New Orleans early in the 1760s, some ten years after being exiled from Nova Scotia for refusing to take an oath of allegiance to the new British authorities. They are first mentioned in New Orleans in 1764, when four families arrived from New York; a year later Aubry wrote that "we do not speak of them in the hundreds any more, but in thousands." Most of them soon left New Orleans for the country, the greatest concentration being on the rich farmland bordering the Bayou Teche west of New Orleans. In the city one sometimes meets their descendants early in the morning around the French Market, bargaining over their produce in an outlandish patois, which is the delight of French philologists.

The history of the Acadians is personified for most people in Longfellow's poem *Evangeline*, the story of the Acadian maiden who loses her lover Gabriel in the departure from Nova Scotia and wanders for many years searching for him in the Mississippi Delta, where so many of her compatriots had settled, to find him many more years later dying in an alms house in Philadelphia. The story was suggested to Longfellow by Hawthorne. Longfellow never visited "Acadiana"—Evangeline country—to check the origin of Hawthorne's version, at the unromantic conclusion of which the real heroine, Emmeline, finds her lover comfortably married and settled in St. Martinville, the modern center of the cult.

There is a stately and magnificent live oak in St. Martinville where Evangeline is supposed to have waited for Gabriel. Huey P. Long made a famous and characteristic speech there in his 1928 campaign for governor: "Evangeline is not the only one who has waited here in disappointment . . .," implying that his Acadian audience had been waiting there for social reforms; "your tears in this country, around this oak, have lasted for generations. Give me the chance to dry the tears of those who still weep here."

The descendants of another group of immigrants are also to be found occasionally in the French Market, to which they come from their narrow farms along the river and Bayou Terre aux Boeufs (there used to be water buffalo in the Delta) to sell their farm produce. These are the Isleños, many of whom live in inaccessible communities—albeit only a few miles from the city—and speak little or no English. The Isleños were encouraged by Governor Galvez in the 1770s to immigrate from the Canary Islands to what is now St. Bernard Parish, allegedly one of the richest fur-trapping areas in North America.

Most of these immigrants, Isleños and Acadians alike, helped in the long-delayed agricultural development of the colony. Dr. John Sibley, traveling downriver to New Orleans at the end of the century, commented on the fertility of the new farms on either bank: "Nothing is put in the ground that don't grow in the most luxuriant manner." In the 1790s a further boost was given to New Orleans' cultural and social life and to Louisiana agriculture by the arrival of refugees from the former French island of San Domingo (now Haiti), where a successful slave revolt led by Toussaint l'Ouverture in 1792 ousted the wealthy planters who had given the island a name for luxury and gracious living. Other immigrants in New Orleans retained their national groupings for a while—Austrian and Dalmation butchers, Catalan tavern keepers, for instance—but they are now assimilated into the melee of races. "All this can be called mixed merchandise," commented the Frenchman Berquin Duvallon somewhat cryptically. And beyond New Orleans the vast wilderness was at last being slowly explored and settled by Americans.

Immigration went a long way toward solving the manpower problems that had dogged French development of the colony; it also raised fresh problems, of which the uncontrolled ambitions of American settlers came to be the most serious. Not only was there the floating population of boatmen come downriver with agricultural produce from the plains, but there were also a number of Northern merchants with an eye for a good risk and few sentiments of loyalty to inhibit them. Several of these had settled in New Orleans since early in the 1770s; one of the first, and most respectable, was Oliver Pollock, who won Spanish trust when he supplied O'Reilly's troops with much-needed flour in 1769 and who spent the War of Independence in New Orleans as purchasing agent for the American forces. But Pollock's happy relations with the Spanish authorities were exceptional, and the officials were soon as suspicious of the Americans as they had been of the British. Hence the encouragement given by governors Carondelet and Miro in the 1780s and 1790s to the dissident General James Wilkinson in Kentucky to secede from the seaboard states.

The so-called Spanish Conspiracy stems from Wilkinson's visit to New Orleans in 1787 ostensibly to "promote trade" between Kentucky and New Orleans. His real business, however, was to enlist support for his secession claims. One of the principal intriguers in New Orleans was the merchant Daniel Clark, "of large wealth and possessions," who had arrived the previous year from Philadelphia and who was to become a thorn in the flesh of several New Orleans governors. He built up a considerable fortune as an import merchant under Spanish rule, was Wilkinson's agent and also American consul, and later claimed to have done more than any other individual to persuade Jefferson to buy Louisiana.

Governors of this period were in a quandary, wanting to extend New Orleans trade while safeguarding Spanish rule in Louisiana. Some officials argued for free trade; the settlers—who outside New Orleans were increasingly American—were no longer content to be fobbed off with exclusively Spanish goods and were more likely to support Spanish rule if allowed to do their shopping wherever they liked. Good relations were not going to be promoted by such measures as the prohibition in 1791 of the import of popular boxes, clocks, and coins stamped with the figure of a woman in white holding the banner of "American Liberty." On the other hand, prosperity certainly had the effect of undermining law and order in the city itself. "The gangrenous irregularity of the city" was becoming a favorite topic of criticism. New Orleans often seemed a seething mass of ill-disciplined "Kaintuck barbarians" with a remarkable facility for spending and losing their money in a city already famous for its gambling. "It is said, that when the Kentuckians arrive at this place, they are in their glory, finding neither limit to, nor punish-

ment of their excesses." By the end of the century, there was reckoned to be a floating population of some three thousand Americans
in a total of eight thousand in New Orleans.

Over the years, this inevitably posed a considerable problem for
the maintenance of tranquillity. Governor Carondelet was obliged
to impose a highly unpopular chimney tax to finance street lighting
and the policing of the city by watchmen to guard against the wave
of petty crime that followed the opening up of Mississippi trade.
Partly because of its unpopularity and partly because there were few
chimneys in such a climate, the tax was later changed to one on
bread and meat. The latter was apparently a most successful commodity to tax, Louisiana having already earned the reputation of
consuming more meat than any other country in the world; New
Orleanians should "truly be called carnivores," noted one observer.
Other attempts to police the city included the firing of cannon at
eight on winter evenings, and at nine in the summer, as a signal for
all sailors, soldiers, and blacks to go home; any found out after curfew
were put in jail.

The city had changed drastically both in appearance and character since the withdrawal of the French. From a crumbling settlement of wooden cottages it had become, by the turn of the century,
a "stylish Mediterranean town" of about fifteen hundred houses.
The change was due largely to two fires which destroyed the old
French town in 1788 and 1794. The 1788 fire was the most devastat-
ing, reducing the greater part of the town to charred embers in a few
hours. It began on Good Friday when the wind blew candles in a
private chapel against the curtains. A London newspaper, imbued
with the strong anti-Catholic prejudices of the period, described the
fire as starting in the house of a "zealous Catholic, who, not satisfied
with worshipping God in his usual way, had a chapel or altar erected
in his house . . . which he had illuminated with fifty or sixty wax
tapers, as if his prayers would not ascend to heaven without them."
The fire spread instantly among the wooden buildings.

The fire of 1794 was concentrated in the commercial district, so
that the cost of the damage far exceeded that of the earlier fire. Even
so, a new ordinance on firefighting (which ordered all carpenters and

joiners, "be they whites or negroes", to go to the scene of a fire with
all the tools necessary to stop it spreading) noted "the little inclina-
tion existing among individuals to lend the necessary help." Instructions that houses must be built with tile roofs were regarded with
typical New Orleans disdain for the law until fashion changed and
other building materials became cheaper than wood.

The city's attitude toward firefighting improved with the years
and, during the nineteenth century, voluntary fire companies played
an important part in the social life of the middle and lower classes.
Exemption from militia duty made membership in fire companies
attractive. In the 1850s Bishop Whipple wrote that "this city is
highly favoured in its fire department." Volunteer companies were
formed with all the rigmarole of masonic lodges, calling themselves
by such names as Vigilant, Perseverance, Tom Thumb, and Nep-
tune, with elected officers, initiation ceremonies, and benevolence
programs. Every March 4th firefighters staged lavish parades
through the city; "a grand procession of the natives," as Sir Charles
Lyell, the geographer, put it: "the corps of all the different companies of firemen turned out in their uniform, drawing their engines
dressed up with flowers, ribbons and flags, and I never saw a finer
set of young men." The companies had comfortable incomes, too,
enabling them to invest in real estate and cemeteries and in politics;
by the end of the century the fire companies were part of the
complex political machine that ran New Orleans. Mayor Martin
Behrman, boss of the machine for over twenty years, acquired his
early political experience campaigning for the fire companies in the
1880s.

Needless to say, there was no such organization in 1788 and 1794.
A different kind of political philanthropy did the city a good turn,
however, in the person of Don Andres Almonester y Roxas. Almonester came to New Orleans with O'Reilly, who appointed him to the
profitable sinecure of royal standard bearer. He became the richest
man in New Orleans and the largest landowner, much of his land
being along Bayou St. John. He also leased land on either side of the
Place d'Armes, on which he built rows of stores. He appears to have
had considerable social ambition since his various acts of benevo-

lence toward the city were allegedly undertaken in exchange for promises of titles, honors, or a prominent burial site. But it was largely thanks to him that New Orleans' public buildings got off the ground after the fires. He lent the money to rebuild the cathedral. He partly financed the building of the Presbytère alongside (though his widow refused to continue the payments after his death in 1798). He had already in pre-fire days rebuilt the charity hospital after it had blown down in a hurricane and he also built a leper hospital near what is now Central Park. Almonester is said to have spent nearly three-quarters of his fortune on the city and yet was still considered an upstart. But he did have himself buried near the altar of his cathedral.

The new town was a definite improvement on the old. There were still many gaps in de Pauger's outline, convenient for dumping garbage; the drainage system left much to be desired; the streets were unpaved, so much so that blacksmiths were unknown in the city, the *terre douce* making horseshoes unnecessary. One visitor alleged there was nothing to equal the city's filthiness unless it be its unhealthiness. The population had grown considerably and was busy acquiring the trappings of an urban society. The Bishop of Louisiana reported to Cuba on the arrival of a "mob of adventurers to the colony who know not God or religion" and, even worse, a lodge of freemasons—anathema to right-thinking Catholics—was said to have been set up just outside the city limits. As in most frontier settlements, education was at a premium. Schoolmasters were not easily persuaded to undertake the long and somewhat perilous journey from Europe and probably most New Orleanians, half of whom were reckoned to be illiterate, were none too anxious to pay them an encouraging salary. "No booksellers either," complained Berquin Duvallon, one of the city's harshest critics, and for the good reason that "a bookseller would perish of hunger there in the midst of his books, unless these taught the fascinated reader the art of doubling his capital in a year's time." Everyone agreed, however, that New Orleanians needed no one to teach them how to make money.

Also typical of frontier life was the fact that the city's muddy squalor did not stand in the way of its earning a reputation for a fast, gay life, more pleasure-bent than was acceptable in cities of the United States. "Luxury within a dozen years had made great progress through the colony," wrote Berquin Duvallon; "everything in the town is tinctured with ostentation. An air of expense distinguishes the apparel, vehicles, furniture of the inhabitants. Simplicity has taken flight, parade has usurped its place. This luxury is dangerous in a rich nation, but to regions ever doomed to mediocrity it is mortal poison." Public morals have never been considered the city's strong point, as gleefully stressed by modern travel brochures as it was condemned by nineteenth-century ministers.

Other reports were more favorable: John F. Watson commented on Spanish honesty, lack of ostentation, lack of snobbery and frugality and reckoned the extravagances were being introduced by the Americans. Another visitor who preferred, despite his compliments, to remain anonymous, commented on the city's lavish hospitality; he had scarcely dined at his lodgings since his arrival, which perhaps explains why he was given such gargantuan meals when he was in —"seldom less than eight dishes elegantly dressed; and wine and claret at breakfast, dinner and supper without limitation." As for the New Orleanians, male and female, far from being pallid from their lust for commercial wealth and gambling debauches, they were "universally as hale, fair and fresh-coloured as our own people . . . they say themselves that this is the Paradise of the World."

The political background to this hedomistic "paradise" was less satisfactory. The governor in 1801, Salcedo, was universally acknowledged as a helpless and stupid old man who had virtually surrendered the administration of the colony to his son, "a greedy young man, an uneducated blockhead who disgraces his rank in the army by his daily conduct." It had been clear to the Spanish government for some time that it could no longer maintain New Orleans as a strong bulwark against American pressure. Trading rights had been granted to the Americans in 1795 and in 1800 at the Treaty of San Ildefonso Spain secretly handed Louisiana back to France. As in 1762, the colonists were kept ignorant of the deal though the furore of rumors among all sections of the population kept the city in a ferment.

The details of the Louisiana Purchase have been described elsewhere and do not really concern us here. But it is worth remarking,
in passing, on the strange hallucinatory experience of reading about
the negotiations and the discussions leading up to them—is it real?
one keeps asking. Diplomacy gone wild, it seems: Spain's retroces-
sion of Louisiana to France, a secret that everyone claims to know
about, American diplomats in Paris frenziedly trying to buy vast
tracts of land, and even stranger, Napoleon nonchalantly considering
the sale, the United States Congress mouthing warlike sentiments
about enforcing American control of the Mississippi. But one is
inclined to judge these antics by modern speed of communication
and needs to be reminded that they occurred in a vacuum of time
of which today's diplomats would be very envious.

In March 1803, French ownership of Louisiana was published for
all to see with the arrival in New Orleans of Pierre Clement de
Laussat as French commissioner, charged with taking over Louisiana
from Spain. An ambitious but naive envoy, de Laussat arrived "full
of a zeal for glory and a desire to be useful," and equipped with "the
largest library ever seen in this country." He was quite unaware of
the fate of his new province. Salcedo was replaced by the Marquis
de Casa Calvo, considered more suited to handing over the territory.

De Laussat claimed his arrival excited "the enthusiasm of the
people here; everywhere addresses were made to the First Consul,
the most energetic expressions of thoroughly French devotion."
Rumors of the sale to America he discounted as "an improbable and
impudent lie" but was soon obliged to acknowledge his mistake and
to report the extravagant joy of the Americans when the news of the
Purchase arrived from Washington. "Most of the Spaniards, between joy at seeing this colony escape French domination and the
regret of losing it themselves have the stupidity to show themselves
satisfied," he complained; "the French, that is to say, nine-tenths of
the population, are stupified and disconsolate; they speak only of
selling out and fleeing far from this country."

The last three months of 1803 saw New Orleans *en fête* as never
before, as if the city were determined to refute for once and for all
any imputation that it was not the most affluent spot in the New

World. Casa Calvo and de Laussat entertained each other and leading citizens at huge, lavish banquets, fountains in the Place d'Armes were set flowing with wine, fireworks displays helped to salve the feelings of those who had not been invited to the banquets, and the whole city was bedecked with French and Spanish flags. The hand-over, just before Christmas, to the American authorities, represented by the handsome, young, ham-fisted William Claiborne, was a more subdued affair; de Laussat gave another banquet, but Claiborne, one suspects, was ill at ease among such frivolities. Once again flags were lowered and raised in the Place d'Armes. One onlooker reported that "the American flag remained stuck for a long time . . . as if it were confused at the taking place of that to which it owed its glorious independence . . . It was not until that flag had been quite hoisted up that suddenly piercing cries of 'Huzza' burst out from the midst of one particular group. . . . Those cries made more gloomy the silence and quietness of the rest of the crowd of spectators scattered far and wide—they were French and Spanish and were all moved and confounded their sighs and tears."

Joseph Ingraham, the nineteenth-century traveler and novelist, gave his own idiosyncratic version of the colonial period in New Orleans' history: " . . .the plaything of monarchs, 'swapped' as boys swap their penknives. Discovered and lost by the French, possessed by the gold-hunting Spaniards—again ceded to the French—exchanged for a kingdom with the man who traded in empires, and sold by him for a 'plum' to our government."

4. The Creoles

Nowadays New Orleans regards its French origins with a blissful nostalgia, a Southern characteristic elaborated with Latin exuberance by New Orleanians. The unsuspecting stranger is led through a verbal gallery hung with images of a picturesque little Mississippi town redolent of garlic and olive oil, its citizens dedicated to a tropical version of *la bonne vie*. In the center of every picture is the Creole. The word comes from the Spanish *criollo* and came to mean whites of French or Spanish descent; in New Orleans, where there were never very many Spanish settlers, the word has always had a distinctive French flavor. The mystique surrounding the Creoles of New Orleans is partly the creation of foreign writers of the first half of the nineteenth century but even more of romantically inclined New Orleans writers of the end of the century, who tried to snatch from the forgetful hand of time some of the social and cultural inspiration of prewar New Orleans, investing it with a romance that was conspicuously absent from their own time.

To the majority of New Orleanians, Creole means white. Old established New Orleans mulattoes also refer to themselves as Creole, with every justification since they are also for the most part of French or Spanish descent as well as African. Modern sociologists

have found the term "colored Creole" a convenient way to distinguish between the old colored families and those Negroes who came
to New Orleans after the Civil War—ex-slaves from the plantations.
But the white Creole will never acknowledge his colored kinsman's
claim to the name. As George Washington Cable pointed out, the
term Creole was adopted by, not conceded to, natives of mixed
blood.

The Creole preserved the Frenchness of New Orleans. Just as that
Frenchness is sometimes hard to pinpoint nowadays, and often
seems artificial or unreal, so the Creole is partly a figment of social
snobbery or of a travel agent's imagination. The importance of the
Creole in the New Orleans economy and society faded with the
city's Americanization, though it is due to the few die-hard Creoles
of modern New Orleans that any Gallic flavor remains.

New Orleans remained persistently French during the years of
Spanish rule. Since the Spanish government had only rather nega-
tively assumed the burden of its administration in order to keep the
British, and later the Americans, from pressing too hard on its more
valuable colony of New Spain (Mexico), they were anxious, after
Alejandro O'Reilly's firm suppression of the 1768 rebellion, to con-
ciliate their new subjects as far as possible. French officials were
placed in seemingly important administrative posts, including the
Cabildo, which replaced the Superior Council, although the only
really effective power stayed with the governor as representative of
the Spanish government. Spanish officials married French women;
the first Spanish governor, Luis de Unzaga, married the daughter of
a leading French Creole. The outnumbered Spaniards learned to
speak French as the predominant language. French Ursulines, invet-
erate educators of New Orleans womanhood, refused to admit
would-be Spanish novices "so long as these applicants should remain
ignorant of the French idiom," and Ursuline nuns sent from Havana
to replace their French counterparts and to teach Spanish in the
Ursuline school found their pupils in tears, to be placated only by
continuing their lessons in French. Only in official notices did the
Spanish authorities exercise their prerogative of using their own
language, and even those were duplicated in French. There was

small consolation in the acid comments of the French traveler Berquin Duvallon on Creole pretensions at speaking his mother tongue, which, he claimed, they did "with a disgusting drawling method of pronouncing their words."

The impact of the French Revolution on New Orleans was at first only mild. A few exiles from the Revolution reached New Orleans, including a group of Capuchins from Amiens and Tours. But after war between France and Spain broke out in Europe and trade with France was forbidden in New Orleans, the New Orleanian, his heart dictated by his purse (and by his dislike of Spanish wine), became a fervent republican. In one way the turbulence of Jacobin New Orleans—stimulated by the presence of large numbers of unruly boatmen, who were, according to the Spaniards, infected with the dangerous disease of revolutionary fervor—benefited the city: Governor Carondelet decided he would feel more comfortable if the city were properly lit at night and policed. After 1793 a Jacobin Club was founded in New Orleans, and martial dances were performed to the tune of the "Marseillaise" in the new theater opened by exiles from San Domingo. Carondelet nervously forbade the dances, closed the theater, and arrested overenthusiastic Jacobins, but the unease persisted. By the end of the decade, however, New Orleans Jacobinism had been tempered by the arrival of royalist sympathizers from San Domingo. In 1798 the Duc de Chartres (later Louis XVIII) and his two brothers, the Ducs de Beaujolais and de Montpensier—sons of Philippe-Egalité and great grandsons of the Duc d'Orléans, after whom the city had been named—visited New Orleans in the hopes of reaching Cuba and were warmly welcomed by French and Spanish alike. Only the governor was less than pleased, being obliged to meet the entertainment expenses of some three thousand dollars from his own purse.

The divided loyalties of the city's population toward the problems of France, however, did not lead to any greater warmth toward Spain. "I fear that if war were declared on France," wrote one governor all too accurately in the 1790s, "we would find but few inhabitants of Lower Louisiana who would sincerely defend the country from any undertaking of that nation."

After the Louisiana Purchase, the new American governor, Claiborne, found that the French were far more trouble than the Spanish. Claiborne reckoned the French commissioner Laussat was deliberately agitating his fellow countrymen: "I should not regret M. Laussat's departure from Louisiana," he wrote. "He feels some chagrin at the loss of his Prefectorial authority, and manifests a disposition to interfere in the interior police of the Province." Not that the Spanish commissioner, the Marquis de Casa Calvo, was entirely innocent in this respect, but Laussat had more material to work with. Claiborne, who spoke neither French nor Spanish, was at a disadvantage. "I have discovered with regret that a strong partiality for the French government still exists among many of the inhabitants of this city," he complained to Madison, echoing his Spanish predecessors. Twenty or thirty "young adventurers" had arrived from Bourdeaux and San Domingo "who are troublesome to this society; they are men of some information, desperate fortunes, and inflated with an idea of the invincibility of Bonaparte and the power of the French nation." The Francophile population, in his opinion, was all too easily led astray by such disreputable visitors.

Bastille Day, 1804, was very pointedly observed by the Creole population, the raising of the tricolor acting like a red flag to Americans in town (mostly the boatmen), who tried to tear it down. Claiborne obviously thought both sides were behaving childishly and several times reassured correspondents that the French population was acting from sentimental rather than political attachment to France. (Bastille Day continued to be a major celebration until the early 1900s and is still observed today as an excuse for a party.) His patience was severely tried, however, by the famous "fracas at a Public Ball" over whether the American or French waltz should be played; he was obliged to regulate the order of dances—one French, one American. Even so, fighting broke out on one occasion at a ball when Americans present began singing "Hail Columbia," to be furiously answered by the French singing "La Marseillaise."

As late as 1826, the Duke of Saxe-Weimar commented on the aversion of the French Creoles to the Americans, particularly on the occasion of Washington's Birthday Ball, which was virtually boycotted by the Creoles. "The division between the American and French factions is visible even in the drawing room," he wrote; "the French complain that the Americans will not speak French, will not meet their neighbours even half way in accommodation of speech. The Americans ridicule the toilet practices of the French ladies, their liberal use of rouge and pearl powder."

Between 1808 and 1809, the Francophile fervor of the Creole population was stimulated by the arrival of more than five thousand San Domingo refugees who had originally fled to Cuba from the French-owned island and were now ousted from Cuba as a result of the war between France and Spain. Not only were many of them skilled craftsmen, which New Orleans still needed so badly, but much of the sophistication that came to be associated with New Orleans Creoles dates from this influx. San Domingo Creoles had already been responsible for the opening of the city's first theater and the publication of the first newspaper, *Moniteur de la Louisiane*, in the 1790s; they were now to inspire the taste for culture and refinement that made New Orleans the first city in the United States to have a regular opera season and on which its perhaps slightly exaggerated reputation for gracious living was founded.*

Similarly the city began to cash in on the glamour that the term "Creole" seemed to include; "a Creole chicken, egg or cow is worth nearly twice as much as one from a distant state," wrote a visitor in the 1850s. A more acid commentator—and one much reviled by the Creoles themselves—was George Washington Cable, who wrote that "the spirit of commerce saw the money value of so honoured a title (as Creole) and broadened its meaning to take in any creature or thing or variety or manufacture peculiar to Louisiana which might become an article of sale." The market value of "Creole" is still apparent today; its use puzzles the outsider trying to buy tomatoes, peaches, figs, or watermelons in the French Market ("French" comes a good second in commercial value), all of which are proudly

---

*Even Berquin Duvallon commented on the San Domingo exiles that "Louisiana has profited in this, as well as in many other matters of the greatest importance, from the ills with which that wretched colony has been afflicted."

labeled Creole though not noticeably different from those labeled California or Florida, except to a practised New Orleanians who swear quite seriously to their superiority.

Yet another influx of French refugees occurred after the Battle of Waterloo. Napoleon was already quite warmly regarded in Creole circles in spite of his responsibility for the sale of Louisiana, and the Code Napoléon was and still is the basis of Louisiana civil law, making New Orleans a more litigious city than most, with a double capacity for "interpretation" of the law. Among the political exiles who emigrated to New Orleans from France was Pierre Soulé, an example, by no means as unique as is often implied, of a Creole who played an active part in the American political system. Soulé was imprisoned by Charles X for republican activities, escaped to American in 1825, and later came to New Orleans, where he married a Creole, sorted out the confusion of Louisiana law, and became a prominent Democratic politician.

St. Philip's Theatre was again the scene of rowdy enthusiasm when the news reached New Orleans of Napoleon's escape from Elba. "The jubilee of the city was incomprehensible," wrote Vincent Nolte. The French consul was obliged hastily to don a tricolor, having only a year before worn a white cockade to mark the Bourbon restoration. And there is a popular legend that after Waterloo the Mayor of New Orleans, Nicolas Girod, planned to help Napoleon escape from St. Helena, and had a house built on Chartres Street for the ex-Emperor's use. (The truth seems to be that Girod said Napoleon was welcome to use it if he ever came to New Orleans.) An expedition was about to leave the city to rescue Napoleon in 1820, under the command of Captain Bossier and Dominique You, the latter a pirate turned worthy citizen; but unfortunately Napoleon died before they left. Instead the city showed its admiration by a huge memorial service in St. Louis Cathedral. "Never did that temple have such a large assembly," marveled one of the congregation.

The city's loyalty to Napoleon was later rewarded when one of Napoleon's doctors during his imprisonment, Dr. Francisco Antommarchi, offered the city a bronze cast of Napoleon's death mask (which now sits in solitary, white-elephant splendor in a room in the museum). An area of uptown New Orleans being developed at the time of the gift acquired a rash of Napoleonic victories as names— Jena, Austerlitz, and Marengo among them—and a principal avenue was named after the emperor himself.

With all these encouraging influences feeding the natural Francophilia of the majority of the resident population, it is hardly surprising that visitors to New Orleans continued to be impressed by its Frenchness. In the 1850s Frederick Olmsted drove through the French Quarter from the station to the St. Charles Hotel past "French noises and French smells, French signs, ten to one of English." "Everything was Parisian about me," wrote Henry Didimus in 1845, "and I was in spirit three thousand miles distant from American soil, so easy it is in this the most unique of cities, to pass in a walk of five minutes from Dover to Calais or from New York to Madrid." French was still the language of polite society; those speaking it would argue that the Americans had no polite society, and prominent American families—such as the politician John Slidell and his family—spoke French by preference at home. When William Russell dined with Judah P. Benjamin, the Confederate statesman, on the eve of the Civil War, he found his hosts far happier speaking French. Those who could afford it bought French furniture for their houses and sent their children to school in Paris, while their wives tried their best to keep up with French fashions. Until the Civil War, legal proceedings were more often conducted in French than English, "and it is indispensable for a lawyer to have a free command of both languages."

Many visitors commented on a hostility between the Creoles and Anglo-Americans that has often been exaggerated. Cable is partly responsible for this, as one of the most influential writers about the city in the later years of the century. To the rage of the New Orleans Creole, Cable described him as "handsome, proud, illiterate, elegant in manner, slow, a seeker of office and military commission, ruling society with fierce exclusiveness, looking upon toil as the slave's proper badge . . . and taking but a secondary and unsympathetic part in the commercial life from which was springing the future greatness

of his town." Where there was conflict, it was cultural rather than
political or commercial, and political and commercial conflict by no
means developed on racial lines. The happy combination of the
Anglo-American speculator, such as Edward Livingstone, and the
elegant Creole wife, such as Livingstone's wife, the daughter of a San
Domingo refugee, was not so unusual. There was a spacious middle
ground occupied by both races where racial characteristics were
easily blurred; the Creole successfully copied his neighbor's business
and political acumen, the American his neighbor's refinement and
way of life. On either side of the middle ground were the less
successful, the less refined of either race, who disliked the other's
foreign habits and language and would make no concession.

There were certain wealthy Creoles, however, who did bear out
the derogatory comments, who failed to take advantage of the influx
of speculative wealth, whose misfortunes have been applied far too
generally. Bernard de Marigny is such an example, often cited as
typical of Creole attitudes, rather than as an exception. Marigny was
descended from one of the most distinguished French families of
New Orleans. An ancestor of his, Josselin, came out to Louisiana
with Iberville; another, Antoine Philippe, interrupted his exploration of Louisiana to oppose administrative reforms in the 1750s and
was arrested and shipped to France. His son, Pierre, was responsible
for building up the great Marigny fortune, mainly in real estate; he
entertained the three French princes in 1798 with astonishing splendor and none of Carondelet's misgivings about the cost. Bernard de
Marigny has accumulated a large number of legends, even for a New
Orleanian; they say he used to light cigars with ten-dollar bills, that
he introduced the dice game of craps to the United States—so-called
because the Americans called the Creoles *crapauds* because they ate
frogs' legs and the dice game became craps because the Creoles
played it—that he finally gave up dueling (for which he had a great
fondness) when he challenged a particularly tall man who chose Lake
Pontchartrain as the ground. One story, however, is true: that he
refused to sell his land adjoining and below the French Quarter to
American real estate developers in the 1820s. They went elsewhere
and developed the prosperous American Faubourg Ste. Marie
upriver of the old city. Marigny later tried to develop Faubourg

Marigny (as his plantations were called) himself, but his fortune was by then too depleted, and no one was interested in investing capital in that part of town (nor has been ever since). Marigny's complacency was typical only of a very few Creoles who sat idly watching the development of the city's prosperity; most were as enthusiastic as any American businessman.

"In less than fifty years the influence of all persons of the French race will be utterly extinguished throughout Louisiana," wrote the English visitor G.W. Featherstonhaugh in the 1840s. What in fact happened was that only those Creoles who acknowledged American influences maintained their position. After the Civil War, no one moving to New Orleans from elsewhere in the United States would have needed to learn French; no Frenchman emigrating to New Orleans would make his fortune without learning English. Again, after the war, the impoverished upper class of New Orleans could no longer afford to send its children to France to school; French remained the language of instruction in schools below Canal Street for a while, but the better schools were above Canal Street and there English held sway. Louisiana historians of the old school, such as Charles Gayarré and Alcée Fortier, wrote in French but were translated almost immediately into English.* The decay of Creole society was to some extent typified by the decay of the French Quarter; George Cable described it as "a region of architectural decrepitude, where an ancient and foreign-seeming domestic life, in second stories, overhangs the ruins of a former commercial prosperity and upon everything has settled a long sabbath of decay." Influential Creoles now lived in the Garden District. Spoken French gradually became an elegant anachronism except among a few families. In 1911 the state legislature forbade the printing of official notices in French as well as English; the famous New Orleans newspaper *L'Abeille* ceased publication shortly afterward.

Street names are still given a confusing French pronunciation,

---

*On the other hand, Grace King, one of the city's most affectionate historians, could write of Paris in 1890 that it "seemed so natural, so what we are accustomed to," like "letting out a French opera matinee at every corner" of Royal Street. (*Memoirs of a Southern Woman of Letters*, quoted C. Vann Woodward, *Origins of the New South*, p. 137.)

especially those named after the Muses in the region of Coliseum Square, inspired by the vogue for classical republicanism current in France at the time. A number of societies have been formed from time to time to encourage the speaking and study of French (such as the Creole Association of New Orleans, which was founded in 1886 "to promote the advancement of the Creole race in Louisiana"), but the cause was moved still further from reality when the legislature forbade the use of French as the principal language in schools, and the societies that have lasted longest are those that have concentrated on the social rather than the linguistic tendencies of the city. For it still counts to be of Creole descent. Old ladies of old families are still to be found on Sundays profanely (according to the sabbath traditions of the Anglo-Americans, who were horrified by the gaiety of the New Orleans Sunday) sipping their champagne and addressing each other as *chère* this and *chère* that—Chère Mimi, Chère Marie, Chère Francine—and their descendants may respectfully refer to them as *tante* and *grandmère* or *chère mère* if, according to the younger generation, you can stomach it. Similarly Creole families occasionally adopt a prefix of 'Ti, an abbreviation of *petit* and the New Orleans version of the American junior. There are also a remarkable number of French surnames. French is still spoken in the remoter parts of southwest Louisiana among the Acadians and in some colored communities, but in New Orleans it is American, and within the city one is hardly more likely to hear French spoken nowadays than anywhere else in the United States.

Only—and this is a major exception—only in the food of New Orleans is the Gallic influence unmistakable. Food is a major topic of conversation in New Orleans as in France, and the newcomer is overwhelmed with advice on what and where to eat. Thackeray noted that "New Orleans in springtime . . . seemed to me the city of the world where you can eat and drink the most and suffer the least." The diligence of the American tourist must make the city one of the few places in the world where people queue up outside to eat in a particular restaurant. Walk past a gourmet haven such as Galatoire's (noting as you pass the unpretentious decor—New Orleans' best restaurants have preserved the tradition that it is the food that counts) on any weekday when there is a convention in town (and that applies to most weekdays outside the middle of summer), and see the long line forming at midday, labels on lapels proclaiming identity and profession. Exotic menus compensate for plainness of decor; Indians and Africans have contributed a lavish use of spices to the basic French cuisine—sassafras for the famous gumbo filé (gumbo itself a West African word),* a stew best made from the magnificent shrimps and oysters of the Mississippi Delta, peppers of every shape, size, and color for the hot sauces that are such a relief after the pink, turgid synthetic glues with which Americans elsewhere douse their food. Tourists say food is the main reason for their coming to New Orleans; they leave as soon as they have ticked off and consumed all the famous dishes: pompano ("delicious as the less criminal forms of sin," said Mark Twain), scarlet encrusted crayfish, soft-shell crabs, oysters so abundant that you can eat them in a dozen different ways without the usual qualms that they should only be eaten raw. There is even a chocolate pudding, the recipe for which says the chocolate must be melted in the sun. The New Orleanian's liver is as tough as if not tougher than most French ones, and his appetite as large as any American's; the combination can be alarming.

New Orleans anniversaries introduce small worried municipal officials from France into this former French colony: the two hundred and fiftieth anniversary of the city's founding, the two hundredth anniversary of Napoleon's birth send the city into a frenzy of resuscitating its French in order to greet emissaries from the mother country. The most nerve-racking of such occasions was General de Gaulle's state visit in 1960. One is strongly reminded of Claiborne's language problems, for none of the city council spoke French, and the General had little intention of speaking anything else. There were some uncomfortable moments, which he did little to ameliorate. An avenue was named after him and retained its name even

---

*Basil Hall wrote in the last century of "a very nice mess of stuff which I took to be curry, and envied them accordingly. But I found it was called gumbo, a sort of gelatinous vegetable soup of which, under other instruction, I learnt afterwards to understand the value."

after the General's apparent insults to the United States had stimulated a move to change it. "Many years will elapse before the strong partiality of the Louisianians for their Mother Country will be effaced," prophesied Claiborne. Laussat wrote rather more sentimentally, "May a Louisianian and a Frenchman never meet . . . without giving each other the sweet name of brother."

5. The Filibusters

APART FROM LAMPPOSTS in Canal Street acknowledging "The Spanish Domination" and quaint ceramic plaques in the French Quarter giving the Spanish names of the streets, one would scarcely know that Spain had ruled New Orleans at all, much less for a period as long as the French. New Orleans showed remarkably little gratitude to the country whose easygoing imperialism had at last made the colony's economic and social development possible, preferring to consolidate its relations during the nineteenth century with Latin America, relations which in the new age of revolutions were no longer compatible with friendship for Spain.

The forty years of Spanish rule left no very distinctive impression on New Orleans, and after the details of the Purchase had been cleared up and authority handed over to the French and thence to the United States, there was little to keep Spanish officials in New Orleans. One or two did in fact overstay their welcome, and Claiborne complained that "the intrigues of certain late Emigrants from France and some of the Satellites of the Spanish government have tended to heighten the Discontent in this Quarter." But however much hostility there was to American rule, there was little support for a return to Spanish. Far from it; during the next fifty years New Orleans became a center for anti-Spanish intrigue.

Claiborne's letters give some idea of the atmosphere of suspicion engendered by the Purchase. Spaniards in New Orleans, such as the Marquis de Casa Calvo and his staff, distrusted American territorial ambitions, at this stage the cause of a number of badly organized but troublesome expeditions against Spanish territory, later to be idealized into the "Manifest Destiny" doctrine. Equally the Americans, with some justification, distrusted the Spaniards for their capacity for intrigue. The atmosphere worsened considerably with the arrival of over five thousand French refugees from Cuba; the addition of so many fiercely anti-Spanish exiles into a city already beset with suspicion makes it hardly surprising that so many people considered New Orleans an ideal place from which to launch their revolutions against Spanish rule in Latin America.

New Orleans had first attracted attention in this respect as a haven for pirates and privateers. The distinction between the two is easily blurred. Privateering was eagerly encouraged by governments without navies, who issued commissions, or letters of marque, to individuals to prey upon enemy shipping. Many of those who called themselves privateers during the nineteenth century were taking advantage of the availability of commissions to be obtained from the multitude of revolutions against Spanish rule (which broke out regularly after 1810) to sail under the relative immunity of a national flag, the better to attack the rich prizes of Gulf shipping. Privateering had a long history in the area; Iberville had set up his Gulf colony in order to be able to prey upon Spanish treasure fleets, and he died in Havana of yellow fever caught after raiding the British West Indian possession of Nevis. The Gulf and Caribbean, with their jumble of national possessions, reflected European hostilities with commissioned privateers coming into their own during the Napoleonic wars. Before 1810 most of the privateers flew the French flag, attacking British, Spanish, and American shipping, and using New Orleans as their headquarters. Daniel Clark was appointed United States consul in 1798 partly because American vessels captured in the Gulf by French privateers were being taken to New Orleans, sold very cheaply, and the crews allegedly ill-treated. Not only was New Orleans the only port, for some time, where privateers could outfit their vessels (removing their French flags for the purpose), but, thanks to their easy confusion with pirates and smugglers, it was easy to attract the financial support of the city's merchants, their consciences eased, particularly later in the nineteenth century, by the knowledge that they were contributing to the battle of liberal principles against Spanish dictatorship.

Smuggling, after all, was endemic to the city, the habit encouraged during the eighteenth century by prohibitive French and Spanish trading regulations and customs dues. The Spanish authorities had established a fort at the entrance to Bayou St. John but failed to prevent the infiltration of smuggled goods. How could one prevent smuggling through the maze of swamps and bayous surrounding New Orleans, where a man in a pirogue could wind his way through an underground tunnel of reeds right to the edge of town? The British from West Florida had been the most proficient at supplying the settlers' needs, not only up Bayou St. John: British ships had the right to enter the Mississippi to trade with British possessions above Bayou Manchac and the British maintained two "floating warehouses" opposite New Orleans stuffed with illicit delicacies and sometimes slaves.

The most notorious example of this combination of smuggling and commercial interests was the Baratarian Association. Barataria is an area south of New Orleans on the edge of the Gulf, an area of marsh, lake and half-submerged islands conveniently linked to the Mississippi by bayou. A respectable lumbering settlement was noted there in the eighteenth century, but the land was infinitely better suited to smuggling, and the Spaniards were obliged to build a watch tower on Grand Isle guarding the entrance to Barataria Bay. Early in the nineteenth century, it became the headquarters of groups of smugglers, many of whom claimed from time to time to be privateers acting in someone's national interest, financially backed by the Baratarian Association, which was made up of New Orleans merchants. Smuggling increased after 1808 with the United States' prohibition of the foreign slave trade. Slaves from Africa and the West Indies became one of the principal commodities, smuggled in through the lakes and bayous of the Delta. Louisiana opinion was unanimously in favor of the trade—"they must import more slaves," Claiborne reported, "or the country was ruined." At least one expedition went from New Orleans to West Africa to collect a cargo of slaves after the abolition act was passed, but a far more popular method of acquiring them was to buy them in Cuba and smuggle them in from there. There was a well-known practice of the slave ship anchoring at the Balise at the mouth of the river while the agent hurried to the city to tell the authorities in strictest confidence that he had reason to believe there was a slave ship at the Balise; the authorities would then apprehend the ship and auction its cargo in New Orleans, the "informer" being entitled to half the profits, thus gaining a handsome margin over his expenses. So regular was the trade that there were often complaints of the market's being glutted, but by the 1840s Virginia was supplying Louisiana with enough slaves, so that smuggling them was unnecessary.

While smuggling lasted, the main slave depot was at Barataria, visited by Creole sugar planters who were prepared to pay a handsome price. Vincent Nolte reported that the pirates "had their friends and acquaintances, their depots of goods, etc., in the city, and sold almost openly, the wares they had obtained by piracy, particularly English manufactured goods."

Smuggling was a highly respectable profession in the city, to Claiborne's dismay; once, when he reprimanded a young lady for her family's connection with what would elsewhere be considered a highly dubious activity, she replied that smuggling could not be anything but respectable since at least three generations of her family had been engaged in it. It was impossible to persuade the people of New Orleans that smuggling was immoral, Claiborne told the government. The Baratarian Association meanwhile continued to meet and act quite openly. The members would usually congregate in one or another of the several coffee houses (which were no nearer to being coffee houses than the Baratarians were to being legitimate traders), such as Turner's Coffee House, the Café des Refugies (run by free colored people from San Domingo according to Cable), Maspero's Exchange, which was also, conveniently, an auction house for slaves, and others.

The most famous of the Baratarians, the Lafitte brothers, Pierre and Jean, who are believed to have lived in San Domingo before they took to the sea, came to town regularly.* Nolte describes the brothers parading arm-in-arm in New Orleans streets with Livingstone's brother-in-law; although they were arrested several times, Livingstone always argued their release. Other Baratarians included Dominique You, who later became so respectable as to merit burial in the city's principal cemetery, Vincent Gambi, known as a bloodthirsty Italian, and an attractive-sounding character known as Cut-Nose Chinghizola. From their Grand Isle headquarters they would smuggle captured merchandise up the Bayou Barataria to a halfway house known as the Temple, no doubt on account of the reverence accorded its merchandise by its large New Orleans clientele. Jean Lafitte also had a store on Royal Street under the nose of the authorities.

One visitor to New Orleans complained of the "abominable squealing" made by ungreased cartwheels along the levee past his hotel bedroom; apparently the legislature had forbade them to be greased in the hopes that the smugglers would betray their nightly prowling by the noise they made. Claiborne offered a $500 reward for the capture of Jean Lafitte, who retaliated, according to legend, by generously offering $1,500 to anyone who would bring Claiborne to him. Prosecution was virtually impossible because of the number of leading citizens involved. An expedition against Barataria in 1812 captured the Lafittes, but they were never convicted. Another expedition in 1814 caught Pierre Lafitte again, but again he was never brought to trial. At this point the British approached Jean Lafitte to ask for his help in their campaign against New Orleans, an offer he turned to good advantage when he informed Claiborne of it, suggesting (according to Nolte, on Livingstone's advice) that the Baratarians should be employed by the American forces in return for their pardon. General Jackson's immediate reaction was to have nothing to do with these "hellish banditti," but good sense pre-

*There is no evidence, however, on which to base their alleged ownership of the small cottage on Bourbon Street that calls itself Lafitte's Blacksmith Shop.

vailed. Who knew their way around the Delta maze better than they? They were pardoned after the battle as a reward for their services, though the implication that they should desist from piracy was disregarded. But the end of the war also freed American naval forces for a campaign against piracy from American shores, and the Lafittes were forced to move from Barataria to Galveston in Texas; this too they were eventually forced to abandon, and no more is heard of their piracy after about 1820.

The Baratarians were basically pirates; circumstances made it easy for them to qualify as privateers. From about 1810, the Spanish possessions in Central and South America erupted with revolutionary fervor and wars of independence. New Orleans became the focus of so-called patriotic support—its American character supplying the libertarian ideals, its French character the hostility to Spain, its mercantile character on the lookout for a speculative investment. Although the population of New Orleans condoned and participated in such activities, the United States government was acutely embarrassed, having no wish in the early stages to arouse the already suspicious Spaniards. Equally the government lacked effective means of suppressing these violators of American neutrality. As in the case of the pirates, the government was loath to imperil its relations with Spain but cooperated to some extent with public opinion in disregarding—or at best coping remarkably inefficiently —with violations of the peace between the two countries. These violations are generally known as "filibustering" expeditions. The French word for pirate is *flibustier,* and the filibusters who congregated in New Orleans often had more in common with the Delta pirates than with Latin America patriots.

Until 1821, and the achievement of independence by Mexico, filibuster expeditions supported Latin American independence; after 1821 they were against existing governments, independent or otherwise. Mexico and Texas were the main causes to fire the city's imagination. The Mexican Association was founded in New Orleans about the time of the Louisiana Purchase, led predictably by those ambitious schemers Daniel Clark and Edward Livingstone to plot the "liberation" of Mexico, which together with the western states of the Union would form a separate American nation. Hidalgo, curate of Dolores, raised the flag of revolt in Mexico in 1810 and the next year sent an agent to the United States to collect funds. Support was organized in New Orleans, and a march into Texas from Natchitoches in northwest Louisiana was the first of many filibustering expeditions. Remarkably the expedition got as far as San Antonio before being defeated by Spanish forces.

New Orleans had a ready supply of volunteers to fight for its adopted causes—a large body of unemployed, fed by immigrants and boatmen, and after the demobilization of Jackson's forces, many would-be soldiers found themselves on the street. The villain of George Cable's story "Posson' Jone'," Jules St. Ange, a professional gambler, weighed the merits of gambling versus filibustering to recover his debts. Military tendencies were encouraged by the social popularity of militia companies. Financial backing was easy to find; New Orleans merchants were great speculators (fortunes could be made in less than five years, it was reckoned in that boom city) and made loans to patriotic leaders in return for promises of land and trading advantages. A profitable business was begun in supplying them with arms. Merchants weighed their chances over the tables of Banks Arcade, a huge office building and meeting place just off Canal Street; their deliberations were openly reported in the press and clubs of the city, while the Mexican and other patriots led shadowy lives, anxiously avoiding the limelight. The Spanish authorities maintained an intelligence network, with some success, judging by the failure of several expeditions. For many years the head of the network was allegedly the much admired priest at St. Louis Cathedral, Father Antonio de Sedella, whom Claiborne described as "a very dangerous man" and accused of fomenting the Negroes against the new American government.*

---

*Sedella's saintly reputation certainly jars with authority's opinion of him. Claiborne wrote of the "interruption of public tranquillity by the ambitions of a refractory monk supported in his apostasy by a misguided populace." Sedella had first arrived in New Orleans during Miro's administration as a representative of the Inquisition; Miro had packed him off as soon as he discovered this, but Sedella later returned as an "ordinary parish priest."

In 1819, under the treaty of Florida, Spain surrendered Florida to the United States. (Four years earlier a group of wild New Orleanians had considered capturing Florida from Spain and selling it to the United States, the proceeds of the sale to be spent on arms for the Mexican revolution. Nothing came of the project except a scare for the Spanish authorities.) Under the terms of the treaty, the United States waived its claims to Texas, much to the rage of local liberals. In the next two years, expeditions into Texas were regularly organized in New Orleans, and on one occasion fifty-three people were arrested for planning to make "an irruption" into the area. Little wonder that New Orleans had a reputation for turbulence and "foreign tendencies." During the 1820s and 1830s, thanks to its early involvement in Texas on behalf of Mexican revolutionaries, the city became the stepping-off ground for Texan emigrants. Inevitably the outbreak of the Texan War of Independence aroused boundless enthusiasm in the city. The Mexican government complained to the American that Texans "were daily obtaining from New Orleans assistance of all kinds—in silver and soldiery who publicly enlist in that city carry with them arms against a friendly nation." General Sam Houston came to New Orleans in 1836 to have a wound treated, and Stephen Austin, another Texan leader, was overwhelmed by the violent enthusiasm aroused by his visit the same year to raise funds (he managed to raise $300,000 and wrote gratefully that "the cause of liberty and Texas stands high in this city"). Banks Arcade was full of plans and committees to aid the Texans, a benefit performance was given at the American Theatre, and the city taverns were full of would-be volunteers. "The whole city is like a military station," wrote Austin's cousin, Mary Holley. "The public squares are occupied with tents, recruiting parties—military bands are playing, flags are flying, streets are filled with soldiers." Volunteers, "hastening to the succour of the oppressed but brave and gallant Texans" but also causing a serious problem of law and order, were asked to sign up at the Rising Sun Tavern, situated by the levee conveniently for out-of-work Irish laborers and boatmen waiting for a passage upriver.

New Orleans' support for the war was not entirely disinterested;

Texas as a slave-holding state in the Union would ease the balance of slave states against other, non-slave territories being admitted to statehood elsewhere. At a Banks Arcade meeting attended by Sam Houston, a resolution was passed that "the doctrine which would exclude a new territory because slavery exists in it, conveys . . . an injurious imputation to the slave-holding states already in the Union."

Discontented Latin Americans continued to visit New Orleans to enlist support for attacks on their governments. By far the most disastrous filibustering expedition to leave New Orleans was that of General Narciso Lopez against Cuba in 1851. In the latter half of the century Cuba replaced Mexico as the principal focus of filibustering activity. In New Orleans manifest destiny (already a "motivating factor" in American life but still to be formulated as an official doctrine) became a kind of idealized land grabbing; behind the idealization—the freeing of an oppressed people, the bequest to them of the benefits of American rule—lay the fact of Cuban sugar's competing against Louisiana sugar. Lopez and his exiled companions first came to New Orleans in 1850. Posters advertising his proposed expedition to Cuba were already up around town calling for volunteers. Attempts by the federal government to prevent the expedition's leaving town aroused a storm of protest, and when Lopez was arrested after the failure of his expedition and his return to New Orleans, no one would come forward to bring evidence of his violation of American neutrality, and charges had to be dropped. The following year the news reached New Orleans of a rebellion in Cuba. Citizens were summoned to aid the rebels, military parades were held, and volunteer organizations appealed once again to the city's enthusiasm for putting on a uniform. Cuban bonds were issued to raise money for a new expedition to be led by Lopez. Federal agents were on the point of confiscating the transport vessels and arresting the leaders when the expedition sailed from the port—a fiasco of bad planning as a result of its hasty departure. Less than three weeks later, New Orleans heard that the expedition had been scattered and that an entire company of fifty-one men, all American including its commander, had been captured by the Spanish authorities and executed, and their bodies publicly displayed in Havana. Uproar, of course. New Orleans was in the throes of Know Nothing, or Native American, struggles, feeling against foreigners was running high as a result, and the Spanish consul on this occasion was considered a legitimate scapegoat. The consulate was ransacked and the consul burned in effigy (the consul himself was protected by the famous duelist Pepe Llulla); cigar stores, Catalan taverns, and the Spanish vegetable market were looted. The Spanish government protested, but debate among the Americans established the principle that the government of the United States could not be responsible for the acts of a mob. Resolutions were passed at Banks Arcade to take revenge on Cuba but this time it seems the impetuous citizens had learned a lesson—too many fingers and purses had been burned and Cuba was left briefly in peace.

New Orleans did become, however, the center of the growing national ambition to annex Cuba, toward the end of the antebellum period recommending annexation as adding another slave state to the South. *De Bow's Review,* an outspoken economic review published in New Orleans and frequently voicing the opinion of the city establishment, declared in 1854 that "if we hold Cuba, in the next fifty years we will hold the destiny of the richest and most increased commerce that ever dazzled the cupidity of men."

The Tennessee filibuster William Walker found money and men in New Orleans; he had already led two filibustering expeditions to North Mexico when New Orleans investors, hoping for profitable investment opportunities, interested him in Nicaragua, where a revolution was in progress. In 1855 Walker sailed to Nicaragua with only fifty-eight men, captured Granada, and gained control of the country, naming himself president. He was soon ousted and returned to New Orleans, where he was later arrested for violating the neutrality laws. But filibustering was Walker's life. He sailed again for Nicaragua in 1857, was intercepted by the American navy, and brought back to the United States. In 1860 leading an expedition to Honduras, he was caught and executed by a firing squad.

Major Burke was director general of the New Orleans World Exposition in 1884, where he met Louis Bogran, president of Honduras. Bogram granted Burke territorial concessions, which made him "the dictator, practically, of the mining as well as the fruit shipping interests of Honduras." Burke was also state treasurer and was shortly after exposed as a bond frauder. He had fortunately made his escape to London before being indicted for fraud and embezzlement. Neither Burke nor the Hondurans, however, seem to have been daunted by the charge, for Burke was later to be found settled very comfortably in Honduras, no doubt enjoying the fruits of his earlier contacts. Many and diverse were New Orleans' links with Latin America.

Even after the morality of filibustering declared with such aplomb in Banks Arcade on so many occasions had become government policy and the nerve center had moved from New Orleans to Washington, ex-filibusters used to congregate in dockside bars along Decatur and Gallatin Streets, providing material for starry-eyed romantics. Some of the city's filibustering notoriety still lingers on; since World War I, New Orleans has been a refuge for all kinds of political refugees from Latin America, to whom the city appears the nearest to their Latin environment they will find in the United States—Hondurans, Nicaraguans, Mexicans, and, particularly since Castro's revolution, Cubans. There are enough Spaniards in the Irish Channel for them to have their own cinema—with the pleasantly escapist name of The Happy Hour—and their own Baptist church, the First Spanish-American Baptist Church in Coliseum Square.

There was an earlier reminder of a filibustering past in 1930, when a solemn ceremony was held to dedicate Bolivar Place to Simon Bolivar, liberator of Venezuela, on the centenary of his death; an expedition had been fitted out in New Orleans in 1822 to go to the aid of Bolivar in his battle for independence. Smuggling has its more recent aspects too, the Mississippi Delta proving ideal terrain for bootlegging during Prohibition as William Faulkner recalled; he worked for a bootlegger who used to run a launch down the Industrial Canal, across Lake Pontchartrain and out into the Gulf, where the schooner from Cuba had brought the raw alcohol and buried it in the sand.

But, in general, pirates and privateers, smuggling and filibustering, are part of the noise and sometimes dubious glamour of New Orleans' past and only in the darker recesses of the docks perhaps (less dark but still a reminder is the so-called "smuggle-proof" fence that surrounds the city's free-trade zone) or out on Grand Isle, home of the Baratarians, can one catch a glimpse of the sense of undisciplined adventure which was once so popular. Ties with Latin America are still strong but are prosaically commercial; most of New Orleans' trade is with Latin America and the great banana wharves by the Mississippi Bridge are some of the busiest in the port. The city's reputation as the coffee centre of the United States is not wholly based on the fact that you can buy a decent cup of coffee there; it is also the main importing city for South American coffee. The ceramic street names in the Quarter are a reminder of the past; the unexciting reminders of the present are notices in Canal Street indicating "se habla espanol."

6. The Americans

THE NEW AMERICAN RULERS of New Orleans were by no means cowed by the profound distaste with which they were regarded by most of the Creole population, as well as by many American residents who considered themselves better qualified than Claiborne and his deputy Wilkinson to act as governor of the new territory. As far as local government was concerned, however, Americans living in New Orleans were there to make money ("their limbs, their heads and their hearts move to that sole object," wrote the engineer-architect Benjamin Latrobe) and were, within limits, content to leave the business of government to the Creoles; most of the Americans were there only for six months of the year anyway, abandoning it between May and October to the heat, mosquitoes, and epidemics of yellow fever. "The North Americans live in a retired manner, and centre all their cares in that of returning rich to their native district," wrote the British diplomat Charles Murray; "the better American families, as soon as they have amassed a fortune answering to their expectations, prefer to remove to the north."

The sense of commercial security that resulted from the establishment of American control of the mouth of the Mississippi now began to lead toward the fulfilment of that improbable optimism expressed by such earlier visitors as Father Charlevoix. In 1804 the English ambassador in Washington wrote home of Jefferson's obsession with Louisiana; the President had informed him that "the Influx of Americans and Persons of other Nations into the town of New Orleans . . . has been so astonishingly great, that it had already become almost impossible for them to be accomodated with Habitations of any Kind." So enthused was Jefferson with the city's economic prospects that he hoped the British would think it worth appointing a consul there. The British waited until the Battle of New Orleans finally destroyed any hope they might have retained of ever controlling the Mississippi valley, appointing one in 1816.*

To control the unruly elements and swelling numbers of people in New Orleans, and to reconcile older residents to the fact of American rule was a difficult and delicate job. Even though there were probably few candidates for the post of governor, Claiborne was not an ideal choice.

William C.C. Claiborne was born in Virginia in 1775. He studied law and settled in Tennessee, where he became a territorial judge. In 1802 he was appointed governor of the Mississippi Territory; a year later he was appointed commissioner, along with James Wilkinson, to take over Louisiana. In 1804, after Louisiana had been divided into Orleans Territory and Louisiana Territory, Claiborne became governor of Orleans Territory. In a letter to the authorities, he wrote that the natives of New Orleans were "ill-fitted to be useful citizens of a Republic". In spite of the criticism he endlessly incurred as an appointed governor, he was elected governor of Louisiana when it achieved statehood in 1812, and in 1816 he was elected senator for the new state. A contemporary described him as "of fine personal appearance, but in all other respects, a coarse rude man, and at the same time, very sharp and knowing as most Americans are." He was not calculated to appeal to the New Orleanians. For his part,

---

*The consulate was maintained until 1969 when it was closed down, to the indignation of New Orleanians. "The Empire has decided to go where the action is," wrote the *Times-Picayune,* and that apparently was no longer New Orleans, despite energetic protests lodged with the consulate by the Dames of the British Empire, Transatlantic Parents, and the Brides Association.

Claiborne had few illusions about them; he described them, with the puritanical fervor of a young man in his twenties, as "uninformed, indolent, luxurious," thereby fostering a legend that the Creoles have never really lived down, nor wanted to perhaps. He told Madison he regarded the situation in the city as most insecure; "The materials for a mob are abundant, and it requires all my vigilance to prevent disorders. There are adventurers here from several different nations"—American, French and Spanish—"who possess a great share of national pride, and whose jealousies and resentments might easily be excited.

"The credulity of the people is only equalled by their ignorance, and a virtuous magistrate, resting entirely for support on suffrage and the good will of his fellow citizens in this quarter would at any time be exposed to immediate ruin by the machinations of a few base individuals," Americans for the most part. "I must confess, Sir," he told Madison, "I apprehend more trouble from some imprudent Americans who are here, than from any of the natives." Foremost among such disturbers of the peace in the city were the supporters of Aaron Burr, among them at one point Claiborne's own second-in-command, General Wilkinson. Burr had earlier been Vice-President of the Union but fell from political power after he killed Alexander Hamilton in a duel. Burr hoped to regain power by exploiting, with Wilkinson's help, the discontents of settlers beyond the Appalachians. Encouraged in his plans by New Orleanians he had met in Washington, Burr sailed down to the city in 1805 (arriving Cleopatra-like in "an elegant Barge" with "sails, colours and oars") in the course of an exploratory visit to the western boundaries of the country, during which he raised support by advertising a war of "liberation" against Spain and Spanish possessions, intending to use that support to persuade Western settlers to secede. New Orleans, as the largest and richest center in the South and West, was central to his conspiracy; it was also further from government resistance and attack. Within the city, American residents from before the Purchase, resentful of Federal authority, formed a powerful Burr clique. It included Daniel Clark, American consul in New Orleans before the Purchase; Edward Livingstone, the brilliant, ambitious lawyer from

New York, who had emigrated to New Orleans after being suspected of embezzling city-council funds; Evan Jones, another lawyer; and Wilkinson, who had introduced his friend Burr to Clark. Neither Clark nor Livingstone was adverse to a little conspiracy, though Clark later had cold feet and wrote a vicious attack against Wilkinson and his connection with Burr.

After leaving New Orleans, Burr returned briefly to Washington and then set out once more for the West, sailing down the Mississippi with an expedition of boats and armed supporters, relying on Wilkinson and his other American allies in New Orleans to rally Creole support. Wilkinson, however, had concluded that his chances were too slim and was now backing Claiborne; in New Orleans he ordered the restoration of Carondelet's fortifications (most of which had been torn down for firewood), as much to overawe New Orleanians as to keep out Burr and his supposed army. The city was put under martial law, to the rage of the Creoles, several of whom were arrested. Moreover, it was Wilkinson's men who finally arrested Burr upriver at Natchez. Burr was later tried for treason in spite of his claims that he was putting himself at the head of a filibustering expedition against Spanish rule in neighboring Texas. Wilkinson, who narrowly avoided a trial for high treason himself, claimed to have saved the constitution; no one seems to have listened to his trumpet-blowing, however, and, he retired to Mexico where he eventually died.

Poor Claiborne complained, "England has her partisans, Ferdinand the Seventh, some faithful subjects; Bonaparte his admirers; and there is a fourth description of men, commonly called Burrites, who would join any standard which would promise rapine and plunder." More cheerfully he seized the opportunity to expel a number of unwelcome residents, including the Marquis de Casa Calvo.

"Great exertions have been made (and with too much success) to foment differences between the native Americans and the native Louisianians," wrote Claiborne. "Every incident is laid hold of to widen the breach." Such incidents, less political than Burr's conspiracy, were frequent, many of them ending in duels, a San Domingo pastime that became very much *de rigueur* after the arrival of so many exiles from the island. Human life was a cheap commodity in New Orleans, and social antagonisms pervaded the highest circles; financial disputes were also more easily settled by a duel than by litigation. The German merchant Vincent Nolte, who found himself settling his financial disputes with duels, attributed the popularity of dueling to the character of the city, "a place of refuge for every description of schemers and scamps." Fencing academies were opened on Exchange Alley just off Canal Street, three of them by free coloreds from San Domingo. Everyone had to learn to fight a duel. The well-to-do used rapiers or pistols; and after the robust tastes of the Americans made themselves felt, the bowie knife became popular. Walt Whitman wrote of his character Daggerdraw Bowieknife that "he would cavil upon the hundredth part of a hair if he thought a bit of a fight was to be got out of his antagonist." Fencing masters were said to earn as much by blackmailing prospective victims—not to fight duels with them—as by their teaching. The most famous instructor, Pepe Llulla, a fervent Spanish loyalist (it was he who protected the Spanish consul against the New Orleans mob in 1851), offered to take on any insurrectionist brave enough to accept the challenge; he was believed to keep a cemetery for those he killed, where the St. Vincent de Paul cemetery is now on Louisa Avenue.*

Favorite dueling spots were in St. Antony's Square behind the Cathedral, now a peaceful retreat in the tourist hurly-burly of the French Quarter, or beneath some magnificent live oaks in what is now City Park, which were then behind the Halfway House on Metairie Ridge and were relatively safe from police interference. Duels were often attended by large cheering crowds. "There were more duels than there were days in the year," sniffed Harriet Martineau. "Fifteen on one Sunday morning. In 1835 there were a hundred and two duels fought between January and the end of April . . . all but one of the hundred and two were for frivolous causes." There were remarkably few deaths considering the prevalence of the

---

*The origin of this story lies in the fact that Llulla later retired to a truck farm on what is now the cemetery, where he and his family are buried.

custom; with a knife or sword it was sufficent to draw blood, and dueling pistols were notoriously inaccurate. But there are several laconic inscriptions in St. Louis cemeteries—"mort sur le champ d'honneur," "victime de son honneur," "pour garder intacte le nom de famille."

An anti-dueling association was formed in 1834, but as it was chaired by Bernard de Marigny, who in his younger days was a prolific duelist, it is not surprising that the association had little effect. A court of honor was set up a year later to assess cases that might otherwise be settled by death, but the duel remained the quickest, the most effective, and therefore the most popular form of settlement. The state constitution of 1848 disfranchised duelists but ultimately it was the Civil War and the less chivalrous violence of Reconstruction that eclipsed the habit. The last duel was fought in 1889, the last challenge issued (but not accepted) in the early 1900s.

The boom years of New Orleans, so closely associated with the American purchase, did not really get under way until the British threat to American possession and American trade was finally removed after the War of 1812. The war itself, sparked by British attempts to impress sailors from American ships, had a disastrous effect on the New Orleans economy. Business was at a standstill because of the close British blockade of the river mouth, and the situation within the city worsened in the summer of 1812 when a violent hurricane tore off most of the roofs and wrecked eighteen vessels in the port. Claiborne had little difficulty in raising volunteers for a defense force outside New Orleans, where many of the rural inhabitants were still inspired by anti-British feeling from the War of Independence, but in New Orleans, race again entered into the issue. Creoles refused to serve under American officers and *vice versa.* Rival committees were formed by the American and British communities for the defense of the city. A British expedition arrived in the Gulf in September 1814, conducting a number of engagements with scattered American units in the Delta area. In December 1814 the advance on New Orleans began.

By then the city's defenses had been taken over by Andrew Jackson, already famous for his successes against warring Indians. Jackson arrived downriver from Tennessee with about fifteen hundred men —some volunteers, some militia, the volunteers including the five hundred men of General Coffee's brigade, renowned for their marksmanship. To the New Orleanians, however, they were all "Kaintucks" like the boatmen who made such a nuisance of themselves in the city. The extent of Jackson's bad relations with the city is illustrated by his threatening to burn the city ("to imitate the example of the Russians at Moscow, and consign the whole city to the flames") rather than let it fall into British hands, while the Louisiana legislature meeting in New Orleans debated whether it would not be better to surrender the city to the British before Jackson could carry out his threat. The British had no better opinion of Jackson's backwoodsmen and particularly resented their harassing British pickets at night; an enemy was to them always an enemy, wrote one British combatant; "to us at least it appeared an ungenerous return to barbarity."

The fiasco of the Battle of New Orleans, which eventually took place on January 8th about ten miles below New Orleans at Chalmette, has been described elsewhere many times. A frontal assault by the five thousand British led by their commander, General Pakenham (Wellington's brother-in-law, a relationship much emphasized by the Americans as if marriage should have bequeathed military skill) was to have been assisted by support from the flank but this materialized too late, and the assault on the well-entrenched American forces, hindered by the fact that the British had forgotten their scaling ladders, became a massacre; there were over two thousand British casualties compared with seventy-one American. After the battle the British sent to Jackson asking a truce in which to bury the dead; Jackson replied that he had no dead to bury but allowed the British twenty-four hours in which to bury theirs.

"Never perhaps was bravery more abused by the unskilfulness of leaders," wrote Harriet Martineau, one of many British tourists taken by their American hosts to the macabre memorial at Chalmette. Most of the original battlefield is now beneath the river, but the effect is carefully preserved in an open grassy space, a national cemetery beyond, and beyond that (and the cloud-capped smoke stacks of an aluminum plant) the great moss-draped oaks beneath which Pakenham died of his wounds. A pretty little plantation house contains a museum that explains the victory all too explicitly, with its display of some overconfident Punch cartoons of the period. "One of the most unintelligent manoeuvres in the history of British warfare," wrote a more recent but equally sharp-tongued critic, Winston Churchill. The victory was celebrated in the Place d'Armes with parades and girls dancing through a triumphal arch, beneath which the general was crowned with laurels by Mrs. Livingstone. Jackson paid a special visit to the Ursulines, who had prayed all day on the eighth for his victory. Only the bad relations between Jackson and New Orleans' leading citizens marred the celebrations. The state legislature, fuming at Jackson's high-handed refusal to deal with them in mobilizing the city before the battle, passed a vote of thanks to the troops who had fought in the battle, which blatantly omitted all mention of their leader. In spite of rumors that peace had been signed, Jackson refused to rescind martial law, arrested the writer of an article criticizing his actions, and banished from the city a judge who issued the writer with a writ of *habeas corpus*. The same judge later fined Jackson $1000 for contempt of court, which an enthusiastic crowd at Maspero's Exchange collected for the general; in an unusually generous gesture he asked that it be given to the war bereaved.

January 8th is still commemorated in New Orleans as Jackson Day, organized by the United States Daughters of 1812; a special mass is celebrated by the Ursulines and, as the *Times-Picayune* put it in a recent headline, "Jackson Day Celebrations Blur Vision, Swell Hearts."

Jackson returned to New Orleans in 1828, when he was a candidate for the Presidency, to be given a tremendous welcome in spite of some unpleasant debate in the legislature over the huge bill for his entertainment expenses. Again in 1840, when he was invited for the twenty-fifth anniversary of the battle, he avoided partisan politics by carefully dividing his attentions between Creoles and Americans, staying at the New St. Louis Hotel in the French Quarter and attending the St. Charles Theatre in the American Quarter. During this visit the base for a momument to the battle was dedicated, and sixteen years later an equestrian statue of Jackson was put on top of it and the Place d'Armes renamed after him. Chalmette also has a monument, which has grown as slowly as a redwood tree, and even at the beginning of this century was still a truncated tower; only recently has it earned its claim to be a Southern rival to the Washington Memorial.

With the war ended, New Orleans began money-making in earnest. The blockade was lifted. The first steamboat had come downriver in 1812; in 1827, 287 steamboats arrived. It was a wonder of the New World, which much impressed home and overseas visitors, to see them lined up alongside the wharves, which were piled high with as vast a range of merchandise as could be found in any American port, but especially cotton and sugar, evidence of the burgeoning slave economy of the countryside. "You may search the world over to find the science of money-making reduced to such perfection and become of such all-engrossing influence as in New Orleans," wrote the New Yorker Oakey Hall. The population grew from about eight thousand in 1803 to at least sixty thousand in 1836 (only about half of whom however were year-round residents).

A new city was growing up beyond the confines of the old city to house those six-monthly traders so despised by the regular inhabitants, on what was once the Jesuit plantation. At the end of the eighteenth century, the area had already been divided into streets and squares by the Gravier owners, but at the time of the Purchase, few houses had been built on the lots, and most of the land was more profitably occupied by small market gardens supplying the city with fruit and vegetables. In the early years of the nineteenth century, flatboats and keelboats coming down the river began to find it more convenient to tie up by the batture along Faubourg Ste. Marie, as the area was known after one of the Gravier wives, than to join the seagoing vessels along the older docks. By 1816 the lower end of Tchoupitoulas Street along the river was thriving with the Midwest trade of the Mississippi valley.

The growth of the American Quarter in the 1830s and 1840s was largely due to Samuel Peters and James Caldwell, two imaginative speculators who turned to it as an alternative after Bernard de Marigny rejected their development offers downriver of the old city. Both men, in their very different ways, were typical of the speculative entrepreneurs who founded the city's greatness in the second quarter of the century. Peters, who was from the North, arrived in New Orleans in 1821 from New York where, with considerable foresight, he had worked with a French firm and lived with a French family to prepare himself for this most French of American cities. According to his autobiography, "at that time the city was looked upon as a vast graveyard and that none who went from New England ever returned; and every effort was made by his relatives to dissuade him from so fearful a project. Happily they did not succeed." Instead he made himself a fortune in the New Orleans grocery business in a very short time and married a Creole girl from San Domingo. Caldwell, on the other hand, was English by birth and an actor by profession; he first came to New Orleans in 1820, when he temporarily took over the St. Philip Theatre and staged some English plays where hitherto only French had been the rule. Caldwell himself modestly claimed to have been the first to establish English drama "on a firm basis and correct principles." His ambition was to have a permanent English theatre in the city, and his St. Charles Theatre above Canal Street was later one of the most dazzling projects in the new suburb.

Caldwell and Peters appreciated that the growing American population were becoming less tolerant of the city's conservatism as manifested in the Creole control of the city's development. In spite of the almost total lack of organization and haphazard docking and port facilities along Tchoupitoulas Street, the city refused to extend the wharves beyond the old city. Clairborne, in the early days of American rule, had gone out of his way to placate the Creoles with as many administrative posts within the city as possible, but this state of affairs could hardly continue with the development of a new American-style city above Canal. With the help of other speculators, such as Thomas Banks (the builder of Banks Arcade), Caldwell and Peters bought a large part of the Gravier holdings and proceeded to build their own city in the Faubourg Ste. Marie. By 1824 Caldwell had his first theater there, the first important building in the area. Others soon followed: hotels such as the palatial St. Charles and the slightly more cosy Verandah, banks, shops, offices, and, perhaps most important of all, the New Basin Canal along what is now Poydras Street providing a link with Lake Pontchartrain so that the new merchants no longer had to depend on the clogged waters of the Carondelet Canal. By 1835 the Faubourg Ste. Marie exceeded the old city in wealth and rivaled it in population. Such an expansion was incompatible with the conservatism of the city council. It was estimated one year that a million dollars' worth of damage was done to commerce in the Faubourg Ste. Marie from unpaved streets; Harriet Martineau noticed that ladies walked more in New Orleans than elsewhere, "from the streets being in such bad order as to make walking the safest means of locomotion." Yet when an enterprising American, a Mr. Duncan, imported a few yards of "curb stones" to lay around his property, the authorties decreed that all sidewalks must be built of cypress.*

It was Peters who finally proposed the division of the city into separate municipalities, after his efforts to reconcile the Creoles to innovations and civic improvements had met with total failure. In 1836 the city was divided into three municipalities, hopefully to create "a wholesome spirit of enterprise and emulation": the First Municipality comprising the old French Quarter; the Second Municipality, the Faubourg Ste. Marie; and the Third Municipality, the Faubourg Marigny below Esplanade Avenue, which was rapidly becoming the first home of thousands of Irish and German immigrants. Each municipality had its own administration, its own budget (mainly from wharf dues), and its own police force, and a mayor and council were elected for the whole city. Each "dirties or cleans its own causeways, puts out its own fires with its own reservoirs, fines its own rowdies, and puts itself into debt without the vulgar interference of neighbours." This last was all too easily achieved. The new system was crippled almost from the outset by the financial crisis of

---

*As late as 1949, it was reckoned that only half of New Orleans' streets were paved.

1837; fourteen banks suspended payment of specie and, in an effort to save the city's economy, each municipality issued its own currency in order to have more money in circulation.

Only the Second Municipality made a full recovery from this blow and rushed ahead to ever-greater prosperity; the First and Third Municipalities stagnated—"there is but little change going on in the First and Third Municipalities," wrote Bishop Whipple, "from the fact perhaps that the foreign population of these parts of the city have not so much 'go ahead' in their disposition." Soon the American Quarter had cables and gas lighting in the streets, which had previously been lit by whale-oil lamps slung on chains across the road. The company that provided the gas had been set up by the versatile Caldwell, who hoped to recoup his investments in the second St. Charles Theatre, built after the earlier building had burned down in 1842. There was even some rudimentary drainage. Speculators hurried to the city to buy up and "subdivide" plantations into profitable real estate ventures. New Orleans embodied the American myth of instant wealth, which enticed so many from Europe. Not only impoverished Germans, Irish, and Italians but also marveling tourists found in this Southern city—in spite of their frequent carping at its imperfections—an almost ideal combination of the New and Old Worlds: the new with its vigorous crude expansionism, the old with its slower, more cultured way of life—a contrast that is still valid today. Most enjoyed the contrast. Europeans coming from the North found New Orleans a gayer, more relaxed place by reason of its Latin heritage; others were more aware of the flaws and the unhappy contrast between the expanding American district and the "decayed town of Europe"—decay hastened, according to many, especially Northerners, by Creole shortsightedness. In 1840, for instance, absentee French landlords of Chartres Street, the main shopping emporium of the city, decided to raise their rents by about 15 percent, as a result of which most of their American tenants left to open shop on Canal Street.

It was so cosmopolitan—that more than anything else delighted the visitor. "Here in half an hour you can see, and speak to, Frenchmen, Spaniards, Danes, Swedes, Germans, Englishmen, Portuguese,

Hollanders, Mexicans, Kentuckians, Tennesseans . . . and a motley group of Indians, Quadroons, Africans etc.," wrote William Darby in his Emigrants' Directory of 1817. Overcharacterized accounts are full of swarthy Spaniards, elegant Frenchmen, beautiful Creoles, and the accounts themselves were written by authors from all manner of countries. "New Orleans seems to have been built by a *universal subscription,* to which every European nation contributed a street, as it certainly has citizens." And Oakey Hall wrote, "If ever there is to be a Congress of Nations, let it be held in New Orleans; there will be no mileage for delegates." By the 1840s New Orleans was the third largest city in the Union. The city's *Daily Delta* exclaimed in January 1850; "We have never seen so many people pressing into our city," adding with a touch of spring, "the weather is mild, balmy and spring like, and everybody seems to be smiling and happy. Altogether New Orleans is at present a very gay—it is at all times a pleasant—place." Even that critical visitor the Duke of Saxe Weimar wrote that "no day passed over this winter, which did not produce something pleasant and interesting." Some people had the temerity to complain about the high cost of living but, as one inhabitant told Frederick Olmsted, "What they think treats in New York they consider necessities here." During the winter season the city became, by common consesus, the gayest place in the Union.

Some approved of this gaiety, others strongly disapproved. Bishop Whipple wrote of the "morals" of New Orleans: "I will say they are decidedly bad and I would not desire a young friend of mine to form his character under the influences of this depraved city." Anthony Trollope's mother, who spent three days in the city, thought it offered little that would gratify "the eye of taste" but allowed that there was much "novelty and interest" for the newly arrived European.*

One valid criticism of the city was its lack of education. Most critics agreed that the average New Orleanian was badly educated

*Mrs. Trollope was much criticized for her unfavorable comments, but Mark Twain wrote that "of all those tourists I like Dame Trollope best. She found a 'civilisation' here" which she spoke of "in plain terms, plain and unsugared".

by contemporary standards and deplored the lack of intellectual stimuli in the form of good schools, colleges, or libraries. Oakey Hall bewailed the fact that "taste in the fine arts and love of the belles lettres have hitherto fallen victims to the smell of trade." That earnest bluestocking Harriet Martineau, while admitting the city to be an interesting study, declared that it was the last place "where one who prized his Humanity would wish to live." The situation was partly remedied, however, through the generosity of John McDonogh. McDonogh was a strange character, another of New Orleans legends. He came to the city from Baltimore shortly after the Purchase and swiftly made a fortune in real estate. Having apparently led a riotously gay life amid the city's high society, he suddenly decided he had had enough and retired to the West Bank. Few knew what he did with his money, some of it made rather dubiously from leasing brothels on Perdido Street. Most of his huge West Bank plantation now lies beneath the Mississippi. His professed philosophy, it was discovered after his death in 1850 (and engraved on his tombstone), was that "without temperance there is no health; without virtue no order; without religion no happiness; and the sum of our being is to live wisely, soberly and righteously"—not precepts normally held in high regard in New Orleans. On his death it was also discovered that he had left most of his vast fortune to the cities of New Orleans and Baltimore and their public-school systems, and some forty-five schools were set up in New Orleans under this bequest.

The New Orleans Sunday was another object of attack, particularly from Northerners, such as Bishop Leonidas Polk, who called New Orleans "a city of moral darkness and papal superstition." "It is the Sabbath!" cried Henry Didimus. "Here the noisiest day of the week—so full of strange contrasts, of lights and shadows, crossing and recrossing each other, of the grave and gay, saints and sinners." Not at all like Sundays in New England (Latrobe in 1817 had wondered how the intermarriage of Americans and French would produce a less rigid observance of the gloom of an English Sunday), where such proceedings would be regarded as highly indecent. Sunday was the busiest day of the week. "It is a day of toil, not in business but in pleasure seeking," complained Bishop Whipple in his journal; "this is the day of *military parade* and review . . . a day of pomp and parade . . . It is but a few Sabbaths since that the Reverend Mr. Wheaton of the Episcopal Church was obliged to quit preaching and dismiss his congregation on account of the noise and confusion of the military." "Shops were open and singing and guitar playing in the streets, for which in New York or Philadelphia one would be put in prison," wrote the Duke of Saxe Weimar.

An industrious tourist would be up at dawn to visit the market down by the levee, the most cosmopolitan spot in this contemporary Babel. Then to the cathedral, where the smartest congregation in the city would be wandering in, white and colored. In the afternoon all New Orleans would promenade on the levee opposite the cathedral, or along the shell road leading to the Metairie Race Course, "that celebrated theatre for young men" which is now Metairie Cemetery. Rather late upon the scene was the Crescent City Cricket Club, founded in 1858 to introduce "this manly game" to the South; teams surprisingly were composed of both whites and Negroes. And in the evening there was the opera or the theater, followed by a ball. Even today there is no feeling against entertaining lavishly on a Sunday; after all, "religion ought to inspire cheerfulness, and cheerfulness is associated with religion," went one accommodating argument. Breakfast on Sunday in New Orleans is a noontide feast, with absinthe frappé and mint juleps, grillades and grits, baked bananas, biscuits, and coffee laced with Grande Marnier. Churchgoing has always had an air of party-going; the crowds bustling in and out of Episcopal, Lutheran, Presbyterian, Baptist, and Catholic churches on Sunday mornings along St. Charles Avenue seem to be moving from one temple to another as to a long line of cocktail parties. Services at the cathedral used to be advertised in the American press as worth a visit, and Didimus was not alone in rhapsodizing on the much-vaunted Creole beauty, which could be seen at the Catholic mass on Sundays.

However uneducated the Creole might be considered, it was due to him—and especially to the San Domingo Creole—that New Orleans became such a center for theater and opera in the mid-nineteenth century and the only American city where French opera and plays could regularly be seen ("given in great perfection," according to James Silk Buckingham), many having their American premieres in New Orleans. The first theater in the city was opened on St. Philip Street by San Domingo Creoles, the scene of Jacobin disturbances; the emotional tendencies of the predominantly Latin audience are reflected in regulations issued for their control: "No one will be allowed to throw or to pretend to throw oranges or anything else, be it in the theater or in any part of the hall, nor in a word, shall anyone be allowed to start quarrels with his neighbour or with anyone; nor shall anyone insult anybody or come to blows or speak ill of anyone in order to stir up trouble." The Jacobin activities of the theater by no means ended with Spanish rule, for an act of 1804 ordered that "the orchestras of the hall cannot be subject to fanciful demands of play this or that tune," reflecting the same divisions of opinion between two nationalities as the public balls. The St. Philip Theatre was built on the street of that name in 1807, but was soon superseded by the much larger Orleans Theatre built by John Davies (who first came to New Orleans in 1811 and made his fortune running gambling halls) on Orleans Street and opened in 1819 by the first drama group from France. Performances were said to last with Oriental longevity from six in the evening until two or three the following morning and to include several French plays. The theater was famous for its grilled boxes for those in mourning. In 1820 Caldwell took over the St. Philip Theatre temporarily with his English troupe; his introduction of English drama to the city, with its growing American clientele, was so successful that he proposed building an English theater in Faubourg Marigny. This was among the suggestions rejected by Marigny which Caldwell and Peters then took to the Faubourg Ste. Marie. Here the American Theatre was completed in 1823, seating eleven hundred people. It obeyed local custom by scheduling Sunday performances, but these were mostly attended by tourists and Creoles; the Anglo-Saxon Sabbath died hard, even in a Latin graveyard. Ten years later Caldwell built a second, even more magnificent, theater, the St. Charles, one of the wonders of the New World according to visitors and certainly one of its largest theaters; it was built between May and November in 1835, despite ninety days of continuous rain.

By 1850 there were three English theaters outside the French Quarter. Within the Quarter the Orleans Theatre was known for its superior acting and staging—it employed only European actors, and imported scenery and costumes from France—but the lavishness of the American Theatre kept its four thousand seats filled and its amenities busy; these included a bathhouse next door, a restaurant, and a chess room—"the frequent resort of the gay and fashionable." Actors and audiences had a mutual affection for each other; most famous actors of the prewar period played in New Orleans, and Edwin Forrest, one of the greatest, is said to have given his last performance there, his eyes "moist with the tears of parting friendship."

Opera was the focal point of the New Orleans season. Saturdays and Sundays were the fashionable nights to be seen at the opera, but there were performances four times a week—two grand opera and two *opéra bouffe* (there was vaudeville for the *hoi poloi* on the other evenings). The first French opera house was built in 1816 with Henry Latrobe (Benjamin's son) as its architect but almost immediately burned down, and operas were performed in the Orleans Theatre until 1859, when the French Opera House was built on the corner of Toulouse and Bourbon streets, seating about eighteen hundred. The opera was an immensely popular Creole pastime, and the high level of appreciation apparent in the audience impressed American visitors in particular, accustomed as they were to the rowdy road shows that counted as entertainment in most of the country. Oakey Hall commented on the quality of the music, the attentive, animated faces, the lack of injudicious encores, and especially the elegance of the audience. French opera in New Orleans continued to hold its own after the Civil War, with singers and musicians still recruited from France, though the standard was lower and it was no longer unique in the United States. A photograph of the opera house taken in 1905 shows it very dilapidated, but money was raised for its renovation and a tourist advertisement a year later speaks of "the renaissance of high art" that this apparently heralded.

There is little sign of this renaissance today. There are no theaters in the business district—as the Faubourg Ste. Marie is now known —and the French Opera House met the inflammable fate of so many New Orleans buildings in 1917. Ballet, theater, and opera companies visit the Municipal Auditorium from time to time, but it has to be a real enthusiast who can enjoy the performances to the full in the excruciating discomfort of the auditorium. Mayor Martin Behrman, under whose administration this lumpish building was erected, was asked to have it designed like a Greek temple but replied that there were not enough Greeks living in New Orleans to make it worthwhile.

The 1850s in New Orleans were years of "flush times, high wages, high profits and high prices." Oakey Hall found everyone in the city in 1850 assuring him of the strength of its future. Only a few Job's comforters pointed out how precariously the booming economy was balanced, however apparent this has been to later historians. The superiority of the Mississippi as the main outlet for Western pro-duce, either to the rest of the United States or even to Europe, had already been undermined by the construction in the 1820s of the Erie Canal and its branches, but the effect on New Orleans had been disguised; the drop in Midwest trade had been more than compen-sated for by the staggering development of the cotton and sugar trade. This dependence on raw materials effectively discouraged industrial development; Simon Cameron, later Lincoln's first Secre-tary of War, reported rather harshly in the 1840s that raw materials were cheap enough but manufactured goods excessively costly— "nobody likes to work; all depend upon the negroes." Railways were also competing successfully with the river; during the 1830s and 1840s they were mainly used in the Mississippi valley as local feeders to rivers, canals, and bayous, but by 1850 they were beginning to branch out of the valley and to supplant the river. New Orleans businessmen had virtually disregarded the potential of railways, and the city had none of any importance until after the Civil War. Nor was the economy entirely under the city's control; most of the capital for New Orleans development came from New York. This accounts for the fact that there was no direct New Orleans shipping line to Europe; the cotton on which New Orleans prosperity as a port was principally based was generally taken up to New York by coastal packets. The hundred-mile journey up the Mississippi from its mouth also became less attractive as oceangoing vessels increased in size and were unable to cross the bar at the entrance to the river; to overcome this barrier appeared to demand more capital and more enterprise than New Orleans could command. Perhaps the notorious Southern indolence so beloved of Abolitionists had indeed overtaken New Orleans.

Bishop Whipple put it rather nicely in his journal: "The truth is New Orleans appears to me to be at the extreme of everything, the hottest, the dirtiest, the most sickly, and at times the most healthy, the busiest, and the most dull, the most wicked and the most orderly."

7. Immigrants

"I DOUBT IF THERE IS any city in the world, where the resident population has been so divided in its origins or where there is such a variety in the tastes, habits, manners and moral codes of the citizens"—Olmsted's comment was endlessly echoed by visitors to antebellum New Orleans. Stepping onto the wharves, driving to one's hotel, walking through the market, peering into the gloom of the cathedral, drinking coffee in Banks Arcade—everywhere a babel of tongues, almost none of them fully comprehensible to Northerners. Every American city has been a melting pot of races at some point in its history, but New Orleans' pot had more ingredients as a leading port of entry to America, the promised land of material and moral well-being.

Of the eighteenth-century immigrants to Louisiana who passed through New Orleans, most were agricultural rural people who had been persuaded to immigrate by promises of rich, alluvial land, free of warfare and exploitation. Thus the early colony of Germans were impressed by John Law's propaganda to settle on a concession on the Arkansas River; they soon found farming there an unpleasant, Indian-beset task and returned to New Orleans intending to take ship back to Europe. But, fortunately for the diet of the New Orleanians, they were persuaded to change their minds and settled upriver along what came to be known as the Côte Allemand, spreading out from the river into the swampy backlands, so that today there are a town, a lake, and a Bayou Des Allemands, though the original German family names have long since been Gallicized beyond recognition. The 1760s saw the establishment of the Acadians, another community of farming immigrants who maintain a remarkably close-knit culture to this day; and in the 1770s the Isleños came from the Canary Islands.

New Orleans itself collected its fair share of nationalities during the eighteenth century, apart from the French—among them Austrian butchers, Catalan tavern keepers, and Anglo-American merchants. By the end of the century, several Irish and German families were living in the city, many of them political refugees whose descendants in the mid-nineteenth century were not always best pleased with the more proletarian arrivals from their countries of origin.

The first Irish came to New Orleans after the Irish rebellions of 1790. New Orleans was a particularly popular choice among them because it was Catholic and had no links with Britain. The delightful, though rather unreliable, commentator Thomas Ashe wrote in 1806 that "the Scotch and the Irish absorb all the respectable commerce of exportation and importation"—an exaggerated generalization, though two of the most successful merchants at the turn of the century were Oliver Pollock and Daniel Clark, both of Irish origin. Several of these early Irish immigrants were prominent among the Burrite secessionists of the city; James Workman, later a judge, entertained them at his house and another of them was the Irishman Louis Kerr, who had allegedly "fled from Bengal for his virtuous deeds." Another Irishman was Maunsel White, who made his fortune, like so many, in land speculation and also by patenting a wine sauce, which is still part of the New Orleans gastronomic scene.* By the 1820s a less ambitious type of Irishman was arriving

---

*White first concocted the sauce for Andrew Jackson to commemorate the Battle of New Orleans, hence its name—1812 Sauce. The recipe is as secret as that of Coca-Cola, passed down from father to son and the present head of the family has told his son, but not his wife.

in far larger numbers, wretched rural refugees attracted to New Orleans as a boom city with an insatiable hunger for labor—"dark, swarthy, thin, whiskered, smoking, dirty, reckless-looking men."

The Irish were conspicuous by their numbers among yellow-fever victims and Timothy Flint, a benign Protestant minister from New England, described multitudes of poor Irish being swept away by the disease. The more cruel of the host population claimed that the Irish were responsible for the disease, even brought it with them—one had only to look at the appallingly unhygienic conditions of their trans-Atlantic crossing combined with the squalor in which they lived in New Orleans. The voyage was remarkably cheap because ships bringing cotton from New Orleans to Liverpool used immigrants as ballast for the return journey. The alternative was bricks, but the little the Irish paid for their fare was still more than the bricks sold for in New Orleans. As a result the Irish arrived in greatest numbers in the summer months, debilitated by a long sea voyage with virtually no nourishment, often unable to find immediate employment (in spite of the labor shortage) and enough nourishment, and therefore easy victims for any epidemic that occurred. Of the eleven thousand deaths in the 1853 yellow-fever epidemic, over a third were said to be Irish (who were also the principal source of grave-diggers).

However liable the Irish to die, they played a useful part on the New Orleans labor scene in supplying cheap expendable manual labor. Since the 1808 abolition of the import of slaves, the price of slaves had risen considerably, their value heightened by the demand for their labor on the cotton plantations. A slave was too valuable to be worn out in the heaviest jobs, many of these created by the rapid expansion of the city—the need for drainage canals inside and outside the city, paving streets, and improving levees. Here the Irish came in very handy, often working alongside Negroes or, in the case of the skilled jobs, even working for the free coloreds who made up the majority of the artisans in the city. Irish delvers dug the New Basin Canal, for instance, connecting the American quarter with Lake Pontchartrain between 1831 and 1835; estimates of the death toll ranged from three thousand to thirty thousand, though a ditty of the period seems to strike a plausible compromise:

Ten thousand Micks they swing their picks,
To dig the New Canal,
But the choleray was stronger'n they
An' twice it killed them all.

"Heaven knows how many poor Hibernians have been consumed and buried in these Louisiana swamps," exclaimed a normally phlegmatic London *Times* correspondent. They also replaced slave labor on the steamboats, a mate aboard one of these telling Olmsted that "the niggers are worth too much to be risked below and if the paddies are kicked overboard or get their backs broken nobody loses anything."

The Germans were only slightly better off: there were fewer of them who stayed in New Orleans for one thing. Of the 34,000 Germans who arrived in New Orleans in 1853–54, less than a quarter remained in the city (hardly surprising in view of the 1853 yellow-fever epidemic), the majority continuing upriver to St. Louis. Others only stayed until they had enough money to move elsewhere. There are three discernible waves of German immigration in the nineteenth century: in the years immediately after the Napoleonic wars (as Goethe exclaimed, *"Amerika, du hast es besser!"*), the 1850s after the European revolutions of 1848, and the 1870s and 1880s after the unification of Germany. The middle period was the most conspicuous. The demand for cheap labor created by the abolition of the slave trade gave rise, in the case of European immigrants, to the system of redemption, similar to the indentures of the seaboard states in the early years of American colonization. Prospective immigrants would sell the right to their services to the ship's captain, who auctioned them to the highest bidder on the wharves of New Orleans. Until 1818 even free coloreds had white redemptioners working for them; after 1818 they were forbidden "to purchase or engage the services of white people for a limited time as servants." Thousands of Germans in fact died before they reached the golden shores: "I am not unfamiliar with the sight of human woe," wrote the Baron von Wurstenwärther, about redemptioners voyaging to New Orleans. "I have seen it in many forms, but in no more horrible than on these ships" where the "freights" were jammed in sitting positions in the hold, often without food for the two or three months of the voyage. Successful Germans proved success was possible, however; among the better known were Michael Hahn, who came over as a child with his parents and later became governor of Louisiana after the capture of New Orleans by Union forces in 1862, and Christian Roselius, who arrived as an indentured passenger in 1823, became an apprentice printer and then a lawyer and fifteen years after his arrival was buying a large and expensive house in the Quarter.

But for the most part it was a struggle, and under such conditions immigrants tended to cling to their fellow nationals, desperately preserving their abandoned heritage against dissolution in the melting pot. Churches, militia regiments, benevolent societies, saints' days—all helped the rootless immigrant to feel part of a group, however wretched the other members of the group might appear to an outsider. Older immigrants who now enjoyed a certain social and financial success founded societies to help newer immigrants. James Workman organized the Friends of Ireland in the 1830s to help rebels in Ireland and refugees arriving in New Orleans. The Hibernia Society was set up "for the relief of destitute natives of Ireland." A German Society helped Germans, and the St. Andrew Society helped the Scots. Immigrants who "plunged into this chaos, raw and ignorant, speak no language but an unknown one, know not where to go, have no friends . . . and are quite certain in their own minds, of being cheated" were occasionally caught up by one or other of the relevant societies.

The Church also provided a national home of a kind. For a long time, Catholic immigrants made do with St. Louis Cathedral in spite of the often alien language (during the Spanish administration many of the priests were in fact Irish, the Spanish authorities hoping thereby to convert the wild American boatmen); the somber baroque confessionals, the lurid stained glass, the pastel-shaded plaster saints provided a familiar environment where even today an occasional old woman in black can be seen slipping in out of the glare and heat. In the 1830s, however, the Irish acquired a church of their own. The first St. Patrick's Church, a wooden building, was built in

1833; the present building, erected two years later, was mostly designed by the architect James Gallier and is improbably said to have been modeled on York Minster. Precautions were taken against the possibility of the tower's slipping, by extending the foundations far out into the surrounding land. Until the 1930s it was the tallest building in the city; now it is dwarfed by graceless office blocks. Later, on Jackson Avenue, two Catholic churches were built, one for Irish and one for German Catholics, both run by the Redemptorist brothers (nothing to do with redemptioners except that many of the latter must have been among the congregation). The German church, St. Mary's Assumption, even has an altar and stained glass windows from Munich. Sometimes the desire to have services in a foreign language led to problems. In 1847 a priest was sent to the new suburb of Carollton to organize a congregation, and a site was bought on Cambronne Street for a church. Most of the congregation being German, sermons were given in German; French and American members, were so indignant, however, that sermons were later given in three languages. The issue remained a source of chronic friction, however, until 1871, when the Germans decided to build their own church, Mater Dolorosa, on the other side of the street. Most of the German churches also had schools attached to them.

St. Patrick's and the Redemptorist churches provided sanctuaries not only for prayer but also for coolness and peace compared with their surroundings. This was the notorious Irish Channel. The Irish Channel is a vaguely delineated area that began a little upriver of St. Patrick's, running along behind the wharves. There are a hundred definitions of what this area actually was and is; most probably it originally referred to the three or four blocks of three or four streets running back from the river—Adele Street is a favorite—where now there are only crumbling warehouses and weed-strewn railway tracks. Henry Didimus described the area with deep horror in the 1830s—the streets "filthy, cut by deep ruts, lined on each side with a narrow strip of stagnant water, and bordered with low one-storey, frame-built dwellings whose roofs, old, covered with moss, jutting over the footpaths, and doors and windows of solid timber never open, impart to the whole a most sombre and gloomy appearance." Today's Irish Channel is no more Irish than the French Quarter is French, but it is still a slum. The inhabitants, many of them recent immigrants but now more often from Latin America than from Europe or Ireland, compensate for their failure to make money—the docks are the main employer in these parts—and thus to be absorbed entirely into the American way of life, by preserving national idiosyncracies to this day; you see it in the neighborhood stores, in the clusters of men outside the corner bars, in the women shouting from one wooden gallery to another. And on a hot summer's evening the streets and porches echo with the same confusion of languages that nineteenth-century visitors noted all over the city. Until recently the Irish Channel also preserved its reputation for violence. In the last century it was ruled by rival gangs—St. Mary's Market Gang, the Shot Tower Gang, and others—parading the narrow filthy streets armed with crowbars. In the early 1960s it was considered the worst area for juvenile crime in the city. But it seems to have embarked on a peaceful old age with the arrival of poverty programs and rehabilitation schemes.

There is a rural charm about the channel as if the country origins of most of its inhabitants had seeded themselves in the city squalor. Early in the morning one is woken by cocks crowing (cocks are in fact forbidden in the city, along with cockfighting, but the Irish Channel and the police are equally notorious for their love of legal and political compromise), and there is even an occasional patch of mustard greens, turnip greens, and a stem or two of corn.

National celebrations have always maintained links with home countries. St. Patrick's Day was first celebrated in 1809, a rather sedate performance compared with later occasions. A certain amount of sedateness has always been present; there are a midday mass at St. Patrick's and a banquet in the evening organized by the Ancient Order of the Hibernians and the Ladies' Auxiliary of the Ancient Order of the Hibernians (attended among others by representatives of the Hibernia National Bank, the Hibernia Homestead and Savings Association, Hibernia Real Estate, and the Hibernia Roofing and Metal Works). There is a Gaelic theme for the banquet, and most of the food is green, one lurid menu reading Heather Honeydew Melon Balls, Shamrock Relish Tray, Broiled Gaelic Ribeye Steak, Baked Irish potatoes, Eire Green Asparagus with Cheese Sauce, Hibernia Mixed Green Salad, Lime Parfait with Kelly Green Cherry, Emerald Isle Wine, Irish Coffee Demitasse, Erin Bread and Green Buns. A profitable line of business must be inventing new green foods for expatriate Irishmen. This banquet is attended by all members of the city establishment and other politicians who can squeeze out a drop of Irish blood for the Irish vote is as important in New Orleans as in Boston.

But down along the Irish Channel, there is a more robust affair. One local bar noted for its political involvements is Charlie Parasol's and this is the center of festivities; no aspiring politician can afford not to be seen joining the heroic drinking bouts that begin several days before St. Patrick's Day. Parasol's is an exclusively male establishment, except on certain occasions; on St. Patrick's Day the men deign to appear with their wives, the men in brilliant green bowler hats or caps, green waistcoats and green ties, even a green suit for the really enthusiastic, and their wives are similarly emeraldine. Even teen-age daughters are allowed, large Irish buttocks and beautiful American legs encased in green Bermuda shorts. The highlight of the festivities is inevitably a parade. There is a big seriously commercial affair downtown, but there is also one in the Irish Channel, parading to the local banquet. It is a disorganized affair, to say the least; two or three days of bucolic preparation are not conducive to straight lines and precise chords. Members of Parasol's Corner Club, an octogenarian establishment owning ill-tuned but magnificently polished brass instruments, lead off in antiquated Mardi Gras costumes followed by green mini-skirted schoolgirls from the Redemptorist schools next door to the churches. St. Alphonsus, the Redemptorist church built for Irish Catholics, has a mass before the parade. There is a queen (or coleen, as the *Times-Picayune* insists on calling her), who has already been fêted at yet another banquet a few days earlier. All this leads toward the Seafarers' Union Hall, a chic modern asylum for lonely mariners on Jackson Avenue, a rather antiseptic setting for such a celebration.

The Germans tended to live more downriver of the French Quarter in the Faubourg Marigny, an area very similar in appearance to the Irish Channel, though its inhabitants always seem to have been more orderly; the streets are neater, fewer weeds grow in the gutters, there are tidy little gardens, and it looks calmer. Oakey Hall found it "unmistakable in its French faubourg look" but given over to "the tender mercies of the Dutch . . . and the usual accompaniment of flaxen-polled babies and flaxen-tailed pigs." St. Paul's Evangelical Church, acting as a focal point for the community, used to hold services in German and ran a school for Germans. One has the impression the Germans in New Orleans were perhaps working too hard to waste time on a saint's day. But during the 1850s the custom grew up for German families to celebrate a Volks-und-Schutzenfest, when they would all drive out to Bayou St. John for a gigantic picnic, no doubt well supplied by German brewing families such as the Fabachers, founders of the Jax Brewery, which is such an eyesore along the river by Jackson Square.

The crowding of immigrants into New Orleans in the middle years of the century created an atmosphere of suspicion among the immigrants themselves and in the attitude of the older community to the new arrivals. This was a common situation throughout the country at this time and led in the 1850s to the foundation of the Know-Nothing Party—also known as the Native American Party— the former name derived from the party's answers to queries about its program, to which it would reply that it knew nothing contrary to the constitution and laws of the land. The party believed that the growing corruption of American politics was due to immigrant voters, most of them poor, who would sell their votes to the highest bidder. In New Orleans as elsewhere they became easy tools in the development of machine politics.

The reunification of the city government in 1852 reproduced the same American-Creole antagonisms that had led to the establishment of the three municipalities. Now, however, the protagonists attached themselves to national parties, the Americans tending to vote Whig and the Creoles Democrat, under their leader John Slidell—who is usually credited with first setting up the Democratic machine in New Orleans. Much of Slidell's success, and that of the Democrats in gaining control of the city, was undoubtedly due to clever manipulation of immigrant voters. There was a deal of truth behind the rather tart remark by a visiting Englishwoman, Miss Murray, that "the Irish paupers are so ultra in their politics and so saucy in their manners, that they have given rise to the 'Know Nothing' movement, which, however reprehensible in its mode of proceeding, is only a practical illustration of the impossibility of carrying out the idea of equality." The opposition formed itself into secret societies known as wigwams to combat what it considered the brutishness and corruption of the ruling party. This developed into the Know-Nothing Party—a gigantic secret society with the usual paraphernalia of "signs, grips and gradations of the individual."

The Know-Nothing movement was national in scope, but in New Orleans it lost the anti-Catholicism that characterized it elsewhere. Elections in the city were increasingly violent, and intimidation at the polls was frequent. According to the *Daily Delta*, political contests were "a farce and a fraud, the knife, the sling-shot, the brass knuckles, determining . . . who shall occupy and administer the (public) offices." Rioting broke out in 1854 between immigrants and members of the Know-Nothing Party, which a year later swept the field in elections. In 1856 the party scared would-be opponents at the polls by dressing up in false whiskers and blackened faces. Thomas Slidell, a cousin of John and a Supreme Court Justice, was attacked at the polls and later died of his wounds. Violence begets violence, and the more stable founders of the party were gradually alienated by the new working-class members, who were jealous of immigrant labor, who liked to display their nativism by dressing up as Indians, and whose power was often based on the new ward clubs, which are still a basis for political power in New Orleans today.

The "responsible" citizens of New Orleans, deciding it was time to take the matter into their own hands, formed a vigilance committee to ensure peaceful elections in 1858. The committee had over a thousand members, but apparently the city authorities were totally unaware of its existence until March 1858 when the members seized the state arsenal next door to the Cabildo, barricaded themselves in

Jackson Square, which they nicknamed Fort Vigilance, and insisted on being sworn in as a special supervisory force to police the elections. Their leader was a Captain Duncan who had recently returned from filibustering with William Walker in Nicaragua. The Know-Nothings retaliated by setting up Fort Defiance in Lafayette Square. Both sides organized pickets on either side of Canal Street. The city authorities eventually worked out an acceptable compromise, and remarkably little blood was shed, considering the number of men under arms (many of them ex-filibusterers like Duncan); although the vigilantes were refused permission to police the polls, the elections were the most orderly the city had seen for several years. The Know-Nothing Party remained in control of the city until about 1860, long after it had died out in most of the United States, mainly because of reaction to the large percentage of foreign-born immigrants in the population. In 1860 more than half the white population of New Orleans was foreign-born: 81,000 out of 168,000.

The Civil War, however, healed many breaches between immigrants and older residents. Some said the Irish were rather half-hearted secessionists but William Russell, the London *Times* correspondent, wrote that "the Irish population . . . being without work, have rushed to arms with enthusiasm to support Southern institutions."

After the war the Italians were the most notable arrivals, living mostly in the Irish Channel or the French Quarter. The French Quarter was virtually taken over by Italians in the second half of the nineteenth century and still seems more Italian than anything else. The principal Italian church is there; there is an ice-cream parlor that sells *graniti* and those parching, dry Italian cakes and that is Italian from its noisy marble floor to its dilapidated baroque fan. "Let the dead speak," wrote one Italian New Orleanian, furious that the French Quarter was not be called the Italian Quarter.

The Italian saint's day is St. Joseph's, on March 19th, just two days after St. Patrick's, and the celebrations inevitably take on a certain competitive spirit. Centuries ago a small group of Italians exiled for religious reasons put themselves under the protection of St. Joseph during their journey into exile, promising to build an altar to him every year if they reached their destination safely, which they did. The custom has continued among Italian wanderers, many of whom have also sought the saint's intercession for other problems, and the saint's day has been observed in New Orleans since the 1840s. For several weeks before St. Joseph's Day, the personal columns of the New Orleans newspapers are filled with advertisements inviting the public to visit St. Joseph's altars in private homes around the city, most of them still concentrated in such immigrant areas as the Faubourg Marigny and the Irish Channel. It is a strange experience to go into the small, dark, cottages to find the main room candlelit for the occasion and the family hurrying in and out with laden dishes, the men particularly Italianate. The altars are the most mouth-watering sights, for the main ideal of a wandering Italian seems to be food; the altars become piles of gorgeously decorated delicacies baked for weeks in advance by the families concerned, the biscuits first because they keep, and so on down to the baked catfish, the bewhiskered *pièce de résistance*, balefully glaring at anyone whose fingers become too greedy. The altars are blessed by the priest on the eve of the saint's day, and on the actual day the food is distributed to the poor and to anyone else who happens to turn up.

One of the most delicious altars is erected annually in the Mother Cabrini Convent in the Quarter, by a woman who vowed to build an altar if her daughter recovered from a serious operation, and year after year on her own she has baked bread and mixed and fried and roasted as well as spending a small fortune on the ingredients. There is another altar at the Italian ice-cream parlor. An Italian delicatessen also in the Quarter, the owner now dead for several years and the premises desolately boarded up, used to have a more permanent altar, decorated with candles and flowers all the year around and with food for St. Joseph's; the owner received a papal blessing for praying in front of it for a thousand days.

There is a St. Joseph's parade too, both formal and—in the Irish Channel—informal; the people participating in the parades look remarkably like those who were decked out two days earlier for St. Patrick, and both parades seem an excellent excuse to drain the last remaining dregs of Mardi Gras spirit before they evaporate in the summer heat.

Along with the Italians came, inevitably, the Mafia, whose first foothold in the United States was said to have been in New Orleans. No one knows quite how strong the Mafia is; most people claim it is very strong and avidly gossip about its leaders and their haunts. A closely knit community of Sicilians settled in New Orleans in the 1880s working as dock laborers and in the French Market, "forming a turbulent and lawless element," and the New Orleans Mafia first came to national notice about this time as the result of the heroic efforts on the part of a New Orleans policeman, David Hennessy, to end the gang warfare over waterfront labor between two Sicilian families, the Provenzanos and the Matrangos, the latter allegedly members of the Mafia. Hennessy was responsible for the capture and deportation of the Mafia leader Esposito. In 1891 Hennessy was assassinated on the doorstep of his house. Public outcry led to the arrest of nine Italians, six of whom were subsequently acquitted, the jury disagreeing over the other three. After the trial, when the defendants were awaiting their release in the parish prison, an enraged mob decided to take justice into its own hands and broke into the prison, shooting most of the Italians inside and lynching two outside in the street. In a famous lawsuit with the Italian government, the United States later indemnified Italy to the tune of $25,-000.

Nowadays one reads in the press of the deeds and misdeeds of the leading Mafia family and of the threat that the Mafia are taking over the city's business concerns and the all-important tourist industry. Most of the center of New Orleans belongs to Orleans Parish, but large areas of the new suburbs come into Jefferson Parish, and it is here that the Mafia allegedly have their headquarters. Several of the better restaurants around New Orleans are said to be owned by the Mafia, and there are a number of gambling clubs just over the parish boundary that are alleged to be Mafia-run. Sometimes one feels that New Orleans is Mafia-mad, seeing sinister assassins behind every tourist tout, but the ease with which they evade the law is grudgingly admired; the reputation of the police is by no means blameless, and most people seem to have about as low an opinion of the officers of the law as of breakers of the law.

The Italians remain one of the closest communities in New Orleans. Like the Irish they often vote as a group, and in the early years of this century it was recognized that the "Dago" vote was controlled by the city's political machine. The French market is still run by Italians and is surrounded by Italian shops, and Italian is the commonest language heard in the predawn bustle. All the best barbers are Italian, and many of the small neighborhood restaurants are run by Italians with monumental wives dressed in stately black.

There are many other communities. There are the Dalmatians, most of whom now live in the lower Delta, seamen by origin; they used to own "dustvas," cooperative households in the Faubourg Marigny, and in the 1870s they founded the United Slavonic Benevolent Society, which owns vaults in the Third St. Louis Cemetery and helps Slavs in trouble such as the inhabitants of Buras in the Delta after floods. There are Greeks who have a Greek Orthodox Church (said to be the first built in the United States, in 1866), which attracts the curious to the Greek Easter to eat sweetmeats made in a Greek bakery; and there is a cluster of Greek nightclubs along Decatur Street, where the nostalgic strains of bouzouki music comfort homesick Piraean sailors. The Chinese have the inevitable laundries around town. They also have an elaborate tomb in the Cypress Grove Cemetery; there are vaults arranged on either side of a central covered corridor, with a grate at one end for burning incense—or perhaps for a fire to warm watchers by the tombs. Before the war every expatriate Chinese used to be buried in China, regardless of where he had spent his life, and the Cypress Grove was merely a temporary resting place; every few years the tombs would be opened and the whitened bones collected in a pile, packed in a lead-lined box, and dispatched to China for burial. But since World War II the Chinese have been resigned to life after death as well as before it in the promised land of plenty.

8. The Negroes

New Orleans was multiracial from its earliest days, and Africans were almost as much a part of the scene as the French. At the outset the French colonists decided they were ill suited to laboring in such a climate, a problem that their compatriots in the West Indies had solved many years earlier by importing African slaves to do the work for them. The French in Louisiana tried using Indian prisoners as slaves, but this had no greater success in Louisiana than elsewhere in North America; the Indians were too homesick and could escape too easily because of their familiarity with their surroundings—Bienville tried to counter this by suggesting the exchange of Louisiana Indians for West Indian Africans, ensuring unfamiliar terrain for both groups. Bienville wanted to import Africans from the West Indies as early as 1708, though nothing seems to have been done about it as the time; similarly the charter granted to Antoine Crozat in 1712 allowed him to send an annual ship to Guinea for Negroes, but in 1717 there were hardly more than a dozen in Louisiana.

John Law's attempts to colonize Louisiana, however, included such incentives for farmers as providing them with a labor force, and the Company of the Indies undertook to send three thousand Negroes to Louisiana. The first two ships sent to Guinea under this provision—"to trade only for healthy and well-made negroes"—returned to Louisiana with their cargo in 1719. This was the beginning of a regular trade. In 1721, for instance, the company imported over a thousand slaves into the colony. Slave ships arrived most years from Africa, though many of the slaves died on the way from scurvy, measles, dysentery, and flux. On arrival the slaves were put into a slave corral built opposite New Orleans in what is now Algiers, then known as "The Company's Plantation." Doctors examined them to separate the sick from the healthy, but demand was so great that the sick fetched almost as much as the healthy ones. They were distributed only to such colonists who could supply them with food and clothing and could pay for them—buyers were allowed up to three years' credit and paid $150 for an average male and $120 for a female.

Rules and regulations for slaves were established in a *Code Noir* drafted by Bienville in 1724, based on the code operating in San Domingo. Basically a slave was always considered dangerous because he was deprived of the privileges and ambitions that could be relied on to restrain a free man. Slavery was regarded, according to the early historian du Lac Perrin, as "the greatest of all necessary evils, as well as to those that endure it, as those that are obliged to employ the victims." The *Code Noir* remained in force with slight variations until the Louisiana Purchase. Its provisions were generally more humane than similar codes elsewhere in North America, but the humanitarian features of slavery were gradually eroded during the nineteenth century. The first clause in the code had nothing whatever to do with slaves, ordering the expulsion of Jews from Louisiana, but the remainder followed the title. Slaves were to be taught the Catholic religion; they were to be given Sundays and church feasts as holidays; intermarriage between whites and blacks was forbidden, as was concubinage (the last forbidden with remarkably little effect); no slave might carry an offensive weapon; slaves of different masters could not assemble, and so on. The code laid down rules for the clothing and subsistence of slaves which, meager though they read today, were probably little worse than what the owners themselves enjoyed.

On Sundays and other holidays, slaves were allowed to work for themselves, keeping the proceeds. This provided a thrifty slave with the means to buy his way out of servitude. There seem to have been free Negroes in New Orleans from the earliest years; the first probably came from the West Indies. Blacks in New Orleans used to be carefully distinguished as slaves; free Negroes, of pure or nearly pure African blood; and "free men and women of color," known as *gens de couleur libre,* whose position in society depended on how much white blood they appeared to have. Manumission was quite frequent in the Colonial period—by purchase, by the owner's deed, by legislative act, or by last will and testament. The shortage of women in the early days of New Orleans meant that many white men had slave mistresses, despite regulations to the contrary. Often white fathers would free the slave mothers of their children since by law the child inherited the status of the mother. During the Colonial period, *gens de couleur* were given the same legal rights as the white population; they also fought in the militia and mostly supplied the skilled manual labor the growing town needed so badly.

The Spanish authorities reenacted the *Code Noir.* Ulloa alleviated some of the harsher penalties. Miro, on the other hand, alarmed at the extent of the system of concubinage so prevalent that by 1788 slaves and free coloreds outnumbered whites, legislated against the notorious *femmes de couleur,* forbidding them to wear silk, plumes, and jewels when they went about in public: "excessive attention to dress" would be considered as indication of misbehavior.

Toussaint l'Ouverture's slave revolt in 1792 in San Domingo made a profound impression on local attitudes to slavery. In Louisiana particularly, where many refugees, black and white, eventually came to settle, a stronger fear of the Negro undermined the previous happy-go-lucky relationship between white and black. A slave conspiracy on the Poydras plantation just above New Orleans in 1795 was brutally suppressed; its leaders were hanged and left to rot on gibbets on the banks of the Mississippi. At the time of the Purchase and up to about 1840, the colored population of New Orleans (about one-tenth of whom were free Negroes) outnumbered the white. In spite of efforts to forbid their entry, slaves were still brought in from

San Domingo, often the only means of livelihood for their exiled French owners, who hired them out as laborers. Nevertheless, the influx of San Domingo Negroes, supposedly contaminated with the disease of revolution, combined with the abolition of the slave trade in 1808 to harden lines between white and black. Distrust between the races soon developed to the point where Claiborne disallowed the militia bands of free Negroes, for the idea of arming Negroes was no longer acceptable.

The first colored immigrants from San Domingo, coming in the 1790s immediately after the revolution, were easily assimilated into the easy-going society of New Orleans and added considerably to the quality of life, but in 1808 and 1809 their numbers rose dramatically as they flooded in from Cuba with the outbreak of war between France and Spain. At first it seemed unreasonable, in view of the abolition of the slave trade, not to allow blacks in as well as whites, slaves as well as free Negroes, but the authorities were increasingly nervous that Louisiana slaves might become infected with revolutionary fervor. Their fears had to some extent been justified by a slave revolt in 1805 planned by a white man from San Domingo. It was due partly to the San Domingo revolution that the legislated separation of the races was set afoot, which was later taken to such extremes by the slavery crisis. Claiborne had reported, as an instance of Spanish laxity, that the slaves "were in a shameful state of idleness and want of subordination," and regulations governing slaves were tightened soon after the Purchase. Free Negroes were also treated with more circumspection. It became harder for slaves to purchase their freedom; the economic and political rights of the blacks were gradually eroded; the immigration of free Negroes was restricted and then prohibited. Claiborne had been worried in the first few months of his appointment as commissioner, when he was petitioned by the *gens de couleur* of New Orleans for a grant of full citizenship, no mention of which had been made in Claiborne's act incorporating the city. Claiborne quietened their fears but was secretly afraid they might be incited to revolt by subversive Spaniards; the suspicion had some foundation since Burr for one was counting on their dissatisfaction to gain their support. The same fears arose in 1814 at the time of the projected British attack on New Orleans; to agitation against arming free colored men, Jackson replied that he would employ whom he liked "without enquiring whether they are white, black or tea." Nevertheless, the two colored militia regiments that fought against the British had white officers.

It was the colored refugees from San Domingo who developed the earlier concubinage (or *plaçage)* system so disliked by Miro to the high degree of sophistication noted by all visitors to New Orleans. Interracial sex in the antebellum period has probably been exaggerated but inevitably there was some. Free children of white-slave parents were more likely to congregate in the city, and more Negroes were employed domestically in the city and lived more closely with whites. Both these factors encouraged the system.

The hierarchy of color was very strictly observed: Olmsted listed the gradings of color ranging from the dark socotra through griffe, marabou, mulatto, quadroon, metif, meamelous, and sang-mélé. The quadroon women, the general term for free women of color, were famous for their beauty and for their accommodation to the legal restrictions placed upon them. English visitors idealized the quadroons because of their opposition to slavery; John Silk Buckingham was typical of their many admirers—"they furnish some of the most beautiful women that can be seen . . . with lovely countenances, full, dark, liquid eyes, lips of coral and teeth of pearl . . ." Several (who lent their reputation to the many less competent) were well educated and often well endowed financially as well as aesthetically. They disdained marrying other quadroons, let alone someone darker, their one ambition being "the elimination of black pigment and the cultivation of hyperean excellence and nymphaean grace and beauty," according to George Cable, hoping to beget children lighter than themselves, who might one day "pass" from the restricted life of a colored person to the freedom of a white. Olmsted said, "Of course I do not mean that love has nothing to do with it, but love is sedulously restrained, and held firmly in hand, until the road of competency is seen to be clear, with less humbug than our English custom requires it to be."

The quadroon balls, so celebrated in contemporary descriptions of

New Orleans, were the outward and visible sign at the turn of the eighteenth-nineteenth centuries of considerable prosperity among the free colored community. The *Times-Picayune* commented condescendingly, but with some accuracy, that the free colored people of New Orleans differed from those elsewhere in their relationship with the whites, in their "commendable spirit of emulation." At the top of this mixed society were some extremely wealthy families who owned real estate, businesses, and slaves, the latter always a yardstick of prosperity. They used to be seen at the opera, where special boxes were reserved for them—*loges pour personnes de couleur.* Thomy Lafon, one of the best known, made most of his large fortune during Reconstruction—in real estate. When he died in 1893, he bequeathed property to a host of charities, regardless of their religious or racial affinities. Other distinguished free coloreds were the poet Armand Lanusse, who published *Les Cenelles,* the first anthology of Negro verse in the United States (the poems appeared originally in a magazine called *L'Album Litteraire,* published by free coloreds), and Victor Séjour who went to France to make his name as a playwright and became secretary to Napoleon III. Norbert Rillieux was a colored engineer, educated in France, who invented a sugar process first exploited by Judah P. Benjamin on his Belle Chasse plantation. Pierre Casinave was "the grandest undertaker of funeral splendour in New Orleans"—quite a claim in a city that prided itself on its splendid funerals. Nelson Foucher was an immigrant from Cuba who became a successful beer merchant. This free Negro elite was also bolstered by the Catholic Church, which did not segregate congregations. Ten free Negroes founded the African Methodist Episcopal Church in 1848 to try to win independence from white-dominated Protestantism, which did segregate congregations.

The vast majority of free coloreds, however, provided the skilled, semi-skilled, and manual labor of New Orleans, though from the 1820s white immigrant laborers, especially the Irish, gradually ousted them from their traditional fields of labor; Olmsted noted in the 1850s that "the majority of the cartmen, hackney coachmen, porters, railroad hands, public waiters, and common labourers . . . appear to be white men." The skilled laborers at one time even had their own union, *Société des Artisans,* founded by Victor Séjour, among others. Most of them lived either in the French Quarter or in the Faubourg Marigny (one of the reasons for the negligible development of the Third Municipality was held to be that much of the property was owned by colored people who could not afford to improve it and had no wish to sell). They were Catholic and spoke a curious French dialect heavily larded with African, known as Creole or gumbo French; academics now study this with great intensity as the speaking of it gradually dies away. Free colored women were often employed as seamstresses, hairdressers, and nurses and were particularly prized as the latter ("when a stranger is brought up by the prevailing fever, the first object is to consign him to the care of one of these tender and faithful nurses," wrote Timothy Flint). Negroes were held to be immune to yellow fever, and a colored nurse could earn as much as $10 a day at the height of an epidemic.

In the 1830s and 1840s New Orleans became the greatest slave emporium in the country, the principal market where Virginian slaves were supplied to the Louisiana and Mississippi cotton planters. The South was a "land of expanding slavery" as a result of the expanding production of cotton. Cotton and Negroes were the theme behind so much of the city's prosperity during this period— "the ever harped upon, never worn out, subject of conversation among all classes." De Bow, the New Orleans editor, the great advocate of a slave economy, wrote that "this alliance between negroes and cotton, we will venture to say is now the *strongest power* in the world, and the peace and welfare of of Christendom absolutely depends upon the strength and security of it." Visitors to the city could not help but notice the signs of the trade—the lines of slaves, the auctions, the advertisements, the notices for runaway slaves. Those arriving by way of Lake Pontchartrain often saw caravans of Negroes being brought from the slave-breeding states of the Upper South to be auctioned off in New Orleans. These auctions were held in such places as the Rotunda of the St. Louis Hotel, St. Charles Hotel, or Banks Arcade. Slave depots, display windows, and showrooms were all unashamedly on the main streets of the city; in 1856–60 there were reckoned to be at least twenty-five places for viewing or buying slaves within a few blocks of the St. Charles Hotel, and Camp Street is said to have got its name from "campo di negros"—a slave depot having been in the vicinity since the Colonial period. Stocks of slaves were kept for sale in so-called jails. To the horror of abolition-minded foreigners, a trade directory of the 1840s listed 185 slave traders in New Orleans, 49 brokers, and 25 auctioneers.

Advertisements for slaves often included animals in the same notice; "A number of slaves and thoroughbred horses will be sold at the same time," ran one such notice. Two English ladies, the Misses Turner, were horrified to see a handbill announcing a raffle for, among other things, a mulatto seamstress and a lady's maid. Handsome slave girls were sometimes sold as "fancy girls"; the city could absorb a large number of these, with its floating population of gamblers and "sporting men." Slaves were often bought as an investment —some owned by companies—hired out sometimes at 20 to 30 percent of their market value. Slaves were also used as security.

In general, slaves were well treated by the owners, especially in the city; Americans had a better reputation than Creoles in this respect. Buckingham, a fervent Abolitionist, thought the Negroes better off in New Orleans than in many Northern cities; "the love of ease, which characterises the slaves themselves, is equally characteristic of those in whose service they may be," and owners of slaves "leave much more to their management than is ever confided to the free servants of England." There was a tacit recognition on the owner's part that "the slaves' best protection was their value," and on the slave's part that misbehavior might result in his being sent to the cotton fields, a fate whose grimness is recorded in so many Negro folksongs. There were relatively few cases of ill treatment, the most celebrated being that of Madame Lalaurie, the wife of a doctor who lived on Royal Street in a house now known as the Haunted House because of the souls of brutally treated slaves that still hang around it. Madame Lalaurie was eventually hounded out of the city by the mob for her cruelty. The architect Benjamin Henry Latrobe felt obliged to move his lodgings because of the cruelty of his landlady to one of her slaves and commented that other similar incidents of cruelty were nearly all committed by women; it quite spoiled his enjoyment of the Washington Birthday Ball because "I fancied that I saw a cowskin in every pretty hand gracefully waved in a dance."

Certain outlets were allowed for the Negroes' relaxation, sponsored by slaveowners, of which the most notable was Congo Square, breeding ground of many of the later jazz influences. This favorite with visitors is now a forlorn and bedraggled rectangle of would-be grass in front of the Municipal Auditorium, now called Beauregard Square after one of New Orleans' most respectable heroes. Between the beginning of the century and the Civil War, this was the main gathering place for Africans on a Sunday. Here they would relive their African origins, often under the eye of elaborately dressed chiefs, dance exotic dances such as the bamboula or calinda, playing African drums and sometimes a curious stringed instrument that was said to be an ancestor of the banjo. Songs from Senegal or Guinea, from which many of the slaves or their forefathers had come, were half-chanted, half-sung, deafening the ears and senses of bemused tourists, lulling their own into a forgetfulness of their condition. "I have never seen anything more brutally savage, at the same time dull and stupid, than this whole exhibition," was Latrobe's comment after watching a crowd of five or six hundred people in the square one Sunday. A contemporary guide to the city tried to discourage tourist attentions by describing the gatherings as a "debauch" and "a foolish custom, that elicits the ridicule of most respectable persons who visit the city" but this was not entirely correct; many praised the fact that the slaves were allowed at least this weekly outlet for emotions and were intrigued by the remnants of African culture that appeared there. Such gatherings survived war, emancipation, and Reconstruction but died out around 1885.

Another popular place for slaves on their day off was Rampart Street, still the principal Negro shopping area, and Olmsted's comment, that "the white passer-by might easily imagine himself in Guinea, Caffaria, or any other thickly peopled region in the land of Ham," could still apply today.

Another aspect of the colored population's preservation of their Africanism, closely linked with Congo Square, was voodoo—a belief in possession by spirits and hence ancestor worship—a rather emotive subject in New Orleans, where it still lingers on. Like other facets of Negro society in the city, it was probably introduced by San Domingo Negroes. A weird agglomeration of African paganism with borrowings from Christianity, it seems to have played a larger part in the city's imagination than in its actual life. Most of the voodoo leaders—the papalous and mamalous—were free Negroes; one such was Sanité Dédé, a quadroon woman from San Domingo who sold sweets in the Place d'Armes during the day and was believed to have nightly voodoo meetings in her house on Dumaine Street, some of which were "even" attended by whites. Another leader was Marie Laveau, who died in 1881 and whose celebrated tomb in the St. Louis cemetery is bedecked with small tokens of flowers and ribbons to this day. Marie Laveau is said to have held some public voodoo meetings, though this seems unlikely in view of the element of secrecy essential to the rites. Observers of the New Orleans scene before the Civil War make virtually no mention of voodoo practices; Miss Julia le Grand noted in her remarkable diary in 1862 her horror in hearing about a Negro society called "vaudoo"—"the existence of such a thing in New Orleans is hard to believe." This is not to say that it did not exist, merely that discussion of it only developed in later accounts of the city, influenced by romanticism and anti-Negro reaction. Since Marie Laveau's day it has become a much tamer affair—some call it hoodoo by comparison—with fusty spell shops along South Rampart selling "fear-producing" talismans, "come-hither" powders, bottled love, and special detergent to wash the gris-gris from your front steps—all made in Chicago.*

Negro freedoms were gradually curtailed in the 1840s and 1850s by more rigid enforcement of the rules; there is a touching memento of slavery preserved in Tulane Library, a pass made out to a slave girl named Julia, aged nine, height three foot six inches, to pass and repass at night. Buckingham reported in the 1840s that "in no part

*Lafcadio Hearn, in his story "The Last of the Voodoos," described a free colored man, Jean Montanet, who had been captured as a slave in Senegal, who bought some property on Bayou Road where he practiced voodoo and Creole medicine and lived in great style on his earnings.

of the South . . . do the whites seem to be in greater dread of the rising of the slaves than here in Louisiana." Regulations were published for the behavior of free Negroes toward whites though the enforcement of the regulations is a better indication of how restricted their lives were. The law turned a relatively blind eye, for instance, on Negro churches and the schools for free colored children, of which there were several at one time—colored illiteracy was said to be less than that of white immigrants. In 1842 free Negroes were forbidden entry to Louisiana, which meant fewer children were sent away to schools in Europe or the North—free Negroes arriving aboard ship in New Orleans, for instance, were arrested and jailed for the duration of their stay if they landed. But free Negroes could make contracts, acquire by inheritance, and transmit by will, privileges which were by no means to be found throughout the country.

Manumission also became harder, and in 1857 was forbidden altogether. In the 1840s and 1850s freed Negroes in New Orleans as elsewhere were encouraged to emigrate. Schemes for African emigration were never very successful, but free coloreds had already set an example for emigration, some of them going to Haiti (the Emperor of Haiti even had an agent in the city advertising his country) and Cuba. John McDonogh was a great enthusiast for such schemes. A man with a strict Sabbatical upbringing, he was very dismayed by the custom of allowing slaves to work for themselves on Sundays and devised an elaborate scheme allowing them to work half of Saturdays instead, their earnings being accumulated until they could buy their freedom. With his slaves going to church on Sundays, McDonogh "noticed a remarkable change in their manners, conduct and life in every respect for the better." He also advocated the federal purchase of slaves and their transportation to Africa, arguing that whites and blacks could not live side by side, and in 1842 he sent a shipload of freed slaves to Liberia at his own expense. But generally very few Negroes wanted to return to Africa, and descriptions of Liberia did little to attract them.

There was little Abolitionist fervor among slaves in New Orleans and even less among the free colored, many of whom felt that the abolition of slavery would threaten their own relative security. On the other hand, free coloreds who volunteered for the Confederate army were willing enough, after the capture of the city by Union forces in 1862, to volunteer for the Union army. Benjamin Franklin Butler, the general in command, found the leaders of the colored community his most enthusiastic supporters, entertaining him at lavish banquets in hopes of gaining his backing for Negro suffrage. A bilingual newspaper, *Le Tribune*, the first Negro daily in the United States, was set up by three colored San Domingans with a dynamic Belgian editor, Houzeau, to educate and inform the Negro community as a whole; it was generally published as a weekly but during the suffrage crisis of 1865 it came out daily. It was largely thanks to *Le Tribune* and another Negro paper, *L'Union*, that Negroes won the right to ride on streetcars with whites and to testify in court.

Several free coloreds whose education preserved their leadership of the Negro community as a whole rose to political fame during Reconstruction. Pinkey Benton Stuart Pinchbeck was perhaps the most famous of these—a mulatto whose white father had sent him out of the state to be educated, Pinchbeck became Lieutenant-Governor for thirty-three days during the impeachment of Governor Warmoth and was later elected to the United States Senate, though after three years that august body rebelled against his demagoguery and refused him his seat.* Oscar J. Dunn and C.C. Antoine were other Negroes prominent in Reconstruction politics.

The abolition of slavery led in 1865 to the establishment of the Freedmen's Bureau, to issue guidelines for emancipated Negroes who flocked from the devastated countryside to try to scrape a living in the city. "These poor people could never travel when they were slaves so they make up for the privation now," wrote Mark Twain; out in the hills of Louisiana and Mississippi, one comes across deserted hamlets of Negroes all of whose active inhabitants have left for the city. This influx developed into the now-familiar pattern of

*After Reconstruction Pinchbeck held several minor state appointments—as internal revenue agent and later customs surveyor at the port—but he left Louisiana in the 1890s to live in New York and then in Washington, where he died in 1921. A grandson of Pinchbeck's was Jean Toomer, author of *Cane*, the "supreme creation of the Negro Renaissance" of the 1920s.

country Negroes cramming into the poorer quarters of the city which swiftly became the ghetto slums of today. The old-established free Negroes, living in the Quarter or Faubourg Marigny—the colored Creoles—remained the leaders of Negro society, bolstering their position with the establishment of such respectable bodies as masonic lodges—Odd Fellows, Knights of Pythias—and social clubs copying the white Carnival krewes (such as the Original Illinois Social and Pleasure Club), despising their brethren of the plantations almost as much as did the whites. In the eyes of the latter, however, there was little difference in the degree of color or the generations of freedom: the Jim Crow acts of the turn of the century affected all sections of the Negro community.

The Jim Crow acts established Negro life in New Orleans very much as it exists today. Voting requirements gradually deprived the Negro of his vote; housing, education, employment, and transport were segregated one by one. The notorious principle of "separate but equal" arose from a Louisiana statute passed in 1890, providing for separate railway carriages for whites and coloreds (with the sub-clause stipulating that "nothing in this act shall be construed as applying to nurses attending children of the other race"). This was challenged in 1896 by Homer Adolph Plessy, a New Orleanian octoroon, who one day bought a ticket for Covington on the other side of Lake Pontchartrain, sat down in a white compartment, refused to leave when asked, and was eventually ejected and jailed. The Negro is still reluctant to vote—one sees notices around the Negro areas of town urging them to register—and an intense Negrophobia can still be aroused among the white working class by ambitious politicians. There is only token desegregation in housing, employment, and transport; on buses, for instance, the notices have gone but most Negroes still go to the back. Negroes are still employed in the old tasks of slavery days, in manual labor as stevedores, porters, waiters, and domestic servants.

Education gave the city its fiercest desegregation battle in the early 1960s. It was fought on two fronts: between black and white and between city and state.* The city reluctantly ordered its schools

---

*This has been vividly, if emotionally, described as "one of the nation's most chaotic and violent school desegregations" (Robert L. Crain, *Politics of School Desegregation*, Chicago, 1968).

to obey the Supreme Court order to desegregate, and the state, by cutting off funds, tried to bludgeon city officials into maintaining segregation. White parents opposing desegregation removed their children to schools in St. Bernard and Plaquemines Parish just outside the city boundaries. Four small Negro girls entering the first grade of two white schools in the Ninth Ward were accompanied for a year by Federal marshals.* The battle for the schools reached a climax in Plaquemines Parish. The Archbishop of New Orleans decreed the desegregation of Catholic schools in his diocese; Judge Leander Perez, "boss" of Plaquemines, told his "parishioners" to discontinue contributions to the Church—"quit giving them money to feed their fat bellies. . . ." Negroes, he told his people, were "unprincipled, unmoral, unclean," for which remarks he was excommunicated. Token integration was eventually achieved, and Perez, when he died in 1968, received a Christian burial.

Black and white in New Orleans still lead such segregated lives that the Negro world seems strikingly foreign—and probably always will. Bars in the predominantly white Irish Channel (but where a lot of blacks work, in the docks especially) still have signs up saying "White only" and even where the signs have been removed, Negroes know better than to enter, and benches are provided for them outside. You may go into a supermarket in an ill-defined area like Magazine Street (where a few blocks of Negroes alternate with several white) and recognize instantly who lives in the immediate neighborhood; if Negro there will be the grotesque root vegetables, the cheaper cuts of meat, and the endless notices shouting discounts on every shelf.

Established middle-class Negro society in New Orleans is less obvious. The old colored Creole families cling together, playing their part in the official life of the city, regarded as spokesmen for the black community by white administrators. They live in neat, com-

*The New Orleans School Board nervously left the selection of two schools to a computer, which lighted on the two in the Ninth Ward, an area then (many whites moved out after the crisis and after Hurricane Betsy flooded the area in 1964) of extreme white segregationists, bordering Plaquemines Parish, from which busloads of whites used to come daily to taunt those escorting the children to school.

fortable streets around the gracious green campus of Dillard University* near the lakefront. Their society is as exclusive as that of the old white families, and like them they buttress their traditions with carnival balls, long pedigrees, and snobbishness. They are often wealthy and make their money in the same professions as the wealthy whites—law, medicine, insurance, and real estate. They are the educators of the Negro community, heads of schools and colleges, owners of the funeral parlors that stand out like palaces amid the squalor of the Negro slums. And they are the ministers.

The Negro churches are perhaps the most vital part of the Negro world. There were reckoned to be some six hundred Negro churches in New Orleans before the war, and there is no reason to think there are any less now. Negro ministers were ordained from the early days of slavery to conduct services on the plantations—slaveowners found religion as good an outlet as any for frustration. Slaves were also allowed into special pews or galleries in white churches. In New Orleans the Catholic churches seldom segregated their congregations. After emancipation ex-slaves were expelled from white Protestant churches and began to set up their own, emotionalism creeping in under the strain of post-Reconstruction reaction. Negro leaders often became preachers. Since then there have also been innumerable spiritualist and Pentecostal cults, which are often started up by women who get calls to go out and preach and which live and die in a decade. The Church of the Innocent Blood was such a one, founded by Mother Catherine Seals in 1922 just off Flood Street in the Ninth Ward—the guidebook advises all too appropriately not to try to visit it in wet weather. But like many of its kind, its immense popularity was short-lived; the founder dies, the building is deserted, rots, and is pulled down and replaced by another cardboard shack whose occupants know nothing of its predecessor. A longer-lasting one on Felicity Street advertises Prophecy and Healing on Tuesdays. The churches preserve the matriarchy of Negro society; outside the

---

*Dillard University was founded in 1931 as a combination of three earlier Negro institutions: New Orleans University, Straight College, and the Flint-Goodridge Hospital.

churches on Sundays, one sees crowds of women dressed sometimes in white, sometimes in party finery with superbly decorated hats, and occasionally a long fleet of cars will pass, filled with chattering white-robed Negro women who will be a choir of gospel-singers traveling from one church to another.

The teeming life of the city's Negro slums is more conspicuous. The picture of Negro New Orleans at the turn of the century painted by Louis Armstrong in his autobiography is still valid today. A world of gangs, honky-tonks, street fights, prostitution, Charity Hospital and over all a strong, redeeming group loyalty. Violence was and is taken for granted in such areas as the Ninth Ward and Central City, the latter backing onto the stately mansions of St. Charles Avenue. Walking through the streets of a black slum in New Orleans leaves a thousand images in the mind. Memories of nervousness akin to fear, because a white person is so conspicuous and his curiosity so ill mannered, clash with memories of the friendliness and familiarity of greetings. There is the heat in summer, few trees to deflect its force, fire hydrants occasionally turned on for the children to play in (because the city closed the swimming pools for six years rather than desegregate them). There are the smells: of endlessly stewing gumbo (made of okra, which was introduced via the West Indies from Africa), of overflowing trash cans and inefficient drainage, of cheap cosmetics from the beauty parlors that play such a large part in the local scene, of frying catfish. There are the shops—corner grocers with their collection of strange fly-blown sweets, the vegetable shops selling piles of watermelons, pumpkins, sweet potatoes, and overripe bananas. And on Rampart Street the tawdry costume shops, their windows glittering with sequined dresses tarnished by too many Mardi Gras, and the voodoo shops smelling evocatively of decay, where you can buy love potions, gris-gris, and John the Conquering Root (you chew this and are supposed to spit the juice at passing women, who are instantly attracted to you), Dragon Blood Sticks and Five Finger Grass, the dusty bottles playing far more effectively on the imagination than the ridiculous voodoo dolls sold to tourists on Royal Street complete with pin for stabbing. And there are the people: old men and women sitting on the galleries of their wooden houses, houses and humans alike showing the effects of age; hugely fat mothers rocking and chatting on the steps surrounded by hordes of children; men of all ages loafing on street corners or squatting with their backs against a wall; women with heads wrapped in newspaper to preserve their straightened hair against a downpour. In the Ninth Ward one sees women picking weeds beside the medieval squalor of Tupelo Canal; they will stew these for supper. Here is a picture of New Orleans as invested with the exotic, the innuendo as a Breughel scene, far more forceful in its impress on the stranger than endless romances of Southern belles, duels, and Creole gallantry.

9. The Big Easy

THE ECONOMIC AND INDUSTRIAL WEAKNESS of the South was especially evident in its greatest metropolis, New Orleans. The seceding states had more than a quarter of the total United States population but less than one-tenth the manufactured articles needed even for an agricultural society, and perceptive visitors had long commented on New Orleans' lack of industry. The South, and New Orleans with it, was very dependent on the North. Thoughtful Southerners had been arguing for a more diversified economy for years, but the reliance on slave labor kept it wedded to agriculture.

The secession crisis seldom reached the peaks of hysteria in New Orleans that it reached elsewhere in the South. Business was business and quite sufficient to occupy a gentleman's mind; and apart from the hectic ravings of a Presbyterian minister, Dr. Benjamin Palmer (the most influential and eloquent spokesman for slavery in the city) and the pontifications of such conservative journals as *De Bow's Review*, everyone was content to get on with making money as fast as possible.* On the other hand, it was rare to meet an

*Despite Buckingham's comment on fear of slaves, New Orleans was probably less scared of its Negro population than rural Louisiana; the white population trebled in the twenty years before the Civil War while the colored population was halved.

Abolitionist; the occasional sympathizer might advocate a gradual emancipation but was quick to point to the demoralized and impoverished condition of freed slaves and their ill treatment in the North as an argument against too hasty measures, and this in spite of the number of free coloreds in the city who had obviously outgrown the crippling effects of slavery. Tourists were horrified by the slave dealing they saw all around them in New Orleans but acknowledged the general humanity of the slave-owner's relationship with his slave. Harriet Martineau spoke for many when she wrote that "the stranger has great difficulty in satisfying himself as to the bounds of the unconsciousness of oppression which he finds as the exculpatory plea of the slave holder." That slavery was an evil institution gently practiced was a common verdict.

Modern Louisiana historians point out that the state was only halfheartedly in favor of secession, New Orleans providing most of the Unionist sentiment, its citizens all too aware of the disastrous effects a war, cutting New Orleans off from the produce of the Mississippi Valley, would have on its economy. The secession candidate in the fateful 1860 election won less than half the votes in Louisiana, and New Orleans voted against secession by three to one.* The election was the usual gay exercise of public emotions, and clubs were formed to support the various political factions; there were about forty of them, mostly calling themselves "young" clubs (such as the Young Bellringers), but there was also one Fossil Club composed of "the old gentlemen of the party who have borne the brunt of many a political campaign." Members went around canvassing in fancy dress. Several of these clubs later became bases for recruiting for the army. Lincoln's election acted like a douche of cold water on the politicking of the city. At the state convention that followed Lincoln's election, the secessionists had a small majority and Louisiana ("with sublime imprudence," according to one of the most loyal of its historians, Charles Gayarré) was among the seven Deep South states to secede.

*The official returns were not published until 1970, in the *Journal of Southern History;* the majority for the secessionists was so embarrassingly small that they did not want to risk dissension by publishing the complete picture and significant sections were omitted.

The New York firms on which the New Orleans economy had been so dependent closed their offices and moved their employees north. Opponents of secession were quickly silenced; anyone found guilty of saying the North might win was liable to six months' imprisonment. Battle enthusiasms and recruiting of volunteers were helped by the unemployment that swiftly followed the Union blockade of the Mississippi mouth and the loss of Union produce from the Midwest; the Louisiana Tigers (later notorious, under their ex-filibuster leader, Roberdeau Wheat, for their wild conduct) were said to have been recruited "on the levee and in the alleys of New Orleans," and indeed for the wretched Irish longshoreman, deprived of his own meager means of livelihood, the army was the only alternative. William Russell, one of the most perceptive commentators on the relative strength of the North and the South (and one of the few British to appreciate Southern weaknesses) wrote of New Orleans, which he reached shortly after the outbreak of war: "The streets are full of Turcos, Zouaves, Chasseurs; walls are covered with placards of volunteer companies, there are Pickwick rifles, Lafayette rifles, Beauregard rifles, MacMahon guards and Irish, German, Italian, Spanish and native volunteers." The ladies of New Orleans celebrated the outbreak of war as members of their sex anywhere, making bandages, collecting bundles of sewing from the Ladies Sewing Society, packing up blankets. The whole city felt most heroic.

Because of the conviction that the greatest threat to New Orleans was by land attack, most of these volunteers were dispatched north to join the main body of the Confederate army. The river forts of Fort Jackson and Fort Philip about eighty miles below New Orleans were considered adequate defense against any river attack; and additional precautions were taken by constructing a cunning barrier of driftwood and sunken boats and slinging a chain across between the two banks. This, it was felt, should be well able to cope with any Union navy. It did, in fact, take the Union commander, Farragut, five days to pierce these defenses—in April 1862—and he never actually silenced the forts. Once through, however, there was nothing to stop his reaching New Orleans.

As soon as it was learned that Farragut was through and on his way upriver, panic took over in the city. People began destroying their own property rather than have it fall into the hands of the Union forces. Fifteen thousand bales of cotton were burned on the levee, empty steamboats were set on fire and released on the current, and the contents of the customshouse were piled up at the end of Canal Street to become an enormous bonfire. A less idealistic form of destruction was undertaken by the riffraff and unemployed, who ransacked warehouses along the river. Confederate and state officials hurried out of town by train. "A pitiful affair," wrote Miss Julia le Grand in her diary, adding that the city was without troops except for the "Confederacy guard, a sort of holiday regiment of the well-to-do old gentlemen of the city, who were anxious to show their patriotism on the parade ground but who never expected to fight." Julia le Grand's diary is one of the more detailed contemporary accounts of New Orleans during the occupation, imbued with the hatred and helpless anger of the Confederacy women.

It took Farragut only a day to reach New Orleans from the forts, but it was nearly a week before Union troops landed to take possession of the city, which they were anxious to achieve with as little bloodshed as possible. A small band of Union troops had already landed and raised the Stars and Stripes over the U.S. Mint, a huge temple to Mammon near the levee, but the flag had been almost immediately torn down by a notorious local gambler, William Mumford, who dragged it to Lafayette Square and distributed the tattered shreds among the crowd assembled there outside City Hall. New Orleans may have been only lukewarm in its support of secession at the outset, but the whole city was now fired by enthusiasm for the Confederate cause.

The occupation of the city was put in the charge of General Benjamin Butler, in peacetime an able lawyer from New England. The overall effectiveness of his seven-month rule of New Orleans was marred by its unscrupulousness and vindictiveness; in New Orleans history, he is classed with "Bloody" O'Reilly as one of the villains of the piece and, in the general history of the Civil War, Butler's rule of New Orleans has rather unfairly become "one of the great atrocity stories" of the South.

Butler made his headquarters in the St. Charles Hotel; when he was refused the exclusive use of Parlor 'P', which was usually reserved for notables, he took possession of the whole building. One of Butler's first actions was to arrest Mumford for desecrating the flag; Mumford was later hanged and immediately became a much-needed hero to the New Orleans population. Opposition to Butler's military administration, to Union troops and to the Stars and Stripes was ruthlessly punished by Butler, who became the butt of innumerable ballads and broadsheets proclaiming his evil character. Schools were closed for refusing to use Union textbooks; churches were closed if their ministers refused to pray for the President; citizens were arrested and jailed, often for unreasonably long periods (or exiled on the near-desert of Ship Island in the Gulf) if they walked in the middle of the street rather than pass beneath the Union flag. Butler's most notorious measure was his "Women Order," issued after the women of New Orleans pretended to vomit on Federal troops passing under their windows, adding insult to would-be injury by playing Confederate airs on their pianos. Butler in return ordered that anyone caught in the act should be treated "as a woman about town plying her avocation." This affront to the legendary Southern belle caused a tremendous uproar, which reverberated as far away as the British House of Lords, where Lord Palmerston condemned it as an act without precedent in the annals of war. "An Englishman must blush to think such an act had been committed by a man belonging to the Anglo-Saxon race," he thundered. New Orleans was as prone as anywhere else in the South to idolizing its women, what W. J. Cash has so nicely termed "gyneolatry."

In Butler's favor, he organized a spring-cleaning of New Orleans such as it had never had before or has had since, putting the hordes of unemployed to the task of removing piles of garbage, scouring the French Market, and taking other precautions against the dreaded possibility of his garrison being decimated by yellow fever. The poverty of the city when the Federals took over was horrifying. "Almost the only people visible are shabby roughs and ragged beggars," wrote one Union soldier. "The town is fairly and squarely on the point of starvation." Butler organized rations for as many as sixty thousand people at one point. He also issued labor regulations for the floods of Negroes who poured into the city from the plantations, often enticed (against Butler's order) by Federal officers, in the hopes of finding instant prosperous freedom.

Butler was recalled in December 1862 after creating a series of diplomatic incidents by arresting foreign nationals for aiding the Confederates. His replacement, General N. P. ("No Policy") Banks, was determined to substitute conciliation for Butler's severity. Churches and schools were reopened and other measures taken to gain local support. Already the free coloreds were agitating to be given the vote though, even among the Unionists, suffrage for the Negro was by no means universally accepted.* The 1864 constitutional convention bypassed the suffrage issue while abolishing slavery.

The whites regarded Banks's leniency as weakness; by 1865 ex-Confederates had virtually regained control of Louisiana, passing the so-called "Black Codes" (repealed during Reconstruction but revived with few changes in the Jim Crow acts of the 1890s) in the state legislature against the freedmen. Determined to remove once and for all the danger of Confederate rule, the extreme Radical Republicans reconvened the 1864 convention to try to enfranchise the Negro. In the riots that marked the convention's first session, thirty-four Negroes were killed. An investigating commission later reported that never in United States history had a riot occurred "so destitute of justifiable cause and so fiendish." The riots led to the ruthless Reconstruction Acts of 1867 and 1868, and the 1868 Louisiana constitutional convention confirmed Republican and Negro control of the state by disfranchising large numbers of those who had had anything to do with the Confederacy, and incidentally giving the governor almost dictatorial powers.

The following eight years in New Orleans, to an even greater extent perhaps than in the rest of the South due to the greater

---

*Lincoln himself, writing to Michael Hahn, advocated a qualified suffrage: "I barely suggest . . . whether some of the coloured people may not be let in (to vote) as for instance the very intelligent and especially those who have fought gallantly in our ranks."

concentration of a rootless population typical of a large port, saw a total breakdown of law and order. Elections were a farce, with Democrats and Republicans vying with each other to deceive the populace and were marked by pitched battles between the two factions. The government consisted of carpetbaggers, scalawags, and Negroes. Tourists visiting New Orleans were taken by embittered Democrats to see the state legislature in farcical debate. There was outrageous overspending; the St. Louis Hotel, for instance, was bought by the state for use as a capitol for $250,000 when it had only recently been sold for $84,000. The Democrats concentrated their opposition in White Leagues, similar to the Ku Klux Klan elsewhere in the South, to which almost all leading citizens belonged. Among them were the Crescent City White League and the Knights of the White Camelia, dedicated to the cause of white supremacy, employing the usual rigamarole of secrecy and elaborate ceremonial to attract numbers. The Republicans meanwhile had been so undermined by the ease and scope of graft and bribery that the constitution placed in their hands that by 1871 they had divided into two factions. One was led by the governor, Henry Warmoth (who once exclaimed when tackled on corruption in his administration: "I don't pretend to be honest . . . I only pretend to be as honest as anyone else in politics . . . Why, damn it, everybody is demoralised down here. Corruption is the fashion."), and his lieutenant governor, Pinckney Pinchbeck. The other was led by Customs-House officials with William Kellogg and Stephen Packard at their head.

For most of the Reconstruction period, New Orleans was on the brink of civil war. Riots followed the open break between the two factions at the Republican state convention in 1871; the following January Warmoth's opponents summoned armed support in the legislature, and four thousand armed men gathered on Canal and Rampart Streets shouting, "Down with Warmoth and his Thieving Crew." In March 1873, more than fourteen thousand armed men were enrolled in the Democratic White Leagues in New Orleans to ensure a fair election that year; when challenged by the Republican government on the right of American citizens to bear arms they barricaded themselves at the river end of Canal Street and fought a pitched battle with police sent to disarm them. Known as the Battle of Liberty Place (and commemorated now by an austere granite shaft), it attracted hordes of sightseers, every window along Canal Street filled by craning necks to watch the affray in which twenty-one people were killed. The contested Presidential election of 1876, between the Republican Hayes and the Democrat Tilden, eventually led to the compromise of withdrawing Federal troops from Louisiana, thus bringing the disastrous years of Reconstruction to an end.

But the damage, both moral and political, had been done. The defeatism of the South, which is still so marked today—in distrust of the Federal government—was mirrored in the faces of the populace; a Northern visitor to New Orleans in 1873 exclaimed, "These faces, these faces! One sees them everywhere, on the street, at the theatre, in the salon, in the cars, and pauses for a moment struck with the expression of entire despair." Eight years of rule by *force majeure* reinforced by corruption in every field of the city's government had left irradicable scars; the habits acquired during the occupation and reconstruction have stuck to this day—illegality become honorable.

Violence became a natural characteristic of the New Orleans scene, gunfights succeeding the more romantic and less effective duel. Vigilante groups were common, one of the most notorious instances of their power being the lynching of the Italians acquitted of David Hennessy's murder. Gangs ruled the Irish Channel—the Shot Tower Gang and others. Law officers were equally violent: a coroner is said to have bitten off the tip of his opponent's nose in a street fight; the city pound keeper was known for his tendency to pick pockets and fights; and a deputy sheriff gouged out an enemy's eye with his umbrella. Strikes were often accompanied by violence. A Committee of Public Safety was founded in 1881–82, a vigilante secret society with at least eight branches in New Orleans, its members patrolling districts with shotguns. Several similar groups claimed to be halting political corruption—the Committee of One Hundred, the Law and Order League, Young Men's Democratic Association; the latter even had armed guards at the polling booths for the 1888 election. Although one of the reasons advanced in favor of Negro disfranchisement in the 1890s was that elections would be less corrupt and less violent, this was by no means the case; in 1900, for instance, white mobs ransacked the city, attacking Negroes, and the *Times Democrat* observed that "the bloody horseplay of the mobs is full of instruction for the whole South . . . It is evident that the grand idea of white supremacy has become the stalking horse of anarchy in this part of the Union."

The New Orleans Lottery was symptomatic of the post-Reconstruction period. It is easy to laugh at the lottery now, but at the time it aroused the most heated controversy. New Orleans' predilection for gambling was famous, and there had been several attempts during the Colonial period to restrict it. There had been lotteries in the city before 1868, theoretically for worthy or charitable causes: one was organized in 1798 for the benefit of the theater, another in 1810 to raise money for Christ Church (now the Episcopal Cathedral on St. Charles Avenue), another to finance a masonic temple in New Orleans. But that of 1868 was far and away the most ambitious, "the most colossal private speculative concern in the United States." The lottery was chartered in 1868, to aid state revenues, the organizers undertaking to pay $40,000 to Charity Hospital (and handsome dividends to shareholders) in return for tax exemption. The lottery building was on the corner of St. Charles and Union—"its foundations rest on human misery . . . its windows are washed with human tears; its walls drip with the ghastly moisture of human pain and human blood," ran one typical piece of anti-lottery propaganda. The odds on winning were hopelessly long, but everyone played; there were over a hundred lottery shops in New Orleans alone, and branch offices in other American cities. Annual profits were reckoned at between $8 and $13 million, much of which was spent on fostering its political power in New Orleans and the state; one account estimated the lottery company spent a quarter of a million dollars in the disputed gubernatorial election of 1877 in favor of Francis T. Nicholls. Most Southern institutions of the post-Reconstruction period tried to identify themselves with the "romance" of the Confederacy; the lottery acquired respectability by the organizers (the chief of whom was Charles Howard) persuading the Confederate generals Beauregard and Early to supervise the monthly and daily drawings in the Academy Theatre. This became a famous ritual: the two generals would turn the two drums that contained the numbers, and two blindfolded orphan boys would pick one out. A daily ticket cost one dollar, but one could buy a quarter of a ticket. Monthly tickets cost twenty dollars.

By 1889, when negotiations were opened for the rechartering of the lottery, the company was able to offer to pay the state a million dollars a year. In 1872 George Cable had described the lottery as a "moral leprosy" for which his newspaper was sued, but both New Orleans newspapers were eventually controlled by the lottery, even the *Times Democrat*, which had been an outspoken opponent until it was acquired by Howard. Perhaps the Creoles' legendary gambling instincts would have kept it going, but it met its match in venturing into Anglo-Saxon territory outside the state, and it did not long survive a bill passed in the United States Congress forbidding it to use Federal mails. Something of the hostility evoked by this profitable but highly dubious enterprise was described by a contemporary critic who wrote that it was "lavish in its gifts, ostentatious in its charities and generous in public enterprise but the Church could as well draw its financial sustenance from the bawdy house or the gambler's den and hope to promote vital piety, as can the politics, charity or enterprise of New Orleans draw tribute with self-respect from the lottery swindle."

Economically the city was flourishing again; river traffic reached a peak in the last quarter of the nineteenth century, later declining from competition with railways that New Orleans was only now beginning to develop. Eads's jetties at the mouth of the river allowed ships of any size to reach the port. Meanwhile the atmosphere of moral and political stagnation that dogged New Orleans in the last decades of the century were blamed exclusively on the war and Reconstruction. Mark Twain commented how the war dominated conversation—"in the South the war is what A.D. is elsewhere; they date from it." Southerners ignored the fact that the stagnation was a visible threat before the war.

Politics in New Orleans had been a popular game since the Know-Nothing period and became an unhappy farce during Reconstruction, a tendency that it was hard to shrug off. The Democrat defeat of the Republicans in 1874 established the Democrats as the single party in the state, dedicated like the White Leagues to white supremacy and in New Orleans to the dominance of the city in state politics. The rivalry between city and state that has characterized New Orleans' relations with the rest of Louisiana ever since, could be said to have begun with the debate on moving the capital from New Orleans in the 1820s; Sir Charles Lyell, who was in New Orleans at the time, suspected that "a spirit of envy and antagonism of country against town lies more at the bottom of the matter than (the legislators) were willing to confess." The battle was really joined, and has been going hard ever since, in the 1890s and especially with the foundation in 1897 of the Choctaw Club to ensure Democrat control of New Orleans, New Orleans' control of the state, and to eradicate the Negro vote, the latter achieved over the next few years by the Jim Crow acts. In its own words, the organization was aiming "to assist the voters . . . in selecting their administrators," which it did with remarkable success.

The Choctaw organization was by far the most efficient and effective in the history of New Orleans politics—efficient as an organization, not as a city administration—one is very struck by the inadequacy of city government in New Orleans since the Civil War. According to Bryce, New Orleans is among half a dozen or so American cities where "ring-and-bossdom" have thrived most successfully. The Choctaws ruled the sordid side of politics as well as providing a headquarters for the city machine, New Orleans' version of Tammany Hall. In the state they maintained their power through an alliance with the so-called Bourbons, the planter aristocracy.

The Choctaw Club premises were suitably located opposite City Hall on the corner of Lafayette Square. Its most prominent member was Martin Behrman, mayor of New Orleans from 1904 to 1920 and again from 1925 until his death the following year (great in life, greater in death, was the dubious praise he earned from his fellow Choctaws). Other members included H. C. Ramoz (who achieved greater fame as the concocter of the famous "Ramoz Gin Fizz," a delectable drink on a hot day) and several members of the all-important Dock Board, which provided "nourishment" for the organization. But the Choctaws were said to have been defeated in 1920 by their rivals' use of dock labor; there were apparently so many workers on the docks that they could not be got out of the way to unload the ships.

Various reform movements came to life in opposition to the Choctaws, all of which were defeated by the elaborate organization of the Old Regulars, as they were also called, and by the working-class roots of the machine, whose rank and file supporters described the reformers as silk-stocking politicians out to preserve their own interests. John Parker was the most determined reformer, establishing a Good Government League in 1910, and ten years later, after that failed to dislodge the Choctaws, the Orleans Democratic Association.

The power of the political machine lay then, as it does now, in its accommodation to the law. It has used its legislative powers to favor special interests; the police have been lenient in enforcing laws (the "unobtrusive non-observance" of Sunday closing laws used to be a famous case in point) in return for votes; there has been a "friendly" regulation of public utilities and the customary manipulation of tax assessments. But it has been pointed out interestingly that New Orleans has been spared large-scale graft, due mainly to heavy city expenses such as drainage and flood control.

Such adaptation of the law appeals to a large number of New Orleanians who have a reputation for a pleasant disregard of the laws of their city, these being more honored in the breach than in the observance thereof. In the years before the Civil War, New Orleans had one of the highest crime rates in the country, rising to a peak during the winter months, and especially noted for the number of swindlers. Mayor Freret in 1842 decided against allowing police patrols to enter public places of amusement because it would encourage habits of dissipation; and Henry Didimus commented that the police had a rather questionable reputation even within New Orleans and their name outside "is held synonymous with midnight robberies and assassinations." There are plenty of examples today of an easy accommodation between law and the citizen; the explosion as well as the purchase of fireworks is forbidden in the city—as a rather quaint example of this—but enough are let off on New Year's Eve to persuade the uninitiated that war has broken out. Gambling is forbidden but every corner store in areas like the Irish Channel is said to be a betting shop in disguise, and pinball machines provide an easy way around the law. Would-be reformers in the city are discouraged from political action by the overwhelming power of the machine.

The Choctaws were eventually outwitted by Huey P. Long. Long first stood for governor in 1924, battling against the established political hierarchy (dominated by New Orleans) with a program of taxing the already vast oil investments in the state to provide better schools, housing, and roads; his defeat on that occasion was very largely due to the power of the Choctaws. Long was never enamored of New Orleans nor the city of him, which may be why the only road named after him is a dismal thoroughfare in Gretna on the West Bank. To begin with, however, he needed Choctaw support and repaid them for it by financing roads and schools in the city. In the long run he determined not to be dependent on the city, and by 1934 relations between the Long machine and the Choctaws were so hostile that the state militia was sent into New Orleans to supervise elections that year. So intense became his dislike of the city's politicians that he determined they and the city should benefit as little as possible from the bridge over the Mississippi named after him, siting it well above the center of the city. Despite his Dixie demagoguery and his total disregard for the political niceties of democracy or the political sensibilities of his opponents, he did launch the state and New Orleans into a modernization of its education, transport, and other fields where the political patronage was valuable. Opponents to Long base their arguments on the thesis that the ends do not justify the means. After Long's assassination in 1935, his successors maintained the manner without bothering about the substance of his politics—Long himself had predicted that "if them fellows ever try to use the powers I've given them without me to hold them down, they'll all land in the penitentiary." The administration of New Orleans under Mayor Maestri in particular set a pattern for crime and corruption that staggered even New Orleanians. Maestri, who was mayor for seven years, was rather more unprincipled than most politicians to decorate the New Orleans scene; he is said never to have made a speech because he was so self-conscious about his Italian accent and the fact that he left school after third grade. In 1939 the scandal broke with the arrest of the President of Louisiana State University in New Orleans, followed by the indictment of over two hundred others, mostly on the Federal charge of defrauding the mails, a favorite way of arrest when state law fails to operate against its suspected criminals. There were four suicides, and the Shushan airport on Lake Pontchartrain had to be renamed because of the involvement of its namesake Abe Shushan, who was accused, among other things, of having made a handsome killing on its construction.

Since then, politics in New Orleans and in Louisiana have been fought on pro- and anti-Long tickets, with enough Longs on the scene to keep the issue alive. Huey's brother, Earl, was governor twice until he had a mental breakdown; Russell Long, Huey's son, is one of the two Louisiana senators in the United States Congress; the other senator is another of Huey's aides, Allen Ellender. Within New Orleans the issues are still subordinate to the machine and the professional politicians who emerge from it or in opposition to it. Reform movements are still set up to purify the city's politics, but their deliberations achieve very little.

After the Civil War, New Orleans declined from being one of the six most important cities in the country to one of the most important in the South—a position now being effectively challenged by Houston and Atlanta—the war a convenient scapegoat for a situation that would probably have occurred anyway. Her prewar reputation still drew the tourists who found the city as raffish, gay, gourmet, and even exotic as before. A German visitor exclaimed in 1869—politically as disturbed a year as any—that "everywhere is gaiety and laughter. Everyone is happy, refreshing himself from the week's work and obtaining new strength." Men still made fortunes but there were many other places where they could do equally well if not better. New Orleans acquired the narrow-minded provincialism of the South, which previously she had avoided due to the large immigrant population. This provincialism still prevails today and in some ways is one of the most likable things about the city. Wealthy parents will send their children to Northern prep schools and Ivy League colleges safe in the knowledge that they will return to the nest, which they do, complaining about the city's administration and politics but inseparably linked not only by family but also by the realization that it would be hard to find its attractive hedonism elsewhere. And the vast middle class has often not been outside the South, if indeed outside Louisiana. There are even enough people who have never been outside New Orleans to merit the city authorities raising a mound of earth in Audubon Park, known as Monkey Hill, so that children shall know what a hill looks like.

Like the rest of the South, New Orleans indulged in romanticism and sentimentality about its past that is still a habit today—"practical common-sense, progressive ideas, and progressive works, mixed up with the duel, the inflated speech, and the jejune romanticism of an absurd past that is dead," wrote W. J. Cash and, he might have added, the inflated histories. The one author of the postwar period with a more rueful approach was George Washington Cable; "his sympathies ranged upon the pro-Southern side of the issue, and his convictions drifting irresistibly to the other," eventually persuading him to flee the South and live in New England.

The city itself had changed little in appearance during the war, despite—or because of—the poverty and wretchedness of most of its inhabitants. "The dust, waste-paper littered, was still deep in the streets," wrote Mark Twain, "the deep trough-like gutters along the curbstones were still half full of reposeful water with a dusty surface" —rather like New Orleans today. But as a visitor in 1887 pointed out, "the city is not nearly as unhealthy as it ought to be with such a city government as they say it endures." Mark Twain thought it better lighted than any other city in the Union; presumably not a single street lamp has been added since most of the city is flooded by Stygian darkness after nightfall.

A popular travel agency description of modern New Orleans is "the city that care forgot"—all too accurate a judgment. Endless energy and money are spent on entertainment while the city's existence is nearly strangled by the boring inadequacies of the port, the welfare system, and education. One old city musician once remarked, "It used to be if you had a mind to, you could go any place in the city and get a job on Monday morning because you'd be the only person that felt like working." While wharves and warehouses disintegrate into the river, the city council and leading businessmen will spend hours and millions of dollars on a Superdome for the city. This *cause célèbre* is to rescue the city's tourism from the doldrums into which it has been cast by the superior attractions of its rivals, Atlanta and Houston.

New Orleans has always had a sporting turn of mind. At the beginning of the century, it was famous for its gambling, horse-racing and prostitution. Boxing has also played a large part in the city. Until 1890 it was illegal; a fight planned in 1889 was kept a close secret, the governor prepared a militia group to prevent it, and those who bought tickets boarded a train without knowing where they were going (Mississippi, as it turned out). In 1890, fights with gloves on were legalized in Louisiana, supervised by police and only in athletic clubs. It was a sport peculiarly well suited to the city's gambling instincts. Jazz bands used to publicize events around the town on horse-drawn wagons; the city became the national boxing mecca, and in 1893 was the scene of the longest boxing match in history—seven hours and fourteen minutes. Many ex-boxers still have nightclubs in New Orleans, reminders of a dim though not so distant past.

Football arouses almost as much interest in New Orleans as Mardi Gras. For several years the city was without a professional team, to its dismay, but recently a Texas oil millionaire set up a team that won the hearts, minds, and purses of the New Orleanians. The Saints, as the team is called, are a greater addiction during their brief autumnal season than the Olympics, the Monte Carlo Rally, and the World Cup all put together. Hence the enthusiasm for a domed stadium that can be heated and air-conditioned and have games all the year round. A game of football is far more worthwhile than modernizing the port.

The Saints team is obviously not the only thing New Orleans has to thank oil for. South Louisiana supplies about one-third of the total United States production of oil and gas, and New Orleans is the state headquarters for all the firms involved. As early as the 1820s, water well-diggers were irritated by finding gas instead of water. The first well was discovered at Jennings in northern Louisiana in 1901. It is easy to forget about the existence of this city-saving commodity; the oil people live far out in brash new suburbs, the tankers and oil barges are out of sight on the river, and there is little of the paraphernalia of oil industry itself. But the belching smoke stacks of chemical and oil plants are nowadays almost as symbolic of the Mississippi as white pillared plantation houses once were—and still are in tourist brochures. Approaching New Orleans on the freeway, one sees the high-rise buildings crowned by oil-company signs and in the narrow, dark streets of the business district that they overshadow are such outlandish concerns as Tideland Navigational Concerns, Dynamic Drilling Tools, Drilco Inc., Offshore Exploration Company; classifications in the telephone directory cover eight closely printed pages. Most of the production, particularly in the vast offshore fields at the mouth of the river, is in the hands of the major oil companies whose directors dine at the Petroleum Club and drink at the Offshore Lounge while their counterparts in the older New Orleans business world go to Antoine's and Arnaud's—the modern version of the American-Creole split. But many of the older families who are still wealthy can only afford to have their daughters be carnival queens — a fair gauge of wealth—because of a substantial income from oil often in the form of royalties on oil produced on their property. Oil has also been a useful political weapon; Huey P. Long's first major fight was with the big oil companies who were getting so much for so little out of the state. Robert Maestri was accused of receiving over a million dollars from oil interests, and more recently oil has been the profitable basis of power for Leander Perez in Plaquemines Parish, oil companies being allowed to operate in the area only on Perez' terms.

It is very easy to criticize the New Orleans way of life, and outsiders have done this from the beginning of its existence, their accounts often as prejudiced in one direction as New Orleanians' accounts of themselves are in the other. Its hedonism, romanticism, and pattern of illegality are common to the South rather than unique to New Orleans. One of the most delightful things, however, about New Orleanians is their imperviousness to criticism. They know things are not quite what they should be in the city—the port sinking into the river, the corrupt administration, the disgraceful slums, the backwater that nobody seems interested in (except tourists), least of all its bosses.* But these are the unattractive aspects of an otherwise most satisfying sense of leisure, which is coming to be increasingly prized rather than laughed at. There is something more than the merely sensual in Harriet Martineau's description of how "we walked under the long rows of Pride of India trees on the Ramparts, amidst the picturesque low dwellings of the Quadroons, and almost felt the glow of the moonlight, so warm, so golden, so soft as I never saw it elsewhere." The New Orleanian is not—cannot be—a worrier like so many Americans; life is not that serious. The pursuit of pleasure does indeed play a large part in the life of New Orleans from the very poor to the very rich, and it is a rather successful pursuit. A liberal attitude toward human frailties is no bad thing.

---

*James Silk Buckingham commented in the 1850s: "What is deeply to be regretted is, that the municipal authorities seem to want the moral courage to pursue, apprehend and punish those among them who are detected in the commission of crime."

PART TWO

THE PLACE

"New Orleans has at first sight a very inspiring and handsome appearance beyond any other city in the United States in which I have yet been."

—Benjamin Latrobe

10. The River

VIEWING THE MISSISSIPPI at New Orleans, one needs imagination and a few vital statistics to create from the turbulent muddy water eddying under the magnificent bridge a vision of its superiority to other rivers—its superiority in size, and in its power of life and death. Unlike most rivers it is narrower and deeper the nearer it comes to the sea, little over half a mile wide at New Orleans, over ninety feet deep below Baton Rouge. "There are no pleasing associations connected with the great common sewer of Western America," wrote Captain Marryat, "which pours its mud into the Mexican Gulf, polluting the clear blue sea for many miles beyond its mouth. It is a river of desolation." An American, Samuel Cumings, author of a navigation manual on the river, wrote more affectionately that "no thinking mind can contemplate this mighty and restless wave, sweeping its proud course from point to point, curving round its bends through the dark forests, without a feeling of sublimity." Inevitably there is truth in both these extremes: the Mississippi is indeed a muddy and polluted sewer for millions of square miles of America, but one is easily overawed by the scale of its activity, a mental image more impressive than the visible one.

The river once had many names: Mech-se-be, Malbrancia, Michisepe, Chucagua, Tamalisieu, Tapatu, Ochechitou, Spiritu Sancto, and Colbert, among them. But a version of an Indian name is the one that has stuck. It is 2,470 miles long, of which nearly 2,000 miles are navigable. The Mississippi drains an area extending from the Allegheny Mountains on the east to the Rockies and from Canada to the Gulf of Mexico. It has four main tributaries—the Ohio, the Missouri, the Arkansas, and the Red River—and several distributaries, of which the Atchafalaya, Bayou Teche, and Bayou Lafourche used to be the most important. Mark Twain estimated that the annual mud deposit brought down by the river to the Gulf would make a mass a mile square and 241 feet deep; nowadays it is said to dump two million tons of silt a day. Statistics are always relative, however; the Mississippi is at first glance one of the least impressive of rivers and, in spite of New Orleans' dependence on its presence, it is so concealed behind levees and wharves that it is easy enough to forget its existence.

But go up on the Greater Mississippi Bridge—bridges are the best place to get a view in New Orleans, and this one is 175 feet above the water—and something of the scale of the river may communicate itself. Its speed for one thing; right under the bridge, eddying along the levees of the west bank, hurtling toward the mouth at many miles an hour. The speed is accentuated by the river's being so straitlaced by the levees and wharves that hide it from the city, forcing the stream to delve a remarkably deep channel. One recent winter a coast-guard vessel was sunk in a collision in mid-channel just above New Orleans; the icy cold, speed, and depth of the river was such that it took divers several weeks to locate the wreck, which was eighty-five feet below the surface.

Early in the eighteenth century there was considerable skepticism about La Salle's high valuation of the river. "Is it to be expected that, for any commercial or profitable purpose, boats will ever be able to run up the Mississippi, into the Wabash, the Missouri or the Red River? One might as well try to bite a slice of the moon," wrote Cadillac. Nevertheless, the river was the reason for the foundation of New Orleans; it provided a sheltered inland harbor with access to the vast hinterland that La Salle had claimed for Louis XIV.

Men-of-war could escape from Spanish vessels into one of the three main passes at the mouth of the river; trading vessels could tie up at New Orleans without the danger of attack that was always present at the Gulf ports. In the eighteenth century there was little of the great river traffic that developed a hundred years later, but the Indian canoe known locally as a pirogue was already being used for the small trafficking between the city and outlying settlements such as the Germans upriver and along the Bayou Lafourche and Bayou Teche, and convoys of pirogues began to ply between the Illinois lands and New Orleans. Water was virtually the only means of communication.

By the end of the eighteenth century, the opening up of the Midwest by American farmers migrating from the Atlantic states led to the beginning of the river trade. In 1795 the Treaty of San Ildefonso gave the Americans the right of deposit in New Orleans, and the flatboats of the "Kaintuck" boatmen became a common sight along the levee just above the city, while the riotous behavior of the boatmen at the end of their journey became a nagging harassment to the population and government of the city.

Flatboats were developed from rafts of logs that could drift with the current down the Ohio River from as far away as Pittsburgh and Cincinnati—"long, narrow, black, dirty-looking, crocodile-like rafts," sometimes with a rudimentary superstructure to protect cargo and crew. But Aaron Burr's flatboat in 1805 was sixty feet long with a fourteen-foot beam; it cost $133 and had four rooms—a dining room, two bedrooms, and a kitchen with a fireplace—quite a splendid craft. By the 1830s the flatboats had become the huge pine rafts described by Mark Twain—"an acre or so of white sweet-smelling boards in each raft, a crew of two doz. men or more, three or four wigwams scattered about the raft's vast level for storm quarters." They could be steered to a certain extent by huge oars but generally relied on the flow of the river, a fairly unreliable and unmaneuverable means of travel, as a result of which it was reckoned over a third of the flatboats never reached New Orleans. If they did, and when their cargoes of furs, grain, and so on, had been sold or handed over, the crews generally broke them up on the levee, sold the timber, spent the proceeds in the already legendary brothels and gambling saloons of the New Orleans waterfront, and then set off home, usually crossing Lake Pontchartrain and following the Natchez Trace, a famous Indian and later pioneer trail, which ran from Natchez as far as Washington. Sometimes, particularly in the low season, crews would try to take their boats back upstream, a grueling nine-month voyage, battling against the current, often pulling the boat along the bank from one tree to another—known as bushwhacking—or poling it through the shallow shore waters.

Flatboats became quite sophisticated before they were eventually surpassed by the steamboat, carrying as much as three thousand tons. Arks, broadhorns, keelboats, mackinaws, and scows are some of the names given to later variations of the flatboat, versions that acquired a shallow keel, occasionally even a sail, and, in the case of the ark, an overall superstructure resembling its original namesake. A mackinaw was made of hand-hewn planks fastened together with wooden nails, flat-bottomed and sometimes as much as fifty feet long and twelve feet wide. Keelboats could not carry as much as a flatboat but they were the only ones that could be satisfactorily poled upstream, they moved faster, and sometimes two or more would be tied together—when Vincent Nolte came downriver in 1812, he had two keelboats tied together and made one his living quarters for the voyage—with a cabin, kitchen, and dining room—while on the other he loaded several hundred bags of flour to sell in New Orleans, thus enabling him to cover the cost of the journey and set himself up in business in the city. Arks varied in length from eighty to ninety feet and from ten to twenty feet wide, were square-ended with slightly curved roofs—similar to the grain and sugar barges that use the river today—and became the main vehicle for taking the produce of the American interior to the sea. There were also a host of miscellaneous rafts roughly assembled by families migrating down the river.

The boatmen figure among the more lurid legends of American folklore. "Old men and young men, hoosiers [of Indiana], pukes [of Missouri], buckeyes [of Ohio], crackers, greenies, busters and other varieties of civilisation are here exhibited in all the eccentricities of their individual characters," wrote Bishop Whipple of the New Orleans waterfront. Characters, half fiction, half fact, such as Mike Fink and Annie Christmas, lent their notoriety to every boatmen who was generally regarded by landlubbers as dangerous scoundrels. There were famous river and land pirates such as Colonel Plug and John Murrell who robbed boats on the river and returning boatmen on land. New Orleans, at the end of the river journey, saw the worst side of these men, celebrating their safe arrival after weeks of loneliness and danger, and more than once regulations were issued for the better policing of the levee and the city itself from the strangers' depredations, whose poor discipline accounts for the hostility with which the Creoles regarded all Americans.

Gradually, however, the keels and flats, arks and scows were superseded by the steamboat, the great harbinger of riches for New Orleans. The first steamboat to come down the Mississippi was the appropriately named *New Orleans* designed by Roger Fulton and owned by him and Edward Livingstone. It set off from Pittsburgh at the end of 1811 and reached New Orleans on Christmas Eve, which was declared a public holiday to mark the occasion. The whole city crowded to the levee, while Nicholas Roosevelt, who had supervised the construction, gave rides to Chalmette and back to those who could afford it. The steamboat later made weekly trips between Natchez and New Orleans, averaging an upstream speed of three miles an hour. On the strength of the *New Orleans'* performance, Fulton and Livingstone were awarded a monopoly of steamboating on the Mississippi for eighteen years and for every boat of seventy tons that they built within three years they would be allowed a four-year extension to the monopoly. Any infringement of the monopoly was to be fined $5,000. In 1814, however—the same year the *New Orleans* struck a snag in the river near Baton Rouge and sank—Henry Shreve built the *Enterprise* and brought it down to New Orleans with ammunition for General Jackson. Livingstone tried to have the vessel impounded, but the United States Supreme Court eventually ruled his monopoly illegal.

Shreve's design was much more efficient than Fulton's; Shreve had his engines above deck instead of below, one either side of the deck so that one paddle wheel could go ahead while the other reversed—a more maneuverable vessel, particularly upstream, than the *New Orleans*. The early steamboat was not very practical as a boat, the main objects in its design being speed and capacity; the seaworthy steamboat was still a long way off.

At first they were principally designed and used for freight, but this was gradually augmented by passengers, especially with the numbers of immigrants wanting passages upriver. The boats became more and more lavish in their furnishings, and there can have been few sights more impressive to the riverside inhabitants who flocked to welcome each arrival than that described by Thackeray, "a huge, tall, white pasteboard castle of a steamer . . . every limb in her creaking, groaning, quivering." "The dark at night was a great fire-work," he wrote, and one can imagine the Stygian blackness of the river lit up by sparks from the roaring furnaces, which earned them the sobriquet of "swimming volcanoes." Some were less glamorous than others, but the most gorgeous displayed a delight in fanciful design to surpass the most baroque Victoriana: "cupolas and domes and observatories to match," wrote Oakey Hall, two towering funnels with decorated ends like paper fingers on a ham, "a fanciful pilot house, all glass and 'gingerbread,' " painted paddle boxes, flags flying from every conceivable corner and the blazing furnaces, the crowds of passengers, the clanging bells of the ships as they arrived and departed from the landing stages (later replaced by whistles, the recognition of which became a subject of jealous rivalry among the experts)—what a glorious diversion from the dreary farmer's round and small wonder that these ferocious vessels were acclaimed by all and sundry as floating palaces.

In 1817 a German named Flugel traveled on the second *New Orleans*, which had allegedly cost $65,000 to build; it carried 200 tons, was 140 feet long and 28 feet wide. There was an elegantly fitted ladies' cabin, and a swivel gun to announce the steamboat's arrival and departure. Passengers were expected to obey the rules: smoking was prohibited in the cabins, and passengers were liable to be fined a dollar for the first offense and 50 cents for each five minutes thereafter; no one could speak to the pilot, and no gentle-

man could lie on his bed with his boots on. Cabin passengers paid
12½ cents a mile upstream, and 6¼ cents a mile downstream.

Steamboat traffic grew fairly slowly at first, in spite of the withdrawal of the Fulton-Livingstone monopoly; in 1816, for instance,
only six steamboats reached New Orleans. But by 1821 there were
287, and four years later the flatboats had been ousted from their
favorite anchorage just above the town and had been forced almost
as far as the small outlying suburb of Lafayette. The passenger trade
on steamboats soon reached such proportions that it virtually ousted
freight (which returned to the arks and keels), the larger vessels
carrying huge parties to and from New Orleans. "A trip to New
Orleans in one of our best boats often resembles a party of pleasure
and combines in its incidents much variety and no small degree of
luxury." "The men of business in the West, and all who are in easy
circumstances, travel often and very extensively, and are thus decidedly acquainted with each other." Half the wedding journeys from
New Orleans were made to St. Louis or Cincinnati by steamboat but
the most popular journey was to go down to New Orleans for Carnival, the celebration of which began as soon as the passengers came
aboard. "Large and cheerful parties thus meet on board the steamboats . . . and it often happens that the greater portion of the cabin
passengers form one circle, in which affability and freedom from
constraint are chastened by perfect decorum and good breeding."
Good breeding was not always apparent, however, particularly to
hypercritical Europeans: "Let no one who wishes to receive agreeable impressions of American manners commence their travels on
a Mississippi steamboat," warned the acid Mrs. Trollope; "for my-
self, it is with all sincerity, I declare I would infinitely prefer sharing
the apartment of a party of well-conditioned pigs to the being
confined to its cabin."

There were two classes of passengers: cabin and deck, the latter
made up of immigrants, returning boatmen and roustabouts, many
of whom paid a nominal fare in return for helping with refueling the
boat—stops were made at least twice a day for this as the fuel
consumption was enormous. Deck passengers had to provide their
own food but cabin passengers were often regaled with the most

sumptuous fare though expected to provide their own claret. Sir Charles Lyell found dinner aboard the steamboat *Magnolia* "only too sumptuous," beginning "with turtle soup, and several kinds of fish, then followed a variety of dishes, admirably cooked, and then a course of cocoa-nut pies, jellies, preserved bananas, oranges, grapes and icecreams."

The cabin passengers, many of them cotton planters on their way to or from New Orleans with large consignments of cotton or the proceeds therefrom, were obvious game for the Mississippi gamblers, a notorious class of gentlemen who ransacked the pockets of aspiring millionaries. One successful gambler, George Devol, outlined his career in his autobiography, *Forty Years a Gambler on the Mississippi*: "A cabin boy in 1839, could steal cards and cheat the boys at eleven; stack a deck at fourteen; bested soldiers in the Rio Grande during the Mexican War; won hundreds of thousands from paymasters, cotton buyers, defaulters and thieves; fought more rough-and-tumble fights than any man in America and was the most daring gambler in the world." Passengers regularly played cards after meals, and professional gamblers would travel as passengers though they risked being recognized by such sharp-eyed regulars as bartenders, who generally came in for a cut of the gambler's takings. Devol claimed to have kept himself in shape for possible fights with impoverished players by exercising with dumbbells. Another famous figure was Major George M. White, one of the few river gamblers to come to a happy, nonviolent end, dying in California at the age of ninety-five. There were said to be between six hundred and eight hundred gamblers operating on the river before the Civil War.

Gambling was not the only hazard facing the steamboat passenger, for navigation on the Mississippi was always a risky venture and accidents were frequent, though less so than the lurid accounts might lead one to believe. "If you will throw a long pliant apple-paring over your shoulder, it will pretty fairly shape itself into an average section of the Mississippi," wrote Mark Twain, somewhat of an expert on the river after several exacting years as a pilot. The shape of the river and the speed of its current made the pilot the most important person aboard the vessel, responsible for knowing the ever-changing course of the stream. So mischievously did the river wander through its soft, sandy bed that Mark Twain reckoned "nearly the whole of that 1,300 miles of old Mississippi River which La Salle floated down in his canoes, 200 years ago, is good solid dry land now." There was a whole vocabulary for the hazards a pilot had to beware of: sawyers, boils, chutes, and snags—to describe the huge tree trunks, whirlpools, fluctuating sandbars, banks that had caved in, any one of which could smash the frail structure of a steamboat. Even today when the river is in flood at New Orleans, "traffic" lights are operated near Algiers Point to prevent two vessels rounding it at the same time; the strength of the current is such that vessels have been known to get out of hand and ram into the levee. The Greater Mississippi Bridge had to be built in winter when the river was lowest and slowest. Exploding boilers was another horrifying possibility; the *George Washington,* Shreve's second steamboat and the first high-pressure boat, was destroyed by a boiler explosion. In 1834 the Louisiana Legislature passed a law providing for the inspection of boilers every three months, and penalties were gradually introduced against overloading and racing, and against captains whose vessels had an accident while they were gambling or watching others gamble.

The famous steamboat races have been ascribed to the sporting spirit but could equally well be put down to the mania for advertising, for, to the owner-captains of the steamboats, the best way of proving the superior qualities of their boats was to outdo competitors. Most steamboats left the New Orleans wharves around five in the afternoon, which made a race almost inevitable for the first few miles. The most famous race was that between the *Robert E. Lee* and the *Natchez* in 1870, establishing a record between New Orleans and St. Louis of three days, twenty-three hours, and nine minutes. The fastest boat on the river, however, was probably an earlier one, the *J. M. White,* which took slightly longer over the route before the Civil War, but then the route itself was longer. Also, as Mark Twain pointed out, the distance between the two cities had been reduced by the new outlying suburbs.

New Orleans was the largest port in the South and in the antebellum period the second largest in the nation, and at the beginning of the nineteenth century the main outlet for Western produce. Trade statistics give some idea of its development: in 1821 exports were valued at $16 million, in 1836 at $43 million, and in 1846 at $77 million. Everyone remarked on the levee scene where port activity was most conspicuous: a forest of masts and funnels, a continuous hooting of whistles, cursing and swearing of Irish draymen, singing of Negro stevedores, the mountains of commodities piled up with little semblance of order and no shelter whatsoever along the river's edge. There was a big trade in tarpaulins until two Liverpool sailmakers, Sam and William Brook, decided to set up shop in New Orleans in 1840, making tarpaulins for the port—the firm is still there. Henry Didimus wrote of the steamboat landing, "Here all is action, the very water is covered with life; huge vessels float upon its bosom, which acknowledge none of the powers of the air, and wait no tide," many of them laden with cotton, "the same precious, gambling, national ruinous commodity . . . huge piles, bale upon bale, story above story, cover the levee . . . unguarded, unprotected, the winds fan it, the rains beat upon it, the sun bleaches it."

Steamboats from upriver and sailboats from overseas tied up in tiers three or four deep, the largest vessels at the upper end of the city in Lafayette, then the steamboats and small vessels, flats by the French Market off-loading fresh vegetables, and coasters down by the lower end of town. Passengers impatient for the first view of the city would disembark at Lafayette and walk along the levee to the port, or through the fields that still lay between Lafayette and the city until about the 1830s. "Steamboats, ships and barges go and come almost every hour," wrote Flugel, complaining as early as 1817 of air pollution; "I am tired of this boat life, the constant smoke etc." Some of the hyperbole of exclamations was explained by one skeptical Englishman, H. B. Fearon, as relief after a tedious and dreary journey downriver, but the atmosphere of commercial bustle, accentuated by not being concealed in sheds, caught the imagination of the most sophisticated, carrying it, according to Buckingham, to the edge of the sublime. In 1836 between sixteen and seventeen hundred steamboats and two thousand sailing vessels used the port. Even trading—in sugar, molasses, coffee, cotton, and rice, the principal commodities—was done on the levee, between Julia and St. Louis streets, and only later transferred to city exchanges.

Increasingly, however, cotton came to take precedence over other commodities, by 1860 totaling 59 percent of all exports handled from the interior. The cotton wharves were at the foot of Canal Street, the center of activity; sightseers in the evening cool, promenading along the levee according to New Orleans custom, never ceased to marvel at the mountains of bales on which the Southern economy was so precariously based. The busiest time was in March and April when the cotton was brought down in bales to New Orleans, taken by drays to the city's steam presses and compressed and repacked for export. In summer the wharves lay virtually deserted, the goods and the dealers abandoning the city to yellow fever. This concentration of cotton wealth was paradoxically one of the causes of the gradual decline of New Orleans as a port, a barely visible decline before the Civil War, only making itself felt after the war had precipitated the ruin of the South. By the 1840s, the heyday of the steamboat traffic, Mississippi valley freight was already beginning to be transported by the newly built canals of the northeast such as the Erie and Ohio canals, which were safer than rivers. Kentucky tobacco and Ohio flour was going direct to New York instead of via New Orleans. Between 1854 and 1858 Western products declined to only 18 percent of the total passing through New Orleans. Most New Orleanians, however, regarded the state of the port with the utmost complacency, refusing to improve upon what it considered an unassailable geographical position and disregarding the "impertinence" of other means of transport in competing with the river, whether canals or the rapidly growing, faster, and cheaper railroads.

Between 1835 and 1842 New Orleans had more banking capital than New York but most of it belonged to New York firms. None of the many shipping lines functioning from New Orleans belonged to local firms. Local merchants were castigated by one newspaper for not establishing direct steamboat links with the Northern states and thence with Europe; a local shipping line was nearly set up in 1836 but called off the following year because of the slump. Most of New Orleans trade, like its shipping, was in the hands of New York firms, hence the dramatic closing of trade on the outbreak of war when most of the main business houses in the city shut up their offices and moved their representatives up North. Similarly nearly all manufactured goods were imported from England or the Northern states. By 1850 New York was actually exporting more than New Orleans, even more cotton.

To this was added the general inefficiency of a port with no warehouses, leaving goods defenseless against the flourishing number of "river rats" (as the hordes of thieves along the levee were known). In one year tobacco losses of $100,000 were reported. There were no public auctions or exchanges; captains arriving with unconsigned cargo had to find their own buyers. The flatboat landing was originally along Tchoupitoulas, and a few warehouses were built there, but the river changed course, leaving a wider batture, and the warehouses were stranded inland, with goods having to be transfered there by dray, which everyone complained was too expensive.

Above all, the port was afflicted by navigation problems at the mouth of the river. The three main passes into which the river divided about thirty miles before reaching the sea were each partially blocked by a sandbar. Since La Salle's discovery of the mouth, the deepest pass has changed four times, depending on the state of the bar at the mouth of each. In the 1720s the French tried unsuccessfully to remove the bar by dragging an iron harrow over it, stirring up the mud, which should then have been removed by the current. In the early 1800s after the development of steam, oceangoing sailing ships used to sail or be towed over the bar and towed up the river by steam towboats (sometimes towing several at a time)—"a tablespoon-shaped piece of timber," according to Oakey Hall, with some of the most powerful steam engines on the water at that period. This was expensive and depended on the whim of the towboats' captains. Pilots were also very unpopular in the early years because no one could enter or leave the river without one aboard and the pilots had no qualms about refusing to go out in difficult weather:

"the many accidents that occur along those coasts would be in part prevented if the pilotage were open to all who had served a suitable apprenticeship," wrote du Lac Perrin.

As ships grew larger, however, it became harder to get them across the bar. Some were irretrievably stranded; some were kept waiting for days before wind and water were strong and deep enough to get them over; some jettisoned their cargoes to reduce their draft; others off-loaded their cargoes to cross the bar and reloaded the other side. Pilots were still blamed for negligence, but even their haphazard standards would not account for the fact that at one point in 1852, for instance, forty ships were aground at the mouth of the river; in 1849 forty-two outward-bound vessels with over 100,000 bales of cotton worth several million dollars were blockaded in the river by mud. Various remedies were suggested; levees to be built out into the Gulf to contain the flow of the river and thereby remove the bars; a ship canal to be cut from Fort St. Philip about fifty miles upriver into the Breton Sound. But nothing lasting was done, and meanwhile the Southwest Pass was dredged regularly and ineffectually every three years, and freight increasingly chose the more reliable passage by rail or northern canal.

Mark Twain, revisiting the Mississippi in the 1870s, wrote that "Mississippi steamboating was born about 1812; at the end of thirty years it had grown to mighty proportions and in less than thirty more it was dead." The decline was relative; the number of boats remained the same but more and more freight was traveling down the new canals from the new cities of the West, which themselves were growing as fast as New Orleans had in the past. Between the outbreak of war in 1861 and the capture of Vicksburg in the summer of 1863, New Orleans trade came to a complete standstill, though it quickly revived after the fall of Vicksburg once more opened up the river between New Orleans and St. Louis. But the war had obliged Western merchants to look elsewhere (if they had not already done so) for freight transport, building railroad lines all over the Midwest to carry their produce to the coast, and the steamboat seemed a slow and inefficient alternative. In an effort to retain the passenger traffic, larger and more glorious boats were built and decorated with a crescendo of steamboat Gothic rather like the super deluxe trans-Atlantic liners of today. The voyage downriver was gradually improved; a Mississippi River Commission was established in 1879, which organized "snag boats" to clear the river and light the navigable channel, making the river "a sort of 2,000-mile torchlight procession," according to a scornful Mark Twain. Even the railroads' success was partially countered by the development of huge towing fleets with tugs dragging six or seven steamer loads of freight downriver at a time.

New Orleans as a port was saved by Captain Eads, a remarkable man who in his youth had made a fortune salvaging steamboats, built gunboats for the Union during the Civil War, built a bridge over the Mississippi at St. Louis to everyone's amazement, and in the 1870s proposed removing the sandbars at the mouth of the Mississippi by a system of jetties. Back in the 1850s, a private engineering firm had tried building jetties, but the river destroyed them as fast as they were built, thus discrediting the idea. "The stupendous jetty fraud," as the *Memphis Avalanche* called Eads's scheme, was highly unpopular in New Orleans, where Eads was branded as a "dabbler in hydraulics" who was delaying the far more hopeful project of a canal. In 1876, however, Eads was given permission to experiment with the bar at the little-used South Pass; he was to finance the attempt himself, to be repaid only if he maintained a channel of thirty feet over the bar for two years. Eads built two walls in South Pass, one either side of the proposed channel; he established the jetty lines by driving piles, linking them with willow mattresses and other material as a foundation for a continuous concrete embankment averaging twelve feet in height. He maintained his thirty-foot channel—against a barrage of skepticism—and New Orleans was at last able to receive the largest oceangoing vessels. The success of the jetties led to an increase in port facilities and railroads finally began to expand. By the end of the century, New Orleans' port was once again second only to New York.

To New Orleanians the port is still the principal headache, as the principal source of revenue. It stretches for miles along the riverfront —there is only one small inland dock—its shabby crumbling warehouses, eventually built early in this century, shutting out the curious from its activity. The division of responsibility for the port is a nightmare: the United States Army Engineers are responsible for maintaining the remarkable depth—seventy to a hundred feet—of the mid-river channel (though the river does their work for them); the state for the depth along the wharves where a dredger is constantly at work spewing rich black mud from the edge into the middle to be swept downstream by the current. The state of Louisiana owns the docks, and the Governor appoints the Board of Commissioners (first set up in 1896). New Orleans owns the "public belt" railroad that encircles the city to reach the port, its engines disturbing the small hours with their piercing whistles.

The public is allowed to walk along the wharves at any time. If you are brave enough to dodge the stevedores and their trailers, the cranes hurtling through the air with their precarious bundles, the holes in the wharf through which you can look down to the brown river surging against the trespassing piles on which the wharf stands, then you can walk the length of the docks from the cotton warehouses at the foot of Napoleon Avenue down to the Army docks below Faubourg Marigny (this is the largest dock unit in the port, begun in World War I and not finished until the war was over). Do it on a Sunday if you are not brave, on a wintry afternoon with the sun setting behind the lumpish International Trade Mart building, throwing a golden light over the magnificent Mississippi Bridge; walk past Indian ships with sad little men hurrying back from hostile night spots to hang their dhotis from the yard arm, past Norwegian and Danish ships with huge disdainful Scandinavians staring over the side, past Chinese ships redolent with rich food smells and hospitable-looking crews, or past scruffy banana boats from Central America, which means nervously scurrying beneath the great steel arms of the banana conveyors ("each with a capacity of 2,500 stems an hour," proudly announces the dock handbook). Or you can walk along the back of the wharves, along Tchoupitoulas, for instance, past the dingy railcars with the peripatetic romance of their dusty names—Route of the Hiawathas, Milwaukee Road, Main Line of Mid-America, Erie Lackawanna. Weeds are everywhere, huge luscious clumps of clover, and the grass between the tracks is greener than anywhere else in the city. The population of Tchoupitoulas is not impressed by such attractions, however; they are black and depressed, with listless children. "Modern Luxury Apartments for Coloreds," runs a notice outside a prefabricated complex of rabbit-hutch buildings. The only respectable buildings are the union offices, modern and plate-glassed.

The port has been modernized, of course, since steamboat days (one of the last steamboats, the *Gouldsboro*, built as a gunboat in the Civil War, ended its days not so long ago as a river ferry from Canal Street to Algiers). Apart from the wharves and the miles and miles of railroad around the city, there is now an Industrial and Inner Harbor Navigation Canal linking the river with the lake below the old city, and a Gulf Outlet opened in 1960, which cuts the route to the Gulf by forty miles but is still as unpopular with ships' captains as bypasses with truck drivers, and the all-powerful river pilots complain of the unreliability of its channel because of marsh deposits. Alone along the banks of the Gulf Outlet stands the giant Michoud complex, where Saturn rockets for the moon launches were manufactured and transported to be tested in Mississippi and to be launched in Florida.

The Industrial Canal is a bleak and dirty waterway, its banks lined by rusty barges and powerful but ugly tugs like middle-aged boxers, and mountains of clamshell, dredged from Lake Pontchartrain and used for the foundations of everything in New Orleans. The barges are the mainstay of river traffic today. In the late nineteenth century they were known as broadhorns, and were partly propelled and steered by manpower. They used to sell goods all the way downriver and were broken up when they reached New Orleans. At the turn of the century they transported grain from St. Louis to New Orleans; grain is still one of the principal commodities handled at the port, and the ugly concrete towers of grain elevators dominate the landscape immediately above and below the city. On the great Intracoastal Waterway, which runs from Brownsville, Texas, to Florida, mostly a few miles inland and therefore protected from sea weather, you see enormous trains of these barges, as many as twenty-four in front of one snub-nosed tug. Others go upriver. When the barge is full, particularly of "bulk liquids"—by-products of the flourishing oil industry along the banks of the lower Mississippi, the rim is almost level with the water. An oriental aroma emanates from the names of these liquids—aromatics, alcohols, kerosene, olefine, solvents, lubricating oils, liquid sulfur—that demands a Masefield's versifying. And the tugs themselves, red-and-white, red or white, the largest of them with a bridge house four or five stories high so that the pilot can see right over all his barges, are in many ways as spectacular as the old steamboats. Some even have retractable pilot houses, which can be lowered for bridges.

The Harvey Canal on the West Bank, which connects the Mississippi with the Intracoastal Waterway, is lined with assembly plants of oil companies—thousands of miles of pipeline, towering rigs laid ignominiously on their sides, barges tied alongside with massive pumping equipment, line upon line of sacks of chemicals and mud for drilling. Sometimes you will see tugs pushing or pulling outlandish constructions on their way to or from the vast oilfields of the Louisiana coast.

The river is invisible most of the time in New Orleans unless one is on a bridge but the port makes itself felt more easily. There is the sound of the port, for instance: the sirens signaling the beginning and end of work, the deep bass of seagoing ships, the alto of the great container trucks as they rumble and hoot their way along Tchoupitoulas, the soprano of the shrill whistles of trains that chug around the railroad or shunt with no apparent objective from one section of the line to another.* The river is so much higher than the city that ships tied up at the docks seem to tower over the streets of diminutive houses. When the river is in flood, you can almost see the decks of the ships. If you are in a part of the town where there are no wharves but only the levee keeping the river out of sight, the ship seems to be running on rails along the top of the levee, effort-

---

*In the nineteenth century, steamboats signaled with a whistle; later the musical steam whistle known as a calliope (after the muse) and, later still, actual calliopes used to be played on board the river showboats by skilled musicians.

lessly gliding across its well-mown turf. When you are on the bridge, the activity may not impress you at first (in spite of Chamber of Commerce reminders that one freighter leaves New Orleans at least every hour), but the speed of what is there is remarkable—barges, ships, tugs, and also ferries, dancing a complicated reel across the current, swirling into the ferry landing like a waltzing Matilda, in winter lurching suddenly out of the river fog.

A dock strike serves to remind the city how dependent its economy and its people are on the port about which New Orleanians are generally rather blasé, rather like coal-mine owners who try to hide the coal dust under their fingernails. A dockside area such as the Irish Channel takes on a new character. In the daytime, when it is usually deserted and quiet except for the women shrieking over their washing lines and the babies playing around the front porch, suddenly men are everywhere, scrubbing, cleaning, painting, pulling to pieces and putting together again. But the evenings are silent, the bars are empty, and even the local supermarket takes pity on its stevedore clientele and curtails its sweet-toothed and expensive temptations. There is an enormous yard down on St. Thomas Street where dock workers are hired every day, where during a strike would-be workers squat beside the railings picking their teeth to while away the workless hours. There is no siren to wake one up in the morning or to warn of the day's end in the evening. There are no ships hooting on the river, and after a while even the train whistle is silent because there is no room on the sidings for any more trains. Only in the idleness and silence of the port are its noise and activity truly felt.

11. Water

THE RIVER HAS its disadvantages, of course, and a good deal of time, energy, and money are spent in New Orleans on coming to terms with them. Oakey Hall wrote that "few cities have as much water over, under, in front, and to its rear" as New Orleans. Miss Amelia Murray called New Orleans amphibious. "The mineralogist is completely baffled in this country," wrote Latrobe; "mud, mud, mud . . . This is a floating city, floating below the surface of the water on a bed of mud." New Orleans is below both Lake Pontchartrain and the river, an average of only one foot above the mean Gulf level.

The first recorded Mississippi flood was witnessed by de Soto in 1542, the year after he discovered it, and Bienville's New Orleans was flooded in the first year of its existence. Bienville's engineer-architect, Le Blond de la Tour, tried to dissuade him from building a city on a site that was so obviously subject to regular inundation; La Tour responded by drawing up the first levee system to be constructed along the river. There had always been a low natural levee along the river, formed by the flood depositing most of its silt along its natural banks; the further from the river source, the less was deposited, with the result that in the low-lying areas of the lower Mississippi Valley, and especially around and below New Orleans, the land is several feet below the river. Two years after Bienville began building his new settlement, the flood was so severe that a levee became essential; but the first proper levee was not complete until 1727, less than half a mile long, though continued on a smaller scale either side of the city. In the Spanish period Carondelet tried firming the levee by planting trees along it, but these were uprooted by boats tying up to them; it was not uncommon either for people to dig away at the levee to get clay for bricks. Even the earliest levees were no more than three feet high. New Orleans residents "who have particular knowledge of the work" were assigned responsibility for sections of the levee during the Colonial period. In 1743 the French authorities decreed that landowners complete their own levees by the following year or pay the severe penalty of forfeiting their lands. Planks, pickets, and piles of Spanish moss were stored at regular intervals along the levee. During the first half of the nineteenth century, cypress slabs were sometimes buried in the levee to help keep it in place but this was no protection against water seeping through animal burrows. Maintenance was haphazard, and crevasses, the term for breaks in the levee under flood pressure, were common. A refinement in levee construction was to build it of shells dredged from Lake Pontchartrain and to reinforce the base by inserting the fan-shaped fronds of the palmetto into the ground.

Floods were regular, however; New Orleans was less often affected than other towns further upriver because much of the force of the flood was spent by the time it reached the city, but when the levee did burst near the city, the havoc was much greater. The Macarty crevasse in 1816 just above New Orleans (in that part of the levee opposite the Macarty plantation where Audubon Park now is) was one of the worst of such floods; afterward Latrobe wrote about the difficulty of finding engineers to go to New Orleans to man his pumping station: "the houses are full of alligators and eels, and mud a foot deep . . . nothing short of a Constantinopolitan plague can follow the inundation." Another flood in 1849 submerged two thousand tenements and left twelve thousand people homeless—"mostly of the humble class of labouring men to whom small losses are heavy burdens." There were flood depths of ten feet in some parts of town.

Although by the middle of the nineteenth century the Federal government was beginning to take an interest in river control, it was more from the angle of navigation, and flood precautions were left to local authorities. Swamp acts were passed in 1849 and 1850, however, allowing riverside states to sell all swamp and overflow lands and to use the proceeds for drainage, reclamation, and flood-control projects. During the Civil War the levees all along the river were much neglected, partly due to a severe flood in 1862, the damage from which was not repaired, and partly because one side would cut the levees against its enemy. In 1879 the Mississippi River Commission began to organize flood control, but the public was more interested in railroads and no money was forthcoming. Right up to the disastrous flood of 1927, flood control continued to depend on levees, partly because by containing the river within its banks the depth of the channel was maintained and it was feared that alternatives or additional measures such as spillways would disperse the strength of the current.

In 1927 a record winter and spring rainfall combined with floods to displace 637,000 people in the Mississippi Valley, inundating about 26,000 square miles; New Orleans was only saved by a dramatic last-minute decision to blast the levee below the city at Caernarvon, flooding most of St. Bernard Parish but saving New Orleans. The idea of cutting the levee to relieve flood pressure was not new; in the nineteenth century, inhabitants of one river bank had sometimes been known to slip across to cut the levee on the other bank to save their own lands, and horseback patrols were sometimes mounted to guard against such inhuman tactics. Obviously something radical had to be done to protect the nation's richest agricultural land from such damage. "Congress quit splitting hairs under the doctrine that so long as the Mississippi remains within its banks it's ours but when it breaks out it's yours," remarked a local politician. It was realized that the levees were merely increasing the force of the water, and nowadays a maze of intricately planned cutoffs, spillways, and dams controls the river, able to cope with a flood 20 percent larger than that of 1927.

One such spillway involves the Atchafalaya River, a distributary of the Mississippi, which was in danger of running away with its parent river (thus abandoning New Orleans and the Delta area to salt water). Today the connection between the Mississippi and the Atchafalaya has been dammed and the latter is only used for the carefully controlled exit of flood waters. Another smaller spillway is the Bonnet Carré about thirty miles above New Orleans, where flood water from the Mississippi threatening New Orleans can be released into Lake Pontchartrain; this has been used three times to save the city from flood. The Bonnet Carré spillway is an open expanse of reeds and grass, the Atchafalaya an impressive maze of lakes and dense cypress swamps, the hordes of mosquitoes and their services to flood control the only common attributes of the two spillways.

The levee is always present in New Orleans. Along the central part of the city it is disguised by warehouses and wharves but further out, above Napoleon Avenue or below the Industrial Canal and along the shore of Lake Pontchartrain, the high grassy bank visibly keeps out the water. A levee board was established in the 1890s to replace the haphazard system whereby city levees were partly the city's responsibility, partly private, and partly that of the dock board; even today the levee board often discovers areas of levee that it was ignorant of, especially in the lower part of Orleans parish. The board has designed a more or less foolproof levee, facing it in sites liable to erosion with concrete revetments effective against wave erosion (though motorboats are forbidden on Bayou St. John, thank goodness, as a further guard against this) and the more insidious but equally dangerous diggings of nutria, muskrat, and crawfish. An eighty-foot muskrat tunnel was once discovered in the lakefront levee; nutria undermine the levee with a series of "caves"; and the crawfish, the delectable "mud-bug" upon which New Orleanians feast in the early summer, does every bit as much damage with his little tunnels, the excavations from which can be spotted all over the place—except nowadays in the levee—in the form of pinnacles of mud, sometimes as much as a foot high, with a hole in the middle.

The river levee is twenty feet above the mean river level, allowing for five feet above the highest flood level recorded. Along Lake

Pontchartrain it is nine and a half feet above the water, allowing for the tidal floods that sweep up the lake during hurricanes and other tropical storms. Between the levee and the river is the batture, land built up by the river's depositing silt against the levee. Sometimes it is more than five hundred feet from the bottom of the levee to the water's edge, land mostly overgrown with cottonwood and willow trees wound together by tenacious creepers, hiding small, still ponds abandoned after the spring flood, wrecked cars, and flood debris. From the earliest years of New Orleans history, ever since there was a levee in fact, the inhabitants of the city have regarded the batture and its treasures as being at their disposal—its woods, its soil, its ground. At the end of the eighteenth century, the batture just above the old city became the favorite landing spot (because of the shallow water) for flatboats and keelboats, where the owners would stack up their cargoes prior to sale.

The batture along the bottom of what are now Canal, Common, and Gravier streets was wider than at most points, due to the action of the river, and when, at the beginning of the American period, the city began to grow beyond the walls of the old French city, the batture became a very promising piece of property. Owners of property behind the levee grew increasingly possessive about the batture on the other side, soon coming to regard it as part of their property although generally content to leave it open to the public. The largest owner, Jean Gravier, fenced his area in, however, and sold some of it to the brilliant and ambitious lawyer Edward Livingstone, who was prepared to do battle for his claim to the batture. Livingstone's ambition was to improve the batture as an investment by building a canal from the river to the basin of Carondelet Canal, thus connecting the river with the lake. In 1807 fighting broke out between his workmen and the local inhabitants digging for their soil and chopping their wood, and the case was referred to the courts, which decided in favor of Livingstone and Gravier. Claiborne took the issue to the Supreme Court, which also declared in Livingstone's favor, but after several years—and a bitter pamphlet war between Livingstone, an early exponent of individual rights and limits to Federal authority, and Thomas Jefferson, who had ordered the batture to be seized as Federal property—Livingstone lost and the batture was declared government property.

Before the Civil War the batture and the levee were prominent features in the tourist's visit to New Orleans. During the daytime on the levee and batture opposite the First and Second municipalities, all was chaos, for this was the center of port activity. But in the cool of the evening after sunset, it became a popular promenade for the fashionable, ladies picking their way in and out of mountains of cotton bales and tobacco, vats of molasses, and sacks of rice. "The Levy is the Walk in the Evening, if it is pleasant everybody is seen walking on it of all Ranks and Colours, joseling One Another without distinction and One scarecly hears a word but French spoken." Young gentlemen new to New Orleans would wander along the levee in search of the allegedy exquisite quadroons, perhaps eventually finding some girl less comely and more accessible than legend would have it, with whom he could live during his season in New Orleans. At night the levee was taken over by less genteel customers while everyone else stayed well away; the batture was a home for boatmen and "river-rats" and the levee was their playground. The explorer Henry Morton Stanley, who as a boy had come to New Orleans from Liverpool and was adopted by a prosperous merchant, described the levee as a haunt for "slung-shots, doctored liquor, shanghai-ing and wharf-ratting." American sailors regularly fought pitched battles with European sailors; Flugel noted in 1817 that crossing the levee to get to his boat late at night was best avoided "since so many persons have been assaulted and several murdered."

There have always been squatters along the levee, whether boatmen from Kentucky or sailors from overseas. Many were steamboat hands and many today are sailors, such as the old man who calls his batture shack "Sailor's Rest" and claims to have owned it for thirty years but to have lived in it a total of no more than three months. At regular intervals these squatters have been moved off; the ground is public property and the public may have access to it but theoretically may not clutter it up with their shacks, which have not changed much in design since the eighteenth century—bits of old boats, logs stranded in the flood, a few broken panes of glass—though the prevalence of rusty corrugated iron roofing is new. Every so often the Levee Board is obliged by the changing course of the river to redesign its levees, and the batture dwellers are moved, literally lock, stock and barrel, off the batture; the press arrives for the occasion and the inhabitants are exalted from the oblivion of their cosy day-to-day squalor to heights of national sympathy, the public regaled with tales of old men and women who have lived there for forty years or more—"but we have our rights too," protest Levee Board officials. The squatters' lives seem extraordinarily precarious. The shanties are built on rickety stilts, and the walls look and often are paper-thin. They are usually surrounded by the eviscerated carcasses of cars and refrigerators but sometimes also by brilliant lilies and daisies, prosperous vegetable gardens, and noisy hencoops. In spite of their proximity to the river, these stilt-houses are high enough—often nearly level with the top of the levee, which is connected with the front door by a gang plank—to resist most floods, and can even withstand hurricanes. They pay no property taxes because the land is government property and they are self-sufficient, living off their gardens, their fishing in the river, and their hunting among the cottonwoods for coon and possum. Of the black community living on the batture, Harriet Martineau wrote rather romantically that "the black man never looks more contented than when he shrouds himself in rank vegetation, and lives in a concert of insect chirping, droning and trumpeting."

The Mississippi is only part of the flood problem of New Orleans. The city has an annual rainfall of nearly 57 inches, several inches of which can fall in one summer storm.* One is never quite dry in summer; with the humidity around 77 percent, New Orleans drips through the summer months, with its luxuriant weeds, grass waist-high, ferns sprouting from every wall, mildew in every cupboard. A rainstorm in New Orleans is a bounteous affair. There is seldom more than five or ten minutes' warning, its arrival heralded by scudding purple clouds, rolls of thunder and lightning, winds tearing the patio banana plants to ribbons. There is no chance of weathering

---

*The maximum recorded rainfall is 85.4 inches, 9 inches falling in one storm.

it, short of virtually swimming. Drainpipes leak, gutters overflow, patios drain into streets, and hopefully streets drain into canals. Then afterward is the refreshing steam, the clean smell, the coolness. To cope with this, and even more with the threat of hurricanes blowing up Lake Pontchartrain, the city has built up a complicated system of canals and pumping stations for surface water that has no direct connection with the river, making New Orleans reputedly a more canal-conscious city even than Venice. Some waterways have now been filled in, such as the Carondelet Canal, which ran from Bayou St. John to the edge of the old city; others, such as the New Basin Canal built by the Americans to compete with the Carondelet Canal, have been covered over and explain the number of wide, spacious roads that cut down the traffic problem in so much of New Orleans.

Bayou St. John is the only natural waterway still visible in the city, though parts of Bayou Metairie, which used to run along the edge of Metairie Ridge, can still be seen in the lakes of City Park. Bayou St. John was the first inhabited part of the New Orleans area and, after the founding of the city, was used regularly by small trading vessels. Not until the early years of this century did New Orleans begin to spread out toward the bayou and only then because the swamps were gradually being drained and reclaimed for building. There is little sign of New Orleans' elaborate drainage system nowadays as one drives around the city. The widest street in New Orleans is appropriately named Canal Street but never actually contained a canal. In 1835 the New Orleans Drainage Company was set up to coordinate drainage, proposing to drain all land between Faubourg Livaudais (now the Garden District) and the lake, but the company collapsed in the 1837 slump. Gradually, however, canals were dug —the Toledano in 1860 to connect with the New Basin Canal, then the Melpomene joined with the Toledano to take water from the Claiborne Canal into the lake. In 1875 the Nashville Avenue Canal drained the low area between St. Charles Avenue and the river. The most important canal is now along Broad Street, the lowest point in the city (there is a drop of twelve to eighteen feet between the riverfront and Broad Street so that canals feeding the Broad Street

Canal move at a good speed); there are five pumping stations along it, and it finally drains into Lake Borgne.

New Orleans was notorious even in the early years of this century for its rudimentary drainage and water schemes. City blocks were known as *ilets* because they were surrounded by water after a heavy rainstorm. Visitors were appalled by the squalor of the city itself, pools of stagnant water everywhere, popular breeding grounds for mosquitoes. The city was supposed to be cleaned by opening the levee to release water onto the streets, which were then swept by slaves, but there seems to have been nowhere for them to sweep the water and refuse. The problem remained insuperable until the invention of more efficient pumps. Streets at the back of town, such as the suitably named Marais Street, were bordered "by a canal of inky-coloured, filthy liquid." Lafayette streets drained into Gormley's Basin, a filthy pond at the back of town, not helped by the soap factories and shanties around its edges. It was reckoned in the middle of the century that there was scarcely an old house that could be safely occupied because of the badly drained land on which its pile foundations rested. Benjamin Butler is credited with being the first to do anything really effective about cleaning up the city, attributing the regular epidemics of yellow fever to its filth and terrified that his small Federal garrison would be attacked by an epidemic. There were no sewers, he complained, only open drains, none of which had been cleaned for years. Waterworks officials were ordered to get all their men onto the streets to clean up, and were helped by a providential rainstorm to clear out the gutters and by a "norther" to blow the muck into the sea from Lake Pontchartrain.

There was no underground drain in New Orleans until 1880, when the St. Charles Hotel built a private sewer emptying into the Mississippi. Several years later the city farmed out the construction of sewers to a private company but progress was slow. By the early 1900s, however, Mayor Behrman could politically extol "the courageous, public-spirited citizens of New Orleans" for "voluntarily" taxing themselves "that the city might be properly drained, that an efficient system of sewerage might be established and that the inhabitants might have an abundant and unfailing supply of pure and healthful water." Some people might have doubts about the efficient system of sewerage; sewage outlets of many older houses are so cracked and leaking today that their contents escape into the main drainage channels that run out into Lake Pontchartrain, especially in the rainy summer season, polluting it to the extent that bathing is forbidden for nine out of every ten days in the summer.

Healthful the New Orleans water may be, but pure it is not; the Mississippi has never been praised for the taste of its water, least of all today with the chlorine content needed to make it healthful. "In a half pint tumbler of this water has been found a sediment of two inches of slime. It is notwithstanding extremely wholesome and well-tasting and very cool in the hottest seasons of the year . . . The inhabitants of New Orleans use no other water than that of the river, which by keeping in jars becomes perfectly clear," wrote Thomas Hutchins in 1784. River boatmen used to let it stand several days in jars on their flatboats before drinking it but then swore by its efficacy in a number of cases. Even today there is something to be said for letting the New Orleans tap water stand a day or two; it loses much of its chlorine taste that way. Some found the water an aperient, others gave it powers of fertility. Berquin Duvallon disliked the taste and the color though admitted it seemed to do little harm, "notwithstanding the river is the receptacle of immense filth and a thousand dead beasts are thrown into it." Whatever the case may be, he added, the Creoles "make a pompous eulogium of it, attributing to it the rarest and most salubrious properties."

A waterworks system set up in 1810 had slaves pumping water from the Mississippi into a reservoir from which hollowed cypress logs conducted "a thin yellow stream" to a few select subscribers. Other inhabitants, then as now, bought water in hogsheads, which had been brought from the "Ozone Belt" on the other side of Lake Pontchartrain. Attempts to dig wells to water fresher than that of the river led to such stories as that told to Buckingham of people digging a well who thirteen feet down came to "a forest of trees, standing upright in their natural position, all without leaves and mostly without branches but the trunks still fresh"—enough to discourage any fresh-water enthusiast.

Mark Twain was greatly relieved when he revisited the city after the Civil War to find that the water at any rate had not changed. "If you will let your glass stand half an hour, you can separate the land from the water as easy as Genesis; and then you find them both good: the one good to eat, the other good to drink. The land is very nourishing; the water is thoroughly wholesome. The one appeases hunger; the other, thirst. But the natives do not take them separately, but together, as nature mixed them. When they find an inch of mud in the bottom of a glass, they stir it up, and then take the draught as they would gruel. It is difficult for a stranger to get used to this batter, but once used to it he will prefer it to water. This is really the case. It is good for steamboating, and good to drink; but it is worthless for all other purposes except baptizing."

Water is always present in New Orleans in spite of the efforts of the Levee Board, the Sewerage and Water Board, and the much-maligned army engineers who, being perhaps the most conspicuous Federal agency in the city, get the full force of the Southerner's dislike of the central government. Particularly is it ever present in the languid humidity of the air; no wonder that anyone born in the city and brought up in such a climate acquires the dubious distinction of being linked with its Creole undertones of idleness and siestas. Only in winter is the dampness occasionally alleviated by a "norther," a blast of clear, icy air blown from the frozen but diligent Anglo-Saxon plains of the Midwest; for a few hours, even sometimes for a few days, the city is stirred by a foreign energy and vitality before sinking happily back to its humid languor.

Proud, civic-minded, and richly historic, New Orleans is the second busiest port in the nation, second only to New York. (Wide World Photos)

New Orleans' famed Canal Street, running toward the Mississippi River. (Wide World Photos)

The levees surrounding New Orleans protect the city and its inhabitants from the sometimes overflowing Mississippi River. (Wide World Photos)

Cotton is among the many products exported through the port of New Orleans. (Pictorial Parade)

Retail vegetable markets line the Decatur Street side of the French Market. (Wide World Photos)

From the air New Orleans appears to be like any other city, but early American history runs rampant through its streets. (Wide World Photos)

Jackson Square, at the heart of the famed Vieux Carré, is the eventual rest stop for visitors. The St. Louis Cathedral is one of the nation's oldest and is still an active parish church today. (Louisiana Tourist Development Commission)

This bronze statue of Andrew Jackson, hero of the Battle of New Orleans, dominates Jackson Square. (Louisiana Tourist Development Commission)

The Little Theater of the French Quarter (Le Petit Théâtre du Vieux Carré), the birthplace of the modern Little Theater. (Wide World Photos)

Characteristic of the French Quarter, this delicate iron lacework gives New Orleans its charming and unique atmosphere. (New Orleans Tourist Commission *and* Wide World Photos)

Basin Street, then and now.
Then: *The arrow, top, points to Lulu White's House of Mirrors, one of the section's most elaborate establishments. At left is the saloon of Tom Anderson, boss of the red light district.*
Now: *Today Basin Street is respectable and undistinguished. Its heyday ranged from 1897 to 1917.* (Wide World Photos)

Chalmette Battlefield, the scene of the Battle of New Orleans in 1815. Andrew Jackson's victory over the British was the greatest land victory of the War of 1812. (New Orleans Tourist Commission)

This antebellum home in New Orleans is typical of the spacious mansions constructed during the prosperous era prior to the Civil War. (Wide World Photos)

The Old Absinthe House in the heart of the French Quarter, now a museum and nightclub. It was here that Andrew Jackson met with the privateer John Lafitte to plan the defense of the city during the War of 1812. (Wide World Photos)

Warrington House, said to be inhabited by the ghosts of Madame Lalaurie's tortured slaves. (Wide World Photos)

A "streetcar" named Desire is now a bus. (Wide World Photos)

The most famous New Orleans event—Mardi Gras. (Wide World Photos)

Not only a city with a past, Louisiana's Super Dome puts New Orleans into the future. Upon completion in mid-1974, this superstructure will house a football stadium, a Madison Square Garden-type arena, auditorium, convention and trade show complex and exhibit hall, entertainment center, and downtown parking complex. (New Orleans Tourist Commission)

New Orleans from the sky with a model of the Super Dome complex. The Mississippi River curves past the city on its way to the gulf, providing New Orleans with the nickname "Crescent City." (New Orleans Tourist Commission)

12. The French Quarter

THE HEAVY SCENTED CHARM of the French Quarter sits hypnotically on the shoulders of modern New Orleans, haunting the business district, in the shadow of whose jagged roofs it lies with memories of a former prosperity. "The ancient part of the city . . . has . . . an imposing and brilliant aspect," wrote Timothy Flint; "there is something fantastic and unique, I am told, far more resembling European cities, than any other in the United States." Nowadays it is harder to see the resemblance, and for the European visitor the French Quarter with all its advertised foreignness may be a disappointment. But it has an elusive picturesque quality effected by the light, say, on a summer evening after a torrential rainstorm or in the cool dawn —a muted misty light casting into relief the ugly, serrated skyline of the business district on the other side of Canal Street.

The Quarter's lack of charm is very evident, however much one allows for the march of time and other excuses: it is overwhelmed with traffic, it has acquired all the tawdry trappings of tourism, crude modern architecture serves every useful purpose except that of pleasing the eye, and here the art of the fake reaches new heights. One senses its helplessness, assaulted by the sight and sound and smell of tourist buses queuing up outside St. Louis Cathedral. But if one goes beyond the cathedral and glances back toward Canal, one sees that the diminution of the Quarter by the businessman's world is half its charm. And in this lower part of the Quarter there are fewer tourist buses, fewer souvenir shops, fewer reminders of a more commercial contemporary world. The fact is that the French Quarter has survived the years and does provide an image of the past that has been obliterated from most American cities. This is perhaps the only reason for being grateful to the distorted historical romanticism of so many New Orleanians, which has undoubtedly played some part in the preservation of the Quarter.

Very little of French New Orleans remains except for the street names. The earliest houses were easily destroyed by fire, hurricane, humidity, and various other endemic disasters that made many contemporaries wonder why the city was founded there in the first place. The decisive reason, the link by Bayou St. John between the Mississippi and the Gulf settlements seemed small excuse for enduring the inconveniences of the site. One would like to think that the aesthete in Bienville influenced his choice; even today the impression of the crescent is extraordinarily strong, its curve neatly completed by the gigantic spider of the Mississippi River Bridge.

The site was chosen and the Company of the West's agreement was won in 1717, but no work was begun until the following year; hence the quarrel that has accompanied every centennial celebration as to which year the city was actually founded. An early settler, Jonathan Darby, described the site as one vast canebrake, and Bienville ceremoniously cut the first cane in 1718 when he arrived with a party of workmen to commence the clearance. By 1721 the settlement had acquired a chief engineer and planner, Adrien de Pauger, who by insisting on rigid adherence to his orderly plan for the new city bequeathed to future generations such a pleasantly symmetrical nucleus. One poor settler who built himself a house outside the proper alignment had his house pulled down and himself sent to prison by the irate de Pauger. The weather solved most of de Pauger's problems with recalcitrant settlers, however, when a severe hurricane blew down most of the houses in 1722.

Those who were assigned lots in the new plan had to surround them with stakes and dig out the tree stumps in the street in front;

later inhabitants were obliged to dig little ditches in front of their houses to drain off the surface water, which lay everywhere in the rainy season. Early prints of New Orleans show the settlement to consist of well-spaced houses, mostly along the riverfront where the land was higher, and centering on the Place d'Armes, now Jackson Square—hemmed in by cypress jungle in much the same way as the French Quarter is now hemmed in by modern port development and high-rise office blocks. An optimistic de Pauger wrote in 1723 that "New Orleans is growing before your eyes and there is no longer any doubt that it is going to become a great city."

The first brickyard was set up about 1725, permitting a rather more enduring form of construction though only by dint of stuccoing the brick to protect it from the excessive humidity. The only building that survives from the earlier days of New Orleans, however, is the Ursuline Convent on Chartres Street, and even there the present building was built between 1745 and 1752 to replace the previous short-lived convent. Today the convent, strong and plain, immediately impresses the visitor with its French accent: the steep slate roof; the large, well-spaced windows; the formal garden, its geometric patterns separated and linked by neat privet hedges like a miniature Versailles; in elegant contrast to the lavishly untidy tropical gardens found elsewhere in the city. Only the porch facing Chartres Street is a reminder of the meddlesome interference of later builders. The convent is second only to the Cabildo in the serenity of its architecture. Scarcely a sound disturbs the Renaissance dignity of its garden, protected by high impenetrable walls. The convent has had an uneasy existence since the nuns moved out in 1824, fleeing before the tide of development that enveloped the Quarter in the early years of the nineteenth century. Later it became the residence of archbishops of New Orleans, and it is now the presbytery of the adjoining St. Mary's Church built for Italian immigrants in 1846. It is strange, with all the noise about historical New Orleans, that this convent, much praised as the oldest building in the Mississippi Valley, has been allowed to deteriorate to that all-too-familiar state of peeling plaster, crumbling floorboards, and echoing, cobwebbed rooms.

Most of the French city of New Orleans was destroyed in the

disastrous fire of 1788. After another more costly though less widely
destructive fire in 1794, the Spanish authorities issued strict building
laws which, like all their laws, were by no means always enforced or
obeyed. The new city was rather feebly fortified; four gates giving
access through the walls—France, Bayou, St. Louis, and St. Charles
—were closed nightly. Contemporaries speculated as to whether the
fortifications were intended to keep out invaders or quell a dissident
population, the implication being that the latter was more likely;
fortunately for the Spaniards, their bulwarks were never put to the
test and the Americans found them in the last stages of disintegra-
tion after the Louisiana Purchase.

The Place d'Armes underwent the most radical changes in the
post-fire city, thanks to the self-interested philanthropy of a Spanish
official, Don Andres de Almonester y Roxas, who was "in early life
a notary, and by various speculations amassed an immense property,
and failed at last to leave an unspotted name behind him." De
Almonester financed the rebuilding of St. Louis Cathedral and the
construction alongside of a new administrative building to house the
Cabildo, and on the downriver side a presbytery for the Cathedral
clergy.

A typical house of the period is one on Dumaine Street, known
as Madame John's Legacy (after a story based on the house by
George Washington Cable), which is thought to have been built
toward the end of the Spanish period and is certainly considered one
of the oldest buildings in the Quarter. It is now a dour house, owned
by a preservation society that cannot afford to open it and cheer it
up; the windows seem permanently shuttered, and the long sloping
roof shading the front gallery sends the would-be visitor to sleep
almost while he looks at it. The main living rooms of the family were
raised onto a first floor over the cellars or shopfront on the ground;
at the back the house extended in a wing along one side of a
courtyard (known as a *garconnière*, housing the children and slaves),
the effect on the street reminiscent of a Mediterranean town but less
often lightened by glimpses of green shady courtyards until the end
of the eighteenth century, most houses in the Quarter were probably
very similar though many also had flat roofs; Dr. Sibley noted that

"the tops of the houses are as their back yards and the women wash, iron, sit to work and the men walk on them and go from the top of one house to the top of another and visit their neighbours without having anything to do with the streets below."

By now the developing prosperity resulting from benevolent Spanish rule led to a number of considerably grander houses, built especially along the levee, where they attracted the attention of visitors welcoming signs of civilization after the rigors of traveling to New Orleans. Nevertheless, Berquin Duvallon was critical of the city and its suburbs, still only an outline, shabby and undistinguished; "it is one of the gloomiest and most disagreeable places in the world, both in its whole make-up and in its details, and in the ugly savage appearance of its environs."

During the early years of the nineteenth century, the Quarter experienced almost as much building as the new American suburbs spreading beyond the old fortifications. The American architect Benjamin Latrobe was one of the most interesting contributors to the new development, as much for his comments on the expanding city as for his architectural achievements, which would no doubt have been more conspicuous had he not died of yellow fever only two years after he first arrived in the city. Latrobe was educated in Europe and trained as an architect in London, a combination that helps to explain how harmoniously his Louisiana State Bank, on the corner of Royal and Conti streets, fits into its surroundings, an expression of mellowed Greek Revival enthusiasm that was never achieved by the monumental mansions of a later date. The Girod House on Chartres Street, with its quaint belfry overlooking a maze of roofs and Brennan's on Royal Street are other examples of this period that fortunately have not been given a face-lift.

But Latrobe was already complaining of the spread of red brick, an Anglo-Saxon taste, in the Quarter instead of the prevailing Mediterranean stucco ("stucco strikes the eye more pleasantly than the dull, sombre red of brick," commented Timothy Flint). But exposed brick was never popular in New Orleans because of the humidity. You do see it here and there, and the contrast is rather pleasant, especially as the stucco is so often in poor condition. It is commonest in the rows of houses that were also popular in the middle of the century, a Northern fashion that was well suited to the Quarter and that gave it an occasional uniformity in contrast to its generally haphazard outline. The most celebrated rows of houses, strikingly built of red brick, are those on either side of Jackson Square, the Pontalba buildings, designed by James Gallier, Jr., at the request of the Baroness Pontalba, who was the daughter of Don Andres de Almonester, the square's original benefactor. These buildings have been quite wrongly described as the first American apartment buildings—a description that ignores the very typical design of the houses as containing the occupants' business premises on the ground floor with their living quarters above. The Pontalba buildings were among the first to incorporate the cast-iron balconies that became such a feature of New Orleans architecture about this time.

Wrought-iron balconies with simpler, more classical designs had been popular since the beginning of the century, the first examples imported from Spain and Mexico, ousting the wooden balconies so unsuited to a humid climate. The wrought iron was itself ousted about mid-century by the more elaborate and fanciful cast-iron designs. A Mrs. Miltenberger built a row of three large brick houses in Royal Street for her three sons—with wrought-iron balconies according to tradition. But one of the sons was in partnership with a Philadelphia iron foundry, and he was responsible for the replacement of the wrought iron by the more fashionable cast iron, which was not altogether in harmony with the buildings.

Several iron foundries were set up on the outskirts of New Orleans. Elaborate cast-iron galleries in many cases extending over the sidewalk and supported by precariously thin pillars (regularly knocked down by today's traffic), make a striking visual impression upon the visitor, who immediately associates them with the Franco-Spanish accent of the district. But they are in fact an Anglo-Saxon addition, a gesture of Victorian romanticism in strange contrast to the almost severe facades they shade so dramatically.

Until mid-century most building in the Quarter was by French architects, who tended to follow European rather than North American building fashions. Benjamin Latrobe's son John, after a visit in

1834, remarked particularly on the Franco-Spanish character of the Quarter, which he found "abounding in the picturesque," although the signs of American influence, "the granite basements and columns of the North, are to be seen intermingled with the quaint and stuccoed fronts of the old Spanish buildings." The St. Louis Hotel, so splendid a climax in the architectural as well as economic and social glories of the Quarter, was designed by French immigrant architects, the de Pouilly brothers, but on a monumentally American scale. The hotel was begun in 1836 but not finished for another two years; Oakey Hall commented that "magnificent intention and gigantic plan stood its godfathers at its first christening and like not a few godfathers were remarkably injudicious." It was the pet project of a group of Creole businessmen, who set up La Compagnie des Améliorations pour la Nouvelle Orleans, with Pierre Soulé as its president. It was designed partly to replace the old Creole business exchange on the corner of Chartres and St. Louis streets and partly "to combine the conveniences of a city exchange, a bank, large ballroom and likewise private stores." The hotel, it was hoped, would revive the flagging economy of the First Municipality and rival the flourishing trade of the other new exchange being built by American businessmen just off Canal Street. Its premises would provide a center of social life—upper floors for gambling, rooms for six hundred guests, American as well as Creole cuisine, expensive subscription balls to be attended by city and country gentry.

All this it achieved, for a while and at a cost of about a million dollars. The center of activity and attention in the stupendous building was its rotunda, decorated with murals by Dominique Canova —a copper-plated dome later discovered to have been built according to Byzantine methods, of earthern cylinders to ensure lightness on such marshy foundations. The celebrated slave auctions were held beneath the rotunda, on a dais with a small wooden railing across the front, which was gradually whittled away by souvenir hunters. But unlike its American rival, the St. Charles Hotel on the other side of Canal Street, the St. Louis never really recovered from the effects of the Civil War; after a brief period as the Louisiana capitol (where white supremacy was successfully reestablished after the defeat of the carpetbaggers in 1876), it was restored and re-named Hotel Royal. It fell on bad ways, however, assisted by a hurricane in 1913, and in 1916 the Federal government ordered its demolition as part of an anti-rat campaign. Fire did a lot of the government's work for it, and lack of interest did the rest, though even in the 1930s the curious could wander round its half-ruined halls, disturbing the bats and pigeons as in some forsaken Valhalla, interrupting the slow munching of mules beneath the rotunda. Nowadays all that remains of the St. Louis are its arches incorpo-rated in the garage entrance of the Royal Orleans Hotel on the same site.

By the 1840s it was rare to find a vacant lot in the Quarter, and most building in the area was a question of remodeling on Greek Revival lines or refacing with a cast-iron gallery, while new building rushed ahead beyond its cramped confines. Affluence was moving to the suburbs, and at about this time Featherstonhaugh wrote that "the old city, which was once the centre of every sort of gaiety and business, is already become gloomy and partially deserted."

After the Civil War, Decatur Street and the other riverside roads were extensively rebuilt. It is curious that once the levee was the smartest place in town, where the grandest houses were, and New Orleans society could be seen promenading there on Sundays. ("A handsome raised gravel walk," wrote Francis Baily, which "in the summertime served for a mall and in the evening was always a fashionable resort for beaux and belles of the place. I have enjoyed many an evening's promenade here, admiring the serenity of the climate and the majestic appearance of the whole river."); while by the 1870s the river could hardly be seen behind a wall of depots, railroad cars, and huge factories. The character of the levee changed with the growth of commerce. Owners of lots along the levee had already watched with helpless rage as commercial developers bought up riverfront lots and extended their huge warehouses along the river. A city administration, eager to revive the city's economy, leased riverfront property along Decatur Street to the railroads, with the right to erect buildings. At the end of the century the joyless brick warehouses were joined by the castellated mass of the Jackson

Brewery, "not a particularly noteworthy example of the brewery style of the day." The sugar industry also moved in; sugar barges from Bayou Lafourche tied up beside the sugar refinery and sugar sheds while sugar dealers swopped prices in the sugar exchange.

While the city's attention was devoted to the river and its uses, the French Quarter languished in decrepitude; old buildings disintegrated and were pulled down and were replaced by the narrow frame cottages known as "shotguns" seen all over the city—cheap versions of Victorian gingerbread. Cable described the Quarter's "solemn look of gentility in rags," a neighborhood "long since given up to fifth-rate shops," a region of "architectural decrepitude, where an ancient and foreign-seeming domestic life in second stories overhangs the ruins of a former commercial prosperity, and upon everything has settled a long sabbath of decay." The inhabitants he described as "occupying their rooms simply for lack of activity to find better and cheaper quarters elsewhere." By the end of the century it had become an Italian quarter.

As the Quarter became more of a slum, so right-minded citizens (none of whom would have considered living there in the early years of this century) felt it was only proper for the crumbling mansions to be replaced by something more representative of the flourishing image of New Orleans they wished to present. In 1905 the huge Civil Courts building was erected on an entire block—everyone thought it best to pull down as much as possible. Actually, in spite of its ugliness, it is worth spending a few minutes wandering along its chilly corridors for a glimpse of the Louisiana world outside New Orleans, for it provides office space for the Department of Wild Life and Fisheries; there is a small museum of Louisiana flora and fauna —birds and snakes molting and moldering behind glass, muskrats and nutria showing their powerful front teeth—and you can buy your duck-hunting licenses there, oyster-bed licenses, and inshore shrimp trawling licenses. An enormous hotel, the Monteleone, removed another block, and a convenient fire on Decatur Street burned down some dilapidated mansions between Bienville and Iberville streets. A preservation-minded group formed the Vieux Carré Commission in 1936 but it has had a hard battle since the war with tourist-conscious city officials, leading to an unhappy truce which allows new hotels to be built ("located in the heart of history") but only along traditional lines. A multistory garage has cast-iron balconies while radiator grills and headlights peer like caged animals out of French windows. The newest hotel even preserves a street-front illusion of being several houses but, unlike its predecessors, has so many basements that the piles driven in to support the building caused foundations to rock several blocks away. It is all a rather dismal but familiar picture.

Tourists come in their thousands to New Orleans and the only time the pressure eases slightly is in the summer months when other parts of America are more inviting than the hard, hot streets of the old Quarter. But within the Quarter the bounds of the tourists are limited: between Jackson Square and Canal Street they are as integral a part of the scene as in Venice, but only the really adventurous and energetic wander below the cathedral. Most activity, too, is concentrated on the four streets running parallel with the river: Decatur, Chartres, Royal and Bourbon. This has always been the case. Chartres was for a long time the main shopping area of the city until outwitted by vaster emporiums on Canal Street; Royal has always had antique shops and cabinetmakers; Decatur has always had the river; and Bourbon Street, one likes to imagine, always provided the light relief.

Royal Street is still the stateliest street in the French Quarter, though the cabinetmakers with their fashionable clientele have now left; this was the home ground of the nineteenth-century cabinet-makers, Seignouret and the Mallard brothers, whose huge mahogany and rosewood beds and couches filled the light, airy rooms of the smart and rich. Past the first block of Royal Street with its paraphernalia of sleazy jukedom are the expensive antique shops and grand houses where even the fakes are well made and the mainly Jewish owners are often descended from several generations of dealers, their Jewishness and consequent aloofness from New Orleans society giving them a cynical perspective and making them suitable links between the two worlds of financial and social snobbery.

A few blocks further down the classy antiques give way to Victorian bric-a-brac, Empire ormolu and Bohemian glass of dubious venue which in their turn yield to gift shops reeking of scented candles and homemade soap, hung with posters and tea towels, paradises for affluent teen-agers and blue-rinsed sixty-year-olds out for a giggle. It is worth trying to tear one's eyes from the shop windows, abandon the struggle for the pavement, to glance up at the houses above the shops, most of which were built in the first half of the nineteenth century. Frederick Olmsted rather unfairly described the newer buildings in the Quarter at the time of his visit as having "the characteristics of the unartistic and dollar-pursuing Yankees." In fact those Americans who built themselves houses in the Quarter in that period adhered with remarkable loyalty to the traditional Creole-planned house, only the facade sometimes resembling a more Northern style. And the unadorned facades of the houses belie their interiors—James Gallier's house further down Royal Street is an excellent example of an unostentatious facade concealing a palatial interior.

In the stuccoed houses of Royal Street you see every conceivable shade of building ("the deep warm, variegated stain" of plaster, said Mark Twain)—faded pink on the building at the corner of Royal and St. Peter (known misleadingly as the city's first skyscraper, which was originally a three-story building with a fourth story added later), next to white, next to beige, next to salmon pink, next to faded brick red—a modern trend—and gray. Dr. Sibley in 1802 noted the elegance of the plastered buildings "looking well and full of People." In the next block most of the houses are built of unstuccoed brick. Then there are some covered with ironwork; the patterns are beautifully fantastic, adding charm rather than elegance to their background. The effect is often too fussy and makes the streets seem narrow and crowded.

The upper blocks of Chartres Street are somber and businesslike, the narrow pavements as often as not downtrodden by vans and trucks unloading goods to the prosaic wholesalers who have long since ousted the once-fashionable retailers. Here again the gift shops take over, fed by passengers from buses in Jackson Square, stocking up on pralines before staggering off to more tourism.

Chartres Street runs into Jackson Square, which has always been the center of the French Quarter, its pleasant symmetry preserved through every vicissitude. Latrobe wrote that the visitor's first impression of New Orleans—and this was very much conditioned by Jackson Square—was of its "very handsome and imposing appearance"; "the public square, which is open to the river, has an admirable general effect and is infinitely superior to anything in our American cities as a water view of the city." It is only fair to add that, on a closer look, he thought the square rather untidy. Originally it served as a parade ground for the garrison, and long after there ceased to be a threat of foreign invasion, making a garrison unnecessary, the local militia used to turn out on Sundays for the benefit of Sabbath promenaders. The church has always been at the head of the square flanked by administrative buildings of one kind or another, with houses and stores down the sides.

The original church, completed in 1726, was burned down in the 1788 fire, and Don Andres de Almonester financed the construction of the new church as well as the Cabildo and Presbytère in the hopes of acquiring a Spanish title for his extensive philanthropy. The church was finished in 1794, described as an example of Mediterranean baroque, which must have delighted new arrivals from that part of the world with its re-creation of the familiar. It harmonized pleasantly with its neighbors until Latrobe capped the side towers with bell-shaped turrets and designed a central clock tower, which was added in 1824 after his death. The extra weight proved too much for the foundations (Latrobe himself describes finding the fabric held together with iron bars), and one of the towers collapsed in 1845. After this the church was virtually rebuilt by Louis Pilié according to the present design, which is not very successful; its whiteness makes a pleasant contrast to the heavy gray of the Cabildo and Presbytère on either side, but it has too many pillars and "étages."

The flanking buildings are unmistakably foreign. They are a very good indication of the relative insignificance of New Orleans in Spanish colonial policy, rather humble buildings compared with the stately offices, religious and secular, to be found, for instance, in

Mexico. Equally they acquire a certain distinction in their present site, only upset by the unnecessary mansard roofs added when the French mansard style was fashionable in the late nineteenth century. The gray sobriety of the Cabildo's arched facade is delightfully alleviated by small wrought-iron balconies, perhaps the handsomest in the city. William Faulkner, in his "New Orleans Sketches," described the Cabildo as a "squat Don who wears his hat in the king's presence, not for the sake of his own integer vitae but because some cannot," and went on, "within the portals Iowa wondered aloud, first, why a building as old and ugly could have any value; and second, if it were valuable, why they had let it become so shabby. 'I bet the city ain't painted it in twenty years. Why don't they·tear it down, anyway? and put up a modern building . . . These people in the South ain't got the pep we have at all.' "

Jackson Square is flanked by the Pontalba buildings which, because of their uniformity, look higher and more massive than most buildings in the Quarter. Shops on the ground floor mostly sell gifts, with pasteboard mammies outside advertising pralines; there is also an unexpected dusty library stuffed full of Louisiana records.

As for the square itself, opinion has always been divided on its appeal. It is an open space, which the French Quarter needs but which, like many such parks, deserved better of its clientele. Back in the 1830s Oakey Hall wrote that it would be best described as a beggars' retreat possessing "a very neat iron railing, one or two respectable aged trees, a hundred or two blades of grass, a dilapidated fountain, a very naked flag staff and a venerable piece of ordinance." He was wrong about the age of the trees, which had in fact been planted not so long before by a mayor concerned with beautifying his city (and also planted the handsome planes and sycamores down Esplanada Avenue). Baroness Pontalba paid for further improvements in the 1850s: a better railing, more shrubs, and a handsome bronze statue of New Orleans' savior, Andrew Jackson, on which the city's captor, Benjamin Butler, later inscribed "The Union Must, and Shall Be Preserved" to the rage of New Orleanians. Oakey Hall's beggars are today's hippies: the prim walkways and benches are occupied by unprim people—layabouts, junkies, the homeless and unemployed, unhappy in the sunshine and flowers, serenaded by the occasional long-haired guitarist.

William Faulkner wrote delightfully of the square as "a green and quiet lake in which abode lights round as jellyfish, feathering with silver mimosa and pomegranate and hibiscus beneath which lantana and cannas bled and bled. Pontalba and Cathedral were cut from black paper and pasted flat on a green sky, above them taller palms were fixed in black and soundless explosion." Unfortunately the artists who have been the most regular *habitués* of the square have never been as artistic as Faulkner; an unkind critic recently described their products as "a little less than art," preserving "the American motto of supply and demand." Subject matter is said to be restricted to Louisiana representation and portraiture, but nudes, however well portrayed, may not be hung in front of the cathedral. Quarter scenes are in heavy demand, and no conventioneer or his wife can leave the Quarter without a charcoal or pastel portrait of him or herself; limp and weary from hot sight-seeing, they sink on to the little canvas stools that stand invitingly by the railings in the shade of the myrtles and allow the "artist" (who wears all the rigmarole of the true Bohemian) to produce an embarrassing unlikeness, watched sardonically by the owners of the ubiquitous hot-dog and ice-cream stands.

Decatur Street runs along the bottom of Jackson Square, between the garden and the river, the most workmanlike street in the Quarter, immersed in the business of the port and discouraging tourist wiles. Within the Quarter one hardly notices the port, except to swear at the huge lorries rumbling from one warehouse to another. But opposite Jackson Square one can clamber up the levee past the brewery and a lonely stone arch built for the city's regiment, the Washington Artillery, to parade through on Sundays. From here one can see the river—rather a squalid view except for the magnificent, aloof Mississippi Bridge, which never seems to come down to earth. New Orleans takes the river so much for granted that it ignores it and thinks all right-minded people should do the same. Equally the huge tankers, grain freighters, and Volkswagen carriers seem to disdain the city as they sweep up the great river, towering over the houses on the other side of the levee.

On Decatur Street is all the paraphernalia of the dockside: the ships' chandlers, the wholesalers—especially fur dealers, visited by wizened French trappers from the marshes loaded with nutria and muskrat pelts—the doss houses (the Eltro Hotel advertises "clean, outside rooms"), the paperback bookshop selling smutty literature. Bars reflect the nationality of their clientele: Fun's Chinese Restaurant (Cable wrote, with an uncharacteristic harshness, that "you see, here and there, like a patch of bright mold, the stall of that significant fungus, the Chinaman"), the Athaenaeum Room and the Greek Club, La Casa de los Marinos (suitably on the site of the popular nineteenth-century filibustering haven Café des Exiles), each politely announcing that "ladies are invited." There is a real French family-style restaurant, Tujague's, black shoeshine boys on a street corner, their grandfathers selling racoon for stew in the winter. In Gallatin Street, the red-light extension of Decatur Street, there are hundreds of bars, one frequented—believe it or not—by the international yo-yo champion for 1937. And beyond is the abandoned and lugubrious United States Mint, outside which Mumford was hanged for desecrating the Union flag.

The French Market, which is also in Decatur Street, was never French; like Creole, French is an adjective applied with romantic abandon to many things in New Orleans, whether or not unique to the city or France, and one eventually ceases to be irritated. During the French period what market there was used to be held in the open beside the levee, where boats bringing produce from the Côte des Allemands could tie up. Particularly in the summer, provisions were often spoiled by the weather, and in 1779 the Cabildo decided to build a wooden shed for the market. The shed was rebuilt rather grandly in 1813 and was restored in the 1930s. There are a fish market, a meat market, and a vegetable market, and the only time worth visiting any of them is early in the morning, though the fish market is always amusing because of the diversity and monstrosity of fish on sale.

The market has always played a large part in the tourist life of New Orleans; people flocked there throughout the nineteenth century to marvel at the variety of produce and of people selling it.

Audubon, who lived in a typical wooden cottage on Dauphine Street from 1821 to 1822, saw on sale in the market in a single day an extraordinary range of birds, from the common mallard to a barred owl. Indians squatted in their shawls selling "bay and sassafras and life-everlasting" (the site of the market was originally an Indian trading post), old Negro women on the levee sold blackberries, Isleños from Terre aux Boeufs sold garlic and sweet potatoes. There would be wagon loads of Spanish moss for upholstery. Latrobe commented on the "strange and loud noise" that greeted passengers disembarking by the market levee. "The articles to be sold were not more various than the people. White men and women, and of all hues of brown, and of all classes of face, from round Yankees, to grisly and lean Spaniards, black negroes and negresses, filthy Indians half naked, mulattoes, curly and straight-haired, quarteroons of all shades, long haired and frizzled. . . . I cannot suppose that my eye took in less than five hundred sellers and buyers all of whom appeared to strain their voices, to exceed each other in loudness." The modern setup is very tame by comparison. Around the edge of the market were "little shows of fat boys, six-legged calves and other monstrosities." Occasionally visitors were more horrified than impressed. Audubon called it the dirtiest place in the United States, and forty years later Butler gave it its first effective spring cleaning, maintaining that yellow fever usually originated in its vicinity—which it often did though not for the reasons that Butler considered. Nowadays the market is very sober, even early in the morning, though in summer it is pleasant to wander down in the early dawn and see the mountains of watermelons and richly polished aubergines, smell the strawberries in April and bursting figs in August; and listen to the conversations—Negroes in their curious Creole patois, perhaps an Acadian greeting another in sixteenth-century French, and everywhere the Italians who run the market.

Tourists still flock to the French Market, partly to buy their souvenirs from the little stores that have cropped up on its fringes instead of the fat boys and partly to indulge in the coffee and donuts that are sold in two continental-style cafés. The coffee is excellent and strong, served with machinelike speed in austere, thick white china cups (which happily reminded Sir Charles Lyell of Paris) by unshaven Gallic waiters in shabby white jackets; one is supposed to accompany the coffee with a plate of fresh donuts, authentic French donuts of batter plunged into deep hot fat, donuts one sprinkles lavishly with icing sugar set in jars on the tables, bought and served three at a time—a gesture to the American appetite.

Down beyond the coffee houses, Decatur Street disintegrates into railroad sidings and warehouses. Parallel to it runs Gallatin Street, (referred to as Louisiana's Barbary Coast at the end of the last century), the seediest end of the Quarter, whose character has changed least with the years. This used to be the playground of such street gangs as the Black Hand and Live Oak, but the gang head-quarters and brothels are slowly being ousted by more up-to-date equivalents—discotheques and drug peddling. And real estate developers are tarting up the worn old houses into chic apartments for bachelors.

The principal red-light district is Bourbon Street, about half a dozen blocks of which consist of a solid line of nightclubs, jazz spots, and strip joints patronized almost exclusively by that uniquely American kind of tourist, the conventioneer, who comes to New Orleans ostensibly to attend a convention but who spends much of his time looking for an easy giggle on Bourbon Street. He will not have to try hard; Bourbon Street is a twenty-four-hour concern, almost as busy during the day as at night. Appropriately it was named after a Duke of Bourbon who had made so much money out of John Law's enterprises that he was able to rebuild his *château* at Chantilly, complete with a zoo and a race track, and give a five-day party for the Regent's daughter. Very little of the city was built as far back as Bourbon Street before the 1788 fire. Its fame dates from the closing of Storyville, the licensed brothel district where jazz first prospered, in 1917. They say one can find sex of all kinds of Bourbon Street—homo, hetero and hermo; the number of male prostitutes allegedly exceeds the female. But the titillation is too easy when the strippers can be seen from the pavement, dancing on the tops of bars, where often the only excuse for entering is to get into the air-conditioning, often advertised as prominently as the bust mea-

surements of the girls. Once Bourbon Street was as dignified as
Royal Street; Judah P. Benjamin, for instance, lived in number 327,
and one can dimly perceive the outline of an elegant house, a typical
town house of a wealthy planter, behind the garish photographs of
the Playgirl Club and advertisements for topless barmaids and wai-
tresses.

Even the bars gradually peter out at the downriver end of the
Quarter. The main residential streets of the Quarter are Burgundy,
Dauphine, Barracks, Governor Nicholls, Ursuline, and St. Philip,
and the end blocks of Chartres, Royal, and Bourbon. New Orleans
is among the very few American cities where one can live comfortably, close to the business district, in an area that has remained
residential for two centuries. The heterogeneous nature of the Quarter's population (listed by a recent survey under thirteen headings
—hippies, bums, artists, bohemians, Negroes, bachelors, students,
wealthy people, poor people, the elderly, families, property owners,
renters—with the proviso that you could belong to more than one
of these groups) is being slowly undermined by the rising popularity
of the area as a place to live. But the mixture is still remarkable. The
back streets of single-story frame cottages, high slate roofs projecting
over the pavement, shading the front porch, where the occupants
will often be seen rocking to and fro in the heat, have a gentle echo
of the abandoned Creole city of eighty or ninety years ago. Even the
strident buzz of Bourbon Street is drowned in the idle silence of its
lower end. Much of the area is still slum, occupied by Italian immigrants or Negro families, often in alternating blocks; hence the city's
reputation for residential integration, though neither group will have
much to do with the other and both are faced with the prospect of
rising rents forcing them out. The houses look older than they are;
uninterested landlords, impoverished occupants, and the climate
work havoc with white wooden houses. The fanciful gingerbread of
their porches and gables may have been an attempt to imitate more
opulent ironwork elsewhere. Some, on the other hand, hide unsus-
pected luxury, *House & Garden* decoration and European antiques;
huge *portes clochères* lead through dark stone-flagged passages to the
courtyards—unfortunately now known as patios—tropical jungles of

overgrown bananas and magnolias, hibiscus and jasmine, gardenias and oleanders, their heavy scents obliterating the exhaust fumes of the street outside.

Along the downriver end of the Quarter runs Esplanade Avenue, once a fashionable street known as the Promenade Publique, still one of the most gracious streets in the city. Most of the houses, separated from each other by narrow passages leading to tiny gardens, were built between 1840 and 1880, reflecting a range of Greek Revival styles interspersed with the rather incongruous mansard fashion more suited to the northern cities of France where it originated. The lack of private greenery is partly compensated for by Mayor Roffignac's avenue of elms and sycamores planted on either side of the street as well as down the middle. Esplanade Avenue still reflects the varied fortunes of the Quarter, some of its houses half-occupied by venerable but impoverished Creole families, others become multi-occupied slums, still others taken over and dressed up with glossy furnishings to the envy of suburban dwellers throughout the country.

There is a very real danger that the Quarter's fluctuating fortunes of the past will be forgotten in the present fashion for bijoux residences and patio parties under the banana palms. The Vieux Carré Commission has reported the dwindling of the Negro population over the last four years as prosperous outsiders move in to renovate the crumbling shotguns. But half the charm of the Quarter, and to a lesser extent of New Orleans, is the heterogeneity of the streets —rich and poor, black and white tend to rub shoulders more easily than in other American cities; it has retained a quaint completeness, despite the years.

13. The American Quarter

THERE ARE STILL two worlds on either side of Canal Street, which separated the French from the American quarter in the nineteenth century—a Brobdignagian world and a Lilliputian one. On one side are the low shabby stuccoed facades of the French Quarter, on the other side the modern towers of steel and glass darkening the Victorian alleyways, the contrast between older and newer as glaring now as it was a hundred and forty years ago when speculators first began investing upriver of Canal Street. Only the "neutral ground" running down the center of Canal Street preserves its impartiality, on lamp posts bearing plaques that refer with equal disdain to French domination, Spanish domination, and American domination.

Canal Street acquired its name from the narrow ditch that ran along the walls of the old French city. At the beginning of the nineteenth century, imaginative speculators saw a great future for Canal Street as the most important street in the city, praising the few large houses scattered along its length for their architecture. These houses were said to vie in excellence with "the boasted granite palaces of Boston." In 1831 the Canal Bank was chartered to raise funds to build a canal which, it was hoped, would supersede the

Carondelet Canal, stagnant and silted up, as a link between the river and the lake; but the canal was never in fact built, and the proud claim that this was the widest street in the country seemed hollow when it became obvious that the width was not to be put to use. The space remains to this day, long after the Canal Bank forfeited its charter in the 1850s by going bankrupt. That the street's appearance left something to be desired is evident from the various efforts made to beautify it. The first of these, published in 1838, was to make Canal Street "an agreeable resort, and public promenade, where all may meet for relaxation and amusement during the sultry heat of summer." During the 1840s Canal Street became the city's main shopping street, after landlords on Chartres Street raised their rents so exorbitantly that the more ambitious shopkeepers decided to start up elsewhere, a whole block (only recently pulled down) being bought and developed by the great Jewish philanthropist Judah Touro. When Touro died in 1854, he left a large part of his vast fortune to a certain Rezin Shepherd who had rescued him from the Battle of New Orleans after he had been wounded; Shepherd offered fifteen thousand dollars of this to the city to beautify Canal Street on condition the street was renamed after Touro. Neither the beautification nor the change of name was effective, however, and the city recognized Touro's unbounded generosity to its hospitals, orphanages, churches, and synagogues by naming after him a small back street in the old Faubourg Marigny.*

Nowadays what was to have been an elegant promenade on the riverfront end of the street is largely taken up with dock palaver and car parks, the space named after Captain Eads of jetty fame. A stark granite pillar nearby marks the Battle of Liberty Place, one of the bitterest revolts in the city during Reconstruction. This end of Canal Street is dominated by the huge Customs House, its designer "an architect only by courtesy," its style "a rather uneducated person's

---

*Parson Clapp wrote of Touro: "the poisonous breath of calumny never breathed upon his fair name as a merchant, the most tempting opportunities of gain from the shattered fortunes which were floating round, not in a single instance caused him to swerve from the path of plain, straightforward, lofty, unbending, simple and magnanimous rectitude."

idea of Egyptian," surrounded by dingy shops, mostly stocking a sordid overflow of cheap wharfside wares, discount clothes, and sleazy jokes, and camera shops with snapshots of sailors on shore leave. Beyond are the grander emporiums, several founded by enterprising Jews. There is Adler's, a would-be Tiffany's of the South, where every New Orleans bride likes to stock her house; Godchaux's, founded by a family of Jewish sugar planters; Maison Blanche, whose catalogues have titillated several generations of rusticated Southern belles. And squashed among them is one of the oldest houses on Canal Street, now belonging to that social pinnacle of New Orleans, the Boston Club.

On the other side of Canal Street from the French Quarter was Faubourg Ste. Marie, the suburb developed on what was originally the Jesuit plantation, bought by the Gravier family after the Jesuits had been dispossessed (it acquired its name from one of the Gravier wives), and subdivided by the Graviers into streets and blocks. An observer at the end of the eighteenth century remarked that "those who live there enjoy good health and the air there is very good and beautiful," but there were not very many enjoying it. The development of the area got off to a late start. In the early years after the Purchase, the dispute over ownership of the batture, the valuable riverfront property where the flatboats were pulled up after their voyage downriver, delayed development. Hence the attempt to develop Faubourg Marigny; not until the War of 1812 had confirmed American control of the Mississippi for once and for all was the speculative finance forthcoming to back development. The Faubourg only began living up to its ambitious layout with the developments of Caldwell and Peters, and of other investors whom they were able to impress with their projects.

James Caldwell and Samuel Peters were an unlikely combination. Although their names are always coupled in the history of the district, it is difficult to imagine them working very intimately—Caldwell, the English actor-manager, whose imagination was caught by the theatrical prospects of the Creole city and who was often carried away into visions of too much grandeur; and Peters, the well-meaning, well-organized grocer from New York, who learned French before he came to New Orleans, married the Creole bride that many considered essential to financial as well as social success in early nineteenth-century New Orleans and invested wisely on both sides of the French Quarter. However incongruous the relationship, it worked; perhaps the incongruity itself persuaded other prospective speculators that there must be something in their suggestions.

As Americans began playing an ever-larger part in New Orleans business, the demand for newer and grander premises and meeting places led to a move away from the old premises on Chartres and Royal streets. In 1831 Exchange Place was cut through to Canal and the new Merchants' Exchange built on it as a rival to the older exchanges dominated by Creole businessmen in the Quarter; it was soon infested by a "talking, money-infested crowd." Before long the cattle pens, pigsties, and market gardens that had all but obliterated the grand layout of the Graviers were themselves being bought up and replaced by the lavish structures so representative of a booming economy. There was Caldwell's American Theatre, one of the earliest buildings in the district, opened before the other amenities had caught up, so that the audiences had to take off their shoes to walk there through the unlit muddy tracks. Banks Arcade was another early building; Thomas Banks, an Englishman, came to New Orleans in 1814 and made his fortune by operating, among other things, a sailors' boardinghouse on the riverfront. His Arcade claimed to be the city's first office building, but its fame was mainly acquired as a meeting place for filibusters planning their Latin-American invasions.

But the American Quarter really only acquired status in the 1840s, when the division of New Orleans into three municipalities freed developers from the rather conservative inclinations of the Creole-dominated city council. Bishop Whipple described the Second Municipality at this time as "the abode of that noble class of human-kind yclept Yankees and here you see the development of that business spirit and enterprise as you can see it in no other place in the Union." The most famous building of this period was the St. Charles Hotel, opened a year after the city was divided in 1837. It was designed by one of the city's most celebrated architects, James

Gallier, and excited even more hyperbole than the St. Louis, which was being built as a rival in the French Quarter. In a famous passage, Oakey Hall described it as "a mammoth pearl thrown before swine," but later more descriptively he added: "Set it down in St. Petersburg and you would think it a palace, in Boston and ten to one you would christen it a college, in London and it would marvellously remind you of an exchange. In New Orleans it is all three, a palace for creature comforts, a college for the study of human nature and an exchange for money and appetite."

New Orleans historians claim that the American hotel—"the caravanserai, immense in size, gorgeous in its furnishings and grand in its table d'hôte"—originated with the St. Charles. There were eight hundred guests staying there the night before it burned down at the height of the New Orleans season in January 1851, though the normal number of beds was nearer three hundred and fifty; the Earl of Carlisle found five hundred and sixty sitting down to dinner, their appetites tempted by seven French cooks and served by waiters of every nationality. The clientele was mostly American, many of them the six-monthly businessmen who fled before the summer's yellow fever, the remainder planters and their families come into the city for the season. Europeans were inclined to be rather rude about the clientele; William Russell described the occupants of the bar "seated with their legs up against the wall, and on the back of chairs, smoking, spitting, and reading." The present vast menagerie is the third on the site; a second building, built after the first burned, was itself burned down in 1894.

Gallier was also the architect for the City Hall of the Second Municipality, which superseded the Cabildo as City Hall for the whole city after the reunification in 1852. It is a delightful neoclassical building, which has recently been renovated from the dilapidation of decades, known as Gallier Hall since the city administration moved to a glass and concrete palace on the edge of the business district. Only during Carnival does the old hall regain some of its official status when the Mayor stands on the steps to receive the acknowledgments of parading royalty. Lafayette Square, which the hall faces on, has not been as carefully preserved as its counterpart in the French Quarter, Jackson Square, and never acquired quite the same fashionable reputation as the latter. Even today it lacks the hippie blessing without which apparently no public park can flourish. It is a dusty plot, shaded by exhausted trees, hemmed in on three sides by bleak administrative blocks, and the sad occupants of its benches appear almost exclusively to be bedraggled mariners shipwrecked on New Orleans' shores.

Lafayette Square marks the end of the business district, the old American Quarter. It is a tightly knit district, a frowning concentration of high-rise buildings divided by narrow windswept lanes. With the older buildings, those skyscrapers of the 1920s and 1930s, one has to walk head-in-air to view the architectural fantasies that must have been designed for the eyes of God and the angels alone so far are they from the eyes of pedestrian mortals. The newer buildings, occupied by oil concerns or banks made rich by oil, keep their glamour nearer the ground: opulent acres of plate glass, behind which black uniformed commissars direct scurrying executives in full public view. A few nineteenth-century buildings remain on Canal, but most of the business district reflects the phenomenon of impermanence as seen in a country where one can sometimes trace three or four generations of buildings on one site in a hundred years.

There is a no-man's-land of slums and spaghettilike overpasses, car lots and derelict building sites, between the downtown business district and the uptown suburbs, but the bone-shaking streetcar rumbles through the area quickly enough and into St. Charles Avenue (past the fantastic oriental portals of the Shriners' Temple), where the gracious somnolence of New Orleans at its best steals over the visitor. For here is the Garden District.

St. Charles Avenue is the main thoroughfare of the Garden District, which was built up in the middle of the last century and still preserves an aristocratic distinction once the prerogative of the French Quarter. The avenue is a double avenue of huge live oaks, densely shading trees whose long branches reach out over the road either side of the streetcar lines ("rude, unbending, lusty" trees, wrote Walt Whitman). Houses on the avenue reflect every classical and Gothic style of the century; Grecian palaces, Charles-Addamslike mausolea, Roman villas, castellated mansions—millionarish quirks designed to transport their occupants as far as possible from the cotton bolls and sugarcane that had made their fantasies possible.

The Garden District lies on the river side of St. Charles Avenue. It is still the most famous and most expensive residential area in the city; New Orleanians plan their lives for years ahead around their chances of buying a house there. It is an enchanting area—there is no better word for it; there is a scent, a shade, a quietude about the great white houses and their gardens that nourishes the soul—particularly after a sweaty, rattled ride out in the streetcar—in a way that more intellectual buildings elsewhere can never achieve. The sidewalk is torn up as if by a minor earthquake by the strong, knotted roots of the live oaks, beneath which little will grow except English ivy and deep blue-green Japanese grass. In the gardens are dark magnolias, whose waxen flowers drop huge petals at one's feet; old ladies in the Garden District still set great store by their magnolia complexions, whose waxen texture so resembles the flowers. In spring one is overwhelmed by the powerful scent of the azaleas, later by sweet olive and jasmine. There never seems to be a month when the perfume of flowers does not hang over the district. Once there were camphor trees along the streets, and the berries squashed underfoot reminded one of grandmotherly chests and old clothes; in the days of yellow fever, people used to collect the berries in little bags, which they hung around their necks in hopes of warding off the noxious fumes.

Every April during the city's Spring Fiesta, certain houses in the Garden District are opened to the public, most of them displaying contents of immense value in their day, however unfashionable now. Among the Victorian bric-a-brac are huge pieces of rosewood furniture made by the cabinetmakers of Royal Street, the most famous of whom were the Mallard brothers, natives of Sèvres, and Seignouret, a wine merchant originally from Bourdeaux. J. B. Priestley decided that whatever else rich antebellum slave-owners had, it was not good taste: "What fortunes must have been spent on this glittering junk and having it shipped and carted, piece by piece, to its place behind the tall white pillars." The image of New Orleans presented by these tours is a typically Southern one of crinolines and those magnolia complexions, families still impoverished by the Civil War, mourning their Confederate dead, their elderly treasures covered with younger dust, "a glimpse of the private lives of orchids and gardenias.". In fact the Garden District is as opulent, and many of its occupants as thriving, now as it ever was.

The district was originally about two miles upriver from New Orleans, part of the small town of Lafayette—"suburbs so radiant with charm," wrote Parson Clapp of his arrival there in 1821, for this was where many voyagers ended their trip downriver. It was built up on three plantations incorporated into the "city" of La-fayette in 1833, the most important of which, the Livaudais planta-tion, had been flooded by the Macarty crevasse in 1816; rather than let the land lie to recover, it was sold to developers. The plantation bordered the river but the streets nearest the levee were taken over by immigrants and boatmen, and only about half a mile inland did the area acquire that grandeur and exclusiveness that distinguish it today. The earliest houses, modeled on those of the West Indies, were known as raised cottages, though cottage is a singularly inappro-priate description for these delightful houses. The main floor was raised on stubby pillars above the ground for coolness and to avoid the damp—foundations being impossible on such land; there was a central passage running through the house from front to back, with rooms going off on either side, and occasionally an attic under the roof for slaves, though these were more often housed in a separate wing at the back. The principal rooms were high ceilinged and lit by large windows shaded from the intense sunlight by wide verandas, known here as galleries, encircling the house. The gardens were designed mainly for shade, huge long-branched trees protecting the owners from the heat (described after a storm by Cable, who himself lived on Washington Avenue, as "so many tearful Lucretias, tattered victims of the storm").

The Garden District proper developed on the fringe of Lafayette, aloof from the dockside bustle, and it was here in the fifteen years or so before and after the Civil War that New Orleans' particular version of Greek Revival architecture flourished on such a grand scale, reflecting the city's prosperity and the grandiose ideas of a nation's enthusiastic expansion. The Greek Revival, a Northern inspiration, turned the rustic charm of the Garden District into a mercantile splendor. Land was cheap, so that houses could afford to be spacious; there were extensive forests to hand, so that houses could be built of wood. The wide shady galleries could be supported by Grecian pillars and elaborated with cast iron, in patterns far more complicated than those of the French Quarter. Inside were mahogany staircases built with South American wood, bronze chandeliers and mirrors from France, and marble fireplaces from Italy. European artists such as Dominique Canova painted frescoes in the halls.*

The center of the Greek Revival in New Orleans ("the sophomoric affectation of Greek forms," according to Cable) was to have been Coliseum Square on the very edge of the Garden District, now sadly dilapidated and dwarfed by the far from Grecian design of the Mississippi Bridge. There were to have been a coliseum and a university (or *prytanium*, hence Prytania Street), and the muses were invoked for their support of the venture by naming approach streets after them—names now quaintly unrecognizable with their Anglo-French pronunciation: one inhabitant of a muse street, on being asked where he lived, replied, "C-L Ten," referring to Clio, the Muse of History. Coliseum Square must once have been delightful, a small park surrounded by the ubiquitous but beautiful live oaks and the houses less monumental than those of the Garden District proper, more in keeping with city life, reflecting a gentler Latin touch compared with the vulgarity of some of the larger, plantation-style houses. In contrast, the Garden District is entirely American. The streets were obviously named by an American—First, Second, Third streets, and so on—and the huge pillared porticos of the later houses, built just before or just after the Civil War, were imported straight from the cotton and sugar plantations, magnificent but too large for their setting.

And yet for all its pretensions the Garden District is the most

*Canova, nephew of the famous sculptor, painted frescoes in two houses in the Garden District as well as in the rotunda of the St. Louis Hotel.

beautiful part of New Orleans. The French Quarter is spoiled by tourists and the intrusion of the docks and has an altogether humbler charm, but the Garden District is carefully zoned off from industry, and those tourists that get as far as the District are isolated in coaches and intrude less. It is an area that is American in the nicest way, sleek and opulent and luxurious like rich women, though more inclined to show its age than the women; cosmetics do a better job of camouflage than coats of paint in such a climate. Staid and serious Negroes walking dogs and children, polishing cars, and watering gardens add to the pleasantly decadent atmosphere.

The Garden District is distinct from its neighbors, St. Charles Avenue and Magazine Street being very marked boundaries. Beyond St. Charles Avenue is the warren of Central City, the densely populated Negro slum; occupants of mansions on that side of St. Charles murmur fretfully about living in a slum and warn their guests about being attacked as they leave at night. Beyond Magazine Street is the Irish Channel, home of immigrants and dock workers. Here and there in the Channel are a few signs of former middle-class aspirations, of which Annunciation Square was the center and stands the most chance of revival. In one corner of the square, for instance, is the rather elegant raised cottage that belonged to H.M. Stanley's patron: Stanley, born John Rowland, came to New Orleans in the 1830s as a cabin boy on a ship from Liverpool and decided to stay, hypnotized, as he confessed in his autobiography, by "the soft balmy air, with its strange scents of fermenting molasses, semi-baked sugar, green coffee, pitch, stockholm tar, brine of mess beef, rhum and whiskey droppings." He was employed and later adopted by a wholesaler commissioner, a Mr. Stanley, a typical middle-class resident of Annunciation Square. An optimistic guide to the city published in 1845 foretold it would one day be the most elegant square in the city, but unfortunately it has become a grubby, dusty playground and the "very tasteful private residences" are for the most part multi-occupied slums. The same fate has overtaken the other large houses in the Channel, whose past reputation for violence and squalor defeats the rare attempt to infuse it with more prosperous life. There used to be large plantation houses along Tchoupitoulas, now ousted by the docks; one family that was devoted to its house but disliked the commercial trend had the house moved by barge to Metairie in the 1920s—to be among the first settlers of that particular suburb.

If you can't afford the Garden District, you go "uptown" beyond the district, the prices dropping gradually the further you progress along St. Charles Avenue. At the end of the Avenue is the district of Carrollton, a suburb originally created by the railroad that ran the length of St. Charles Avenue, on what had been the Macarty sugar plantation. The plantation was bought in 1832 after being flooded by another crevasse only slightly less severe than the 1816 disaster, by a group of investors (among them the politician John Slidell) for residential development. A pleasant resort developed at the railroad terminal beside the river (now beyond the bank). The terminal itself was designed as a Gothic castle; there were floating baths in the river, shooting galleries, bowling greens, a cricket club, and ten-pin alley. The district acquired its name from William Carroll, a governor of Tennessee who first came to New Orleans with Jackson in 1814 and camped with his men outside New Orleans, where Carrollton now is.

The plantations, swamps, and market gardens between Carrollton and Lafayette were gradually bought up and developed. Most streets consist of large rambling houses built after the Civil War; the gardens and their leafy contents are smaller than those of the Garden District, but the houses are often just as spacious. One of the peculiarities of New Orleans is the way houses "of all ranks" are intermingled; "the easy bright democracy of the thing is what one might fancy of ancient Greeks; only, here there is a general wooden frailty," wrote Cable. Uptown New Orleans is interspersed with narrow streets or shotgun frame cottages inhabited by Negroes or poor whites, once housing the domestic labor force of the area. Sometimes, too, there are wide avenues of oaks, symbols of prosperous conservatism. There are several of these avenues around the universities of Loyola and Tulane. Loyola, the Catholic University, is inappropriately Tudor in architecture; one would have thought there might have been some hesitation in using a style associated with enemies of Roman Catholcism. Tulane, next door, is Gothic but also rich enough to include some handsome modern buildings.

Opposite the universities is Audubon Park, the site in 1884 of the World's Exposition and Cotton Centennial, which commemorated the transport of six bags of cotton from Charleston to Liverpool in 1784. It was named after John James Audubon, who lived in New Orleans in the 1820s and saw in Louisiana many of the birds included in his famous *Birds of America*. The park has been ruined by the conversion of the greater part of it to specific activities—the zoo, the golf course, tennis courts and a giant swimming pool (said to be the largest in the South; it had barely been open a year when pools were ordered to be desegregated and those in New Orleans were promptly closed, costing a fortune to reopen five years later).

But the best thing about the park is its oaks, heavily festooned with Spanish moss. Spanish moss is extraordinary stuff. It hangs in long gray-green garlands from the oaks, blown by the wind, draped by birds. Its botanical name is *tillandsia usneiodes* and it is apparently a relation of the pineapple (though the relationship is far from apparent to the nonbotanical eye). It is a plant that feeds on air and, unlike a fungus, is not a parasite; it does no harm to the tree on which it is found, apart from inhibiting foliage by its sheer mass. Sir Charles Lyell wrote that there was enough Spanish moss hanging round New Orleans and the Delta to stuff all the mattresses in the world. The Indians used it as a binder in mud construction, and the early settlers learned from the Indians to use it in upholstery. A pile of Spanish moss makes an exceptionally comfortable mattress. It is still possible, in remote bayous of the Atchafalaya basin, for instance, to see Acadians loading their boats full of the moss, which they dry (it is full of water and thrives on the humidity) and rub off the outside skin, leaving the black fiber to be put to good use.

In describing uptown New Orleans, one inevitably slips into the social jargon that preoccupies so many New Orleanians. The Garden District and Audubon Park are the kingdom of New Orleans society. Here are its meeting places—the Orleans Club, Christ Church Cathedral, Tulane Law School—and mansions. At Mardi Gras when former kings and queens of Carnival are allowed to hang the purple, green, and gold flag of Mardi Gras from their houses, it would be rare to see such flags anywhere except in the vicinity of St. Charles Avenue. Uptown New Orleans wears its wealth and influence with the easy grace of age, and the rest of the city acknowledges its superiority.

14. Suburbs

New Orleans has several generations of suburbs. The Garden District, Carollton, and Bayou St. John are among the earliest— small rural settlements often economically dependent on the city, but, in the case of Bayou St. John and some other settlements based on plantations, isolated from the city by swamp. Three suburbs skirted the crumbling fortifications of old New Orleans at the beginning of the nineteenth century: Faubourg Ste. Marie, from which the nineteenth-century city developed; Faubourg Marigny below; and Faubourg Tremé beyond Rampart Street. Resorts also grew up along Lake Pontchartrain linked to the city by rail, road, or less often by boat. And, particularly beyond Carrollton along the river, in what is now Jefferson Parish, one still comes across narrow frame cottages occupied by impoverished Negroes, which once housed the field hands for plantations long since subdivided into suburbia.

Immediately to the north of the French Quarter, beyond the concrete deserts of car and parking lots that seem to cluster like cancerous growths round the heart of any American city, are the late nineteenth-century suburbs built on what had once been mosquito-ridden swamps, drained around 1900; Marais Street three blocks away from the French Quarter marks where the swamp began. The peeling white stucco of the shotguns and camelbacks has a raffish charm partly due to the proliferation of weeds, which grow up all over the place in the gutters and sidewalks as if longing to return to the morass of a previous existence. The houses have shutters, and the ceilings of the porches are painted an azure blue, supposedly to remind the idler rocking in his wooden chair of the harsh glaring skies from which he is so pleasantly protected. The houses are only picturesque to the stranger; to the city they represent its endless battle with overcrowding slum conditions, often part of the wider issue of where to put all the Negroes who still come into New Orleans from the country in hopes of finding a better life. "Thus they lie," wrote Cable, "deployed in pairs or half dozens, by hundreds, in the variable intervals that occur between houses and gardens of dignity and elegance; hot as ovens, taking their perpetual bath of the great cleanser, sunshine."

The streets have delightful names, a few of them incorporated by one imaginative author into the title of a book he wrote on the subject, *Frenchmen, Desire, Good Children.* In Tennessee Williams' *Streetcar Named Desire*, which takes place in New Orleans, Blanche complains of her difficulty in finding her sister's house: "they told me to take a streetcar named Desire, and then transfer to one called Cemeteries and then ride for six blocks and get off at Elysian Fields." Desire is one of the grubbiest streets in New Orleans; other rivals for this distinction are Pleasure and Treasure, Agriculture and Industry, and a whole series of flower streets from Jonquil to Verbena to Jasmine, which have long since lost what scent they had.

It is a strange world of pinball saloons disguised as corner bars, of half-empty groceries and sno-ball and po-boy stands. The sno-ball is not one of the city's gourmet delights, and it can only have been so named by someone who had never seen a snowball; it is a ball of crushed ice, on to which is poured a choice of rainbow-colored syrups —pineapple, raspberry, lemon, and so on—which bear no relation to the fruit of the name except in color. New Orleanians love them, but rather like Mardi Gras it is something one has to be brought up with to enjoy to the full. A po-boy, on the other hand, is a supreme pleasure, taking the superb American sandwich to superlative heights. Take a "French loaf" (far less dough than real French bread), and slice it lengthwise; stuff it with fried oysters or shrimps or hot sausage or crab or huge slices of ham plus the paraphernalia of lettuce, tomatoes, gherkins, tabasco sauce *ad infinitum* if you wish, and this is the po-boy sandwich and the standard lunch for New Orleanians.

There used to be three principal ways of getting to the lakefront from the city, before these intervening suburbs were built, depending on where one started from—by the shell road following the New Basin Canal if you were in the American Quarter; by Bayou Road to Bayou St. John if you were in the French Quarter, and by rail from the Faubourg Marigny. Nowadays, going this last route, one drives through genteel Gentilly (named after a local plantation) bordering on Faubourg Marigny, rather more pretentious than the slums of Desire, the houses slightly larger with hideous pompous brick ornamentation, jammed close together with barely space for a man to squeeze between ("old-style California bungalows and new-style Daytona cottages"). Elysian Fields (how much better it sounds as Champs Elysées) is one of the main thoroughfares, described in the best novel on New Orleans, *The Moviegoer,* as "very airy and spacious and seems truly to stretch out like a field under the sky." It follows much the same route as the old Pontchartrain railroad though the swamps crossed by the track have long been submerged by shopping centers and bungalows.

The Pontchartrain Railroad Company was formed in 1829 and the railroad completed two years later (apparently the first completed in the United States). In 1832 a steam engine arrived from England and the railroad began operating. The journey was not the most comfortable, one critic commenting that "the lake has its charms but the railroad system of getting there must operate very much against its ever becoming a fashionable retreat for the female portion of the community." It became quite a common way of arriving in New Orleans, however. Visitors from Alabama and points further north and east would cross the lake and describe their first impressions of seeing New Orleans emerge from the cypress swamps that almost engulfed the track. Most were ecstatic, but William Russell, a more dispassionate observer, commented on the "Rows of miserable mean one-storied houses, inhabited . . . by a miserable and sickly population," mostly Irish immigrants.

The terminus by the lake was built on land bought from a Scot, Alexander Milne, who is said to have been a footman in the service of the Duke of Richmond and Gordon; he came to New Orleans in 1776 and made a fortune in brick-making after the disastrous fires of 1788 and 1794. He invested his money in land along the lakefront, believing that this was the direction in which the city would develop. The terminus on his land was originally named Port Pontchartrain, but Milne insisted on its being named Milneburg. He was regarded as a miser during his lifetime, and on his death it was learned that he had made bequests to a number of charitable organizations, establishing two orphanages to be named after him, to one of which Louis Armstrong was sent for a while and where he learned the cornet.

A thriving resort developed at Milneburg. Wharves were built about half a mile into the shallow lake, and a pier with a tavern at the end. There was also the Washington Hotel, "a very handsome café, or hotel, crowded with men," according to Joseph Ingraham. This is where Thackeray ate his celebrated bouillabaisse, "than which a better was never eaten at Marseilles." Milneburg, wrote the *Times-Picayune*, had become "the true republican stamping-ground; only see the crowd trundling out of the [rail] cars, of all sorts, sizes and sexes and descriptions, laughing and elated, and with a determination for fun." Bathing houses were built on the beach and, both sexes would bathe together with great daring; "young ladies are courted and flirt in the bath with as little inconvenience as in a drawing-room." William Russell found a whole village of hotels and restaurants by the Civil War—great white clapboard hotels with sweeping verandas and dance pavilions, lush gardens and band-stands. Special rail coaches were run to the lake at weekends and holidays. There was a bathhouse for free Negroes but slaves were forbidden to use any of the bathhouses. At the end of the nineteenth century, Milneburg became a haven for jazz bands, playing in the dance halls and cafés—"no more the guitar and violin; enter the trombone and snare drums," commemorated by Jelly Roll Morton and others in the "Milneburg Joys."

The railroad closed in 1932 and nowadays Elysian Fields ends up at the Pontchartrain Beach Amusement Park, a windswept expanse of roundabouts and palm trees, the latter out of place in the soggy New Orleans soil. The lakefront has been pushed out some three thousand feet as a flood precaution and the small lighthouse in the amusement park used to be way out in the water. The Washington Hotel (which like its companions has long since been demolished) used to advertise that "reservations by parties may be made to view sunrise on the lake"; this bucolic function has now been taken over by the Church and sunrise services are held there at Easter while the Baptists use the lake for mass immersions. Pontchartrain Beach is a dismal place. After the municipal swimming baths were closed to avoid desegregation, it was thought everyone would flock to the lake. They did indeed at first, only to be told for most of the summer that the lake was too polluted for bathing; most of New Orleans' rain falls —very heavily—in the summer and the sewers overflow into the lake. At the best of times, it is a muddy pond impressive in its size of six hundred square miles (and superbly beautiful at its western end, where the swamps merge with the water) but with an average depth of only thirteen feet. Storms blow up very easily, dashing over the sea wall and lashing the incongruous palms; boats are overturned and a remarkable number of people drown in its deceptive waters every year, a good many of them falling off the steep steps of the levee while fishing or crabbing. "The lake was justly dreaded," wrote Timothy Flint. "The waves are short and the swell of that angry and dangerous character called a ground swell."

Inland from the beach the desolation grows. Right along the lake is an elegantly laid out promenade, but if one leaves this and ventures inland, one soon realizes how wrong Milne was in thinking that this was where the city would expand. There is the huge uninspiring campus of Louisiana State University, there is an army camp and a desert of tall grass and brambles surrounded by barbed wire, where red-wing blackbirds and grackles cavort noisily. Then one comes to the vast soulless housing project on Florida Avenue, a warren of hot concrete in the Lower Ninth Ward, the worst of New Orleans' slums. Beyond, the Industrial Canal, with its mountains of shells dredged up from the lake New Orleans, once again slowly disappears into the cypress swamps and soggy mosquito grass. This is the area of Chef Menteur, a marshy, half-drained suburb named, according to tradition, after an Indian chief exiled to this unhospitable part of the Lake Pontchartrain hinterland because of his uncontrollable capacity for lying.

Recently property speculators have been building new suburbs in this direction, encouraged by the vast Michoud space project to expect hordes of house-hunters. Much of the area once belonged to a successful property dealer, Colonel de Montluzin, who sold his property—on the old Michoud plantation—to a Texan. Parts are said to be "rather high" above sea level compared to the New Orleans average of a foot or so. But the Michoud project, where they built the huge rockets for the Apollo space craft, began economizing and the eastern suburbs suffered, in spite of such enticing and watery names as Venetian Lakes and Lakeview.

The scene is much more spick and span along the lakefront west of Pontchartrain Beach—spacious modern suburbs owned by expensive millionaires. Bayou St. John used to enter the lake here—or whatever a bayou does; in fact, the danger was that the lake would enter the bayou in a storm and, as part of the general program of strengthening and buttressing the lakefront against hurricanes, the bayou was blocked off from the lake. It is now a placid stretch of blue water with wide, grassy verges. It used to be reached from New Orleans along Bayou Road, which followed a ridge of higher land, one of the few roads in the city that does not fit into the regular pattern of blocks and is curiously elusive as a result. It is distinguished from other roads by the occasional country house or raised cottage, almost submerged by later frame bungalows. On Governor Nicholls Street, still in the French Quarter but the beginning of Bayou Road, there is an old two-story plantation house almost invisible behind trees and a high fence, its wide veranda disdaining any Grecian fashions; but another such house, on Bayou Road itself, bowed somewhat to the dictates of fashion with Ionic and Doric pillars and even a stone fountain with a small Cupid on top as a sign of livelier days.

The expanse of water of Bayou St. John takes one quite by surprise. The Duke of Saxe-Weimar noted several handsome plantation houses there in the mid-nineteenth century, "ornamented with columns, piazzas and covered galleries," and of those that still survive some are the oldest houses in New Orleans, and belong to some of the oldest families. Toward the lake these old country houses give way to some very expensive and elegant modern houses with gardens going down to the bayou, prettily pink with crepe myrtle and mimosa trees, decorated with dainty garden furniture and sunshades. Opposite, on the other side of the bayou, is City Park, beautiful with Spanish moss draped on ancient oaks but a very energetic space, even more so than Audubon Park, crammed with every conceivable activity, except that there is little space for meandering.

Up by the lake are the crumbling walls (now carefully cemented in place) of Spanish Fort, built during the Colonial period to prevent smuggling from the British Florida settlements. It was never a very effective check; there were too many smaller bayous wandering out of the lake and, by the end of the eighteenth century, the military character of the fort had yielded to pleasure with "charming dance halls, cafés and billiard parlours," attracting many visitors. Saxe-Weimar, arriving at the Pontchartrain Hotel there, recognized "the darling amusements of the inhabitants, in a pharo and roulette table." A property speculator, Harry Elkin, developed it as a resort, calling it Elkinsburg and selling it with considerable profit to John Slidell.

Beyond Spanish Fort is West End, now the most thriving resort area of the lakefront, known for its fish restaurants, many of them built on piers into the lake like the earlier hotels and dance halls. This is essentially popular eating: most of the fish is deep-fried, muzzled with "French fries," and almost loses any distinctive shape or flavor. And yet . . . even an oyster can be delicious if gently fried, and nothing can really detract from the soft-shell crab where half the pleasure comes from being able to eat the entire creature instead of clumsily forking out morsels. The hard-shell variety are ordered with great abandon by the half dozen. One particular delicacy, seasonal unfortunately, is the crawfish. "Crawfish abound in this country," wrote Thomas Hutchins in 1784; "they are in every part of the earth, and when the inhabitants chuse a dish of them, they send to their gardens where they have a small pond dug for that purpose and are sure of getting as many as they have occasion for." New Orleanians still do this today; one advantage of living in the new suburbs is the swamps around, and the crawfish are easy enough to find, in a wobbly turret of mud in the bayou bank with a hole in the middle down which one dangles a bit of meat in the hopes that they will grab. In the early days of American ownership, Northerners disdained eating crawfish because they thought they were dug up from the cemeteries. Crawfish is an acquired taste: initially the effort required to get at the meat is irritating, and a shrimp seem more worthwhile. But the effort grows less important and the sight of the great blood-red mountains of crawfish more appetizing.

It is worth wandering across the wide drainage canal beyond the restaurants, from Orleans Parish to Jefferson Parish. Louisiana is divided into parishes (from earlier ecclesiastical divisions) instead of counties. New Orleans mostly falls into Orleans Parish, ruled by the mayor and his administration in City Hall. Ever since the separation of Orleans and Jefferson parishes in 1807, it has been a great legal convenience that the mayor has no jurisdiction over the neighboring parishes—either Jefferson or St. Bernard downriver—and Jefferson Parish in particular ("the free state of Jefferson") has taken advantage of the fact that gambling restrictions in New Orleans do not extend into Jefferson. Bucktown, a once-thriving gambling resort just up the lake from West End, has given way to more luxurious saloons further inland. But it retains a picturesque raffishness, cramped and tumbled down, with faded cafés and fishing camps, which stand unsteadily in the shallow waters of the lake.

And now come the modern suburbs, stretching infinitely into the swamps. Where the houses end, the roads continue, while the marshy undergrowth battles against the invasions of property developers, desperately trying to throttle the Tarmac with its creepy fingers before it is too late. A new expressway leads almost to the airport; along it drive-in theaters wait expectantly in the swamp, entertaining drivers with monstrous kisses. The swamp tries to take revenge on suburban gardeners; crawfish dig up lawns, armadillos uproot plants, and mosquitoes attack gardeners at their work.

There is little to distinguish these suburbs from those of any other American city. They are grassy, green, and low-lying; they are comfortable and uninteresting; they have huge, opulent shopping centers. This is the New Orleans that advertises itself as one of the most air-conditioned cities in the United States, strung out along Veterans' Highway and Airline Highway, the latter Huey P. Long's attempt—linking New Orleans with Baton Rouge—to get patronage in the New Orleans area. As *The Moviegoer* said of Gentilly, "Except for the banana plants in the patios and the curlicues of iron on the Walgreen drug store one would never guess it was part of New Orleans."

On the other side of the river, there is another world of suburbia which has really only come into being since the opening of the Greater Mississippi Bridge in 1958. This is Algiers and its offspring. There has been a settlement on the West Bank (as the area on that side of the river is known collectively) ever since New Orleans was founded. In 1717, the Company of the West was granted property there by the Crown; it was known as the Company's Plantation, and there was a corral for newly arrived slaves waiting to be sold. No one seems quite sure how or when it acquired the name Algiers, which does not appear in print until about 1840; perhaps it is a reference to the early slave depot, perhaps to connections with the pirates of Barataria, perhaps to the ruffianly nature of its inhabitants. Oakey Hall described Algiers as "a fitting cognomen for an uncivilised appearing strip of land." But if any of these origins were the case, it seems likely that the name would have been current earlier instead of the various derivations of plantation owners' names, such as Duverjeville and McDonoghville, by which it was known.

Old Algiers still has an attractive small-town atmosphere more like some of the upriver towns, Donaldsonville perhaps or Plaquemines, especially as one swirls across the Mississippi on the ferry and disembarks near the fantastic Gothic courthouse, the red and cream of whose crenellated clock-tower is almost as distinctive a landmark as St. Louis Cathedral on the opposite bank. This was built on the site of the old Duverje plantation house, which burned down in the great fire of 1895. Boatyards sprang up in the nineteenth century with the development of steamboats and the Mississippi trade, an industry that still keeps it going today, the city's only dry dock buffeted by the ferocious current that has eroded Algiers as much as it has added to New Orleans.

Algiers has survived a number of major disasters from cave-ins resulting from the river current (ships often get into trouble around this point, and angry hootings of ships' sirens will indicate that an inexperienced navigator has been swept across another's bows). Boathouses, stores, and a tannery slid into the water in 1844, the worst of the cave-ins, and most of McDonogh's old plantation, including his house, is now beneath the Mississippi. Nowadays Algiers people only see the river from the tops of their low dumpy houses or from the levee, so well protected are they from the river. Fire remained a hazard long after New Orleans had countered this with building regulations, and in 1895 about half the old town clustering round Algiers Point burned down, the disaster compounded by the collapse of a pier near the ferry house beneath the weight of excited spectators and in no way mitigated by the near-lynching of a suspected arsonist. The Southern Pacific Railroad, the largest employer in the town and owner of acres of railway yards, undertook most of the rebuilding. So most of the older parts of Algiers are only eighty years old or so and the apparent age of the buildings is only the aging humidity of the climate.

Algiers' associations with smuggling are almost as long as New Orleans', dating from the time when British frigates ostensibly on their way upriver to British colonies beyond the "island" of New Orleans used to tie up by the Algiers levee for the benefit of New Orleans' inhabitants. In 1814 a canal was dug from Algiers to connect with the Bayou Barataria, considerably simplifying the transport of smuggled goods from the Grand Isle headquarters of the Lafittes and their associates to New Orleans. It was intended to link up with the Atchafalaya river "but when or whether it will be finished is a problem in the womb of time," and in fact the connection was made only in this century via the Intracoastal Waterway. This comes out into the Mississippi through the Harvey Canal and its lock upriver from Algiers. About 1720 a local landowner built a drainage ditch into Bayou Barataria, using German labor from nearby Mechaniksham—modern Gretna. A daughter of the family later married a ship's captain named Harvey, who inherited the plantation and enlarged the canal that now bears his name. Today it is a bustling waterway, its banks lined with dismantled drilling equipment waiting to be transported by barge to the vast oilfields in the shallow lakes and swamps around the Bay of Barataria. It is the sight of so much machinery that implies the bustle for movement on the canal itself always seems a slow and leisurely business—not surprisingly if one watches a tug maneuvering its tow of half a dozen or more barges into the narrow confines of the lock that controls the entrance to the canal.

Mechaniksham was settled in the eighteenth century by Germans from further upriver; its later development was promoted by St. Mary's Market and Ferry Company, which wanted to get the German agricultural produce to the market the other side of the river as easily as possible. There seems no obvious reason for its name, as it was not particularly notorious for runaway lovers like its namesake in Scotland, unless the Scottish Gretna implied a disregard for law —certainly true in this Gretna, which is just inside Jefferson Parish. It is a squalid and unprepossessing slum with plenty of criminal associations. The Mafia is said to have its West Bank headquarters in Gretna town hall, and there is a delightful story of the West Bank Expressway, a wide main road running through the West Bank suburbs, that it ceased to be an expressway after the Mafia insisted on installing traffic lights at frequent intervals to divert people to the restaurants and gambling saloons they allegedly operate in the neighborhood.

The new suburbs, whatever their appearance, have pleasant names: Aurora Gardens, where they ran out of ideas for street names and used those of the French Quarter with the prefix "west" to avoid confusion; Westwego, which boasts it is the only American "city" whose name makes up a sentence; Marrero, with its curious Spanish-style orphanages known collectively as the Hope Haven Institute. Westwego was originally a plantation; during the nineteenth century a canal was built through it connecting the river with Bayou Segnette, Lake Salvador and Barataria. The name Westwego came into common use about the turn of the century, coined perhaps by people going west, to Texas and further. One can paddle by boat through the bayous at the back of Westwego to the Simoneaux Ponds, half-marsh, half-lake, covered in summer with huge lotus lilies that stand up above the water-like parasols and whose stamen are said to be very delicious when cooked. The ponds are one of the best places to see some of the wild life of the Delta, filled with birds, alligators, turtles, nutria, and ducks in winter.

15. Death and Disease

IT IS ALWAYS astonishing that the heyday of New Orleans civilization was only a six-monthly affair: for six months of the year, from October to March, the city was alive with visitors, trade, Carnival —gay and prosperous. For the other six months, during the humid heat of summer, the wharves were empty, the hotels echoed with the rare footstep, and the streets were deserted. Trade came to a standstill as consignments of the previous fall's harvest were finally dispatched; the Creoles left for their summer houses along the Gulf coast; and those six-monthly visitors who swarmed in to New Orleans in the late fall—the men to garner the fruitful yield of New Orleans commerce, their wives and daughters to exhaust themselves in the St. Charles's ballroom—had gone North and East again. During the summer New Orleans "appeared like a deserted city," observed Miss Murray; "all who possibly can, fly to the north or the upper country, most of the shops are shut, and the silence of the street is only interrupted by the sound of the hearse passing through." Apologists for New Orleans said the summer there was no hotter than in other American cities, but it was much longer and was, above all, the bearer of contagious diseases before which all strangers fled.

According to the *Illustrated London News*, New Orleans was built on a site "that only the madness of commercial lust could ever have tempted men to occupy." Many attributed the city's unhealthiness to its filth: Perrin du Lac wrote that "nothing exceeds the filthiness of New Orleans unless it be the unhealthiness which . . . appears to have resulted from it." Mosquitoes were a perpetual menace: they were "so important a *body* of enemies," wrote Latrobe, "that they furnish a considerable part of the conversation of every day and every body; they regulate many family arrangements, they prescribe the employment and distribution of time, and most essentially affect the comfort and enjoyments of every individual in the country." A French visitor in 1831 found a little black boy under the dining-room table to keep away mosquitoes "from under the marbled petticoats of our hostess." Harriet Martineau reported that many ladies in summer used to get into a sack of muslin after breakfast, tied round the throat, with smaller sacks for the arms; others spent the morning sitting on their beds surrounded by mosquito netting. At the outbreak of the 1853 yellow-fever epidemic, a newspaper commented on the arrival of mosquitoes in New Orleans as at least allowing a gentleman to smoke in the presence of ladies. But it was many years before it was fully appreciated just how dangerous the noisy little insects actually were.

Yellow fever was the most drastic of the diseases that gave the city its reputation as the graveyard of the United States. Between 1796, when yellow fever first reached epidemic proportions, and 1905, when the epidemics finally halted, hundreds of thousands of people are said to have died from the dreaded yellow jack. "New Orleans and yellow fever are as inseparably connected as ham and chicken," noted Thomas Hamilton. The disease usually attacked in the late summer, the "sickly season," and most of its victims were "strangers." The causes of yellow fever remained a mystery and a field of unlimited controversy until the early 1880s, but by mid-century the conditions were firmly if not always accurately established by would-be experts.

Yellow fever, which acquired many names during its residence in the United States, was rightly dreaded wherever it appeared. It had attacked several Northern cities before the first epidemic in New Orleans, but by the 1830s New Orleans led the country in the severity of its epidemics. Some said this was the result of the irregular and intemperate lives of the city's inhabitants. Doctors argued among themselves as to whether it was indigenous, induced by local conditions, or whether it was introduced from abroad, by ships coming from Cuba or Central America. The import theory won its case in 1816, and city authorities imposed a quarantine of ten days on all infected ships. But the following year the epidemic was particularly severe, and in 1820 the Quarantine Board was abolished. The import theory was discredited; "medicine lost its effects; the skill of the physician was baffled, and multitudes were carried to the grave," wrote the Louisiana *Gazette*. The uncertainty of public opinion toward the disease is reflected in the fact that the Quarantine Board was reinstated the next year and again abolished in 1825 after another severe epidemic. The business community was wholly opposed to quarantine, the ambiguity of their argument highlighted by the *Times-Picayune*, which favored quarantine as long as it did not interfere with the delivery of valuable cargoes. By the 1850s the indigenous theory was holding sway.

The epidemic of 1853 was the worst in the city's history. There had been no serious epidemic for the previous six years, which partly explains the reluctance of the authorities and the press to acknowledge its existence that summer. The epidemic made its presence felt only gradually; there were several deaths around the city, but none could be linked with another. The press were loath to announce its presence, apparently because of their dependence on advertising, which would fall off the moment the business community caught on to an epidemic; instead they continued to assure their readers that New Orleans was one of the healthiest cities in the Union. A significant meeting of the Howard Association was barely reported in the newspapers, for the Howard Association had been founded in 1837 expressly to organize aid for those left destitute by an epidemic, as well as to collect medicine and to arrange burials and medical aid for victims. Panic did not really set in until the death of a Miss Pearsall, "a highly respectable and accomplished young lady"; this

scared the more influential people, who began crossing the lake. The
Howard Association made a public offer of help and was blamed for
exaggerating the epidemic. But by mid-July it was in full swing,
everyone who could was leaving the city, government had broken
down, and the whole city was a hospital and a morgue.

Descriptions of the epidemic vie with each other in morbidity.
Doctors and ministers built up a literature of ghastly incidents.
"Fever was so bad at the St. Charles Hotel that as soon as a man
arrived and registered his name they immediately took his measure
for a coffin, and asked him to note down in which cemetery he
desired to be buried." People tried to get away on boats going
upriver; there were often diseased passengers aboard, and regular
stops would be made to bury the dead. Immigrants were especially
prone to the disease; ships' captains were asked not to bring them
in the summer, with some justification since most were so debilitated
by the conditions of their voyage that they were terribly vulnerable
to disease. Some of the worst stories of the epidemic came from the
slums of the Irish Channel, where whole families would die in a day,
huddled together waiting for the end in dark, damp hovels. The
fashionable shell road to the lake became a constant procession of
hearses, death carts, carriages, and wagons. Out at the cemeteries
long trenches were dug to take several coffins at a time; even so,
coffins piled up too fast for the grave-diggers to cope, particularly as
the number of the grave-diggers was diminished by the disease. A
favorite and much-repeated story is of the "old and withered crones
and fat huxter women" who sold ice creams at the cemetery gates,
brushing from their merchandise flies that had been drinking
"dainty inhalations from the green and festering corpses." A New
York speculator is said to have shipped a large number of coffins to
New Orleans labeled as pianos. But it is important to remember that
the 1853 summer was worse only in degree than many others during
the century.

In 1853 and other epidemic years, various cures and preventatives
were tried. Cannon were fired in certain parts of the city at sunset
"to clarify the atmosphere and to disintegrate the miasmas." Tar was
burned on street corners. The pollution of the atmosphere, a favorite

argument of the "indigenists," was established daily by flying a kite
with a piece of meat attached, which when retrieved was found to
be covered with "living, moving, vermiform, animaculae." As Parson
Clapp, author of the most famous account of the epidemic, wrote,
"we have no doubt that hundreds perished from mere fright produced by artificial noise, the constant sight of funerals, darkness and
various other causes." The effects of the tar and the cannon were
indeed so depressing that the authorities eventually forbade them,
the *Weekly Delta* suggesting that they should be replaced by a band
playing in the streets "to elevate the minds and raise the spirits of
the suffering patients."

Patients were bled, purged, and dosed with quinine. Inevitably
there were shelves full of fraudulent concoctions, which could be
bought by the anxious, but most reliable doctors advocated no medicine except castor oil in the early stages; this it was hoped would
prevent the accumulation in the stomach of the dreaded black
vomit, the appearance of which was often closely followed by the
death of the victim. Oyster broth was was said to be good for
convalescents, the only cheering food in the list.

There were some eight thousand deaths from yellow fever in 1853
(only eighty-seven of whom were native New Orleanians)—"the
most awful catalogue of mortality." Business recovered as soon as the
city was declared free of it in October, and with the recovery of
business came the old refusal to take full precautions against a
repetition. Quarantine was recommended only for obviously "un-
sound subjects and filthy vessels." One doctor proclaimed yellow
fever to be a member of the typhus family and the handiwork of
oppressive governments. The New York *Tribune* tried to prove it a
consequence of slavery while the *Daily Delta* blamed it on white
people doing the work of slaves. A long report by a sanitary commission appointed to investigate the epidemic concluded that the causes
of the disease were in New Orleans itself, in particular in the distur-
bance of the soil for canals, pipes, new buildings, and railways; hence
the susceptibility of the immigrants, many of whom worked on such
projects. In the 1850s, at the height of the Know-Nothing campaigns, some said they favored epidemics because it kept down the

number of immigrants. Another cause was the foul air: "There is a peculiar air hanging over and constituting that of large cities," and New Orleans air was more peculiar and unhealthy than most.

There were other epidemics in 1854, 1855, and 1858. During the Civil War the city was relatively free of yellow fever, thanks to an effective quarantine and spring cleaning by General Benjamin Butler, but the disease returned with the restoration of trade immediately after the war, and 1867 was another bad year. The last bad epidemic was in 1878. By the 1880s quarantine had been extended to the forty days of its name, a lazaretto had been built three miles below the quarantine station to isolate patients, and the germ theory was being developed—ships were defumigated with carbolic acid and later sulfuric acid. Sulfuric acid was more successful than had been hoped because, as well as removing germs, it was poisonous to mosquitoes. Mosquitoes had been considered as a possible source of the disease, but not until 1881 were they considered as carriers. Even then the theory was virtually ignored until Walter Reed traced it to the female stegonyia mosquito in Cuba. Once the theory proved correct, the answer was seemingly easy: pour oil on stagnant water to destroy the larvae, and fumigate the air with sulfur to kill the mosquitoes. New Orleans did little about the matter until an epidemic in 1905, after which the disease was successfully eradicated.

Cholera was dreaded quite as much as yellow fever though it was slightly less of a scourge. The two worst cholera epidemics were in 1833 and 1849. In the latter year one-seventh of the city's population died of cholera. People were advised to wear flannel next to their skins "as a certain means of keeping perspiration active" (a superfluous extreme during the New Orleans summer) and to carry vials of *vinaigre des quatre valeurs*. In residential areas such as the Garden District, camphor trees were planted outside houses, and the aromatic berries carried in a bag round the neck.

Modern mosquitoes around New Orleans carry no fatal diseases and are severely controlled by mosquito authorities, who have light meters set up round the city by which they can measure the fluctuating mosquito population; when it gets too high, they muster an impressive army of trucks, airplanes, and boats to spread insecticide.

Even so, suburban gardens on the swampy outskirts of the city are noticeably bleak and uninteresting, the reason being, according to the owners, that it is too warm to work in them and there are too many mosquitoes to make it worth sitting in them. Alfresco evenings in suburbia are to be avoided unless a barbecue acts as a smudge.

As soon as an epidemic appeared, most well-to-do inhabitants of New Orleans left the city. Even if the summer was relatively disease-free, it was pleasant to escape from the damp heat that hung over the city from May to September. Some city dwellers went just to the other side of the lake, to the "Ozone Belt," Covington, Mandeville, and other small settlements of the great pine forest. Others went to the Gulf coast—to Pass Christian, Bay St. Louis, Gulfport, or Biloxi, to spend the summer beside the sea in large, cool houses even more palatial than those they had temporarily abandoned in New Orleans. Often they carried the disease with them, so that it swept through these small towns with the same ferocity as in New Orleans. During the 1878 epidemic in New Orleans, there was nearly a sea battle between Louisiana vessels and those of Mississippi, the latter trying to prevent those coming from New Orleans from landing in Mississippi and spreading the disease.

For the poorer classes of New Orleans there was no escape; they were far more afflicted and could ill afford what little medical attention was available. The lucky ones went to Charity Hospital which, eulogized Timothy Flint, "has a moral beauty of the highest order. It is probably one of the most efficient and useful charities in the country." "An index of indigence," was another more prosaic description. About 1736 a sailor named Jean Louis left about $2,500 to found a charity hospital. Although the horror of yellow fever was as yet unknown in New Orleans, the miasmatic mists of the surrounding swamps inevitably took their toll of the struggling population, particularly of the many homeless who were obliged to make the streets their dwelling place on first arriving in the colony. A house was bought and the original bequest was augmented by fines imposed by the Superior Council. Later the hospital moved to larger, though ill-placed, premises on the swampy edge of town. This building was blown down by a hurricane in 1779 and was rebuilt by the wealthy Spanish official Don Andres de Almonester, who endowed it with a perpetual income from the stores at the corner of St. Peter and Levee streets.

In the hospital, as many as five thousand were treated in a year; even without an epidemic, seven to eight hundred died there each year, less than one-fifth of whom had been born in the United States. During the 1853 epidemic Charity Hospital had six dead carts constantly coming and going between the hospital and its cemetery, Potter's Field, where the poor and vagrants were buried.

Death has generally been treated with great ceremony in New Orleans, except during epidemics. The city had a reputation for its funerary pageants in memory of the famous dead, such as Henry Clay and Napoleon. New Orleans was a city where "the undertaker looks with as much periodical anxiety to the season of his harvest as the speculator in cotton does to his," wrote G. W. Featherstonhaugh. Funeral houses in New Orleans are huge; the white palace of Bultman's Funeral Home (*"Everybody's* buried by Bultman's") has black Etruscan vases outside, and the proprietors themselves, who live in an only slightly smaller house next door, are surrounded by necropolic remains—coffee tables made from tombstones, bits of carved marble and inscriptions dotted around the house and womenfolk who are so thin as to resemble the skeletons who were once Bultman's clients. Even today funeral processions wind a stately path through the traffic, headlights ablaze, permitted to ignore all traffic lights so that one may be caught for a long while watching the sleek black limousines glide past on their way to a cemetery.

New Orleans cemeteries have acquired a distinction all their own, based primarily on the difficulty of burying a person beneath the ground in a floating city. Interment below ground was in fact forbidden early in the nineteenth century, with the rise in the death rate commensurate with a rise in the living rate. So the cemeteries developed like cities, vast floating necropoloi of castellated, creeperstrewn tombs; some are stark and puritanical as befits their purposeful occupants; others, gently crumbling in somnolent decadence. J. B. Priestley thought that cemeteries in New Orleans suggested "a mouldering antiquity beyond that of the Valley of the Kings at Luxor."*

In most parts of the city, except the high ground near the levee, it used to be impossible to dig a grave because no sooner did one dig than the hole filled with water and the coffin would float on top. One cemetery, St. Louis No. 3, formerly known as Bayou Cemtery, used to be so easily flooded that it was a common sight for the sextons and undertakers to be paddling round in pirogues, coffin amidships. So everyone except Jews and indigents was buried above ground: the poor man's graveyard at Potter's Field used to be a grassy expanse, and the Jewish cemeteries have the graves marked by marble or granite slabs laid flat on the ground as in other dryer parts of the country. No one cared about Potter's Field, but the Jews had problems when their cemetery was flooded; in 1849 the Protestants lent them their vaults for temporary burials until the floods subsided.

But everywhere else the tombs are above ground, temples dedicated to the dead. The old ones are ragged and sown with weeds, cracking at the foundations; the new ones, in serried ranks of gray granite, are eloquent arguments in favor of cremation. Some of the tombs are those of individuals, most belong to families, and some belong to clubs, associations, societies, whose members have bought the right to be buried there (many of these groups were formed exclusively for that purpose). The tombs are usually built in two parts: the upper part, divided into several chambers, is where the coffins are interred, and beneath is a vault into which all the bones are eventually transferred after a certain number of years. This principle is found in family tombs, large society tombs, and even in the so-called ovens, ranges of vaults usually built into the walls of the cemetery.

The oldest cemetery is the St. Louis Cemetery on Basin Street, established in 1788; once it was larger, but part is now occupied by neighboring housing projects and another part by Basin Street. It covers little more than an acre of land, on what used to be a cypress

*In *Harper's*, May, 1958

swamp beyond the city walls. The water level is here about a foot below the surface, so burial above ground was the only answer. Modern subsurface drainage has caused many of the tombs to sink; they are crowded in according to no plan whatsoever. Narrow, intricate paths wind in and out the monuments of Creole families, the path in places littered with a disintegrated cupid or saint half-washed away by rain, looking as dead as the occupants of the tomb they were designed to decorate. Tombs were built of plastered and white-washed brick, and the entrances closed with marble slabs. There is little space for epitaphs on the tombs, only generations of families. None of the tombs is particularly distinctive except those that are outstanding for their size. New Orleans talks a lot about the cemetery's history but takes little active interest in it and though the guidebook describes the noteworthy people buried there, only the stout, voluble guardian of the cemetery can find them for you.

As the population of the city grew, so did the number of deaths, and in 1823 a second St. Louis cemetery was consecrated behind the first, which by then was so crowded and therefore considered so unhygienic that the mayor had already forbidden burials in the summer. In the second cemetery the more elaborate tombs—huge Grecian temples, Egyptian pylons, obelisks, and Gothic chapels among them—testify to the greater prosperity of the city. Dominique You, the pirate associate of Jean Lafitte, is buried here; when he died, so great was his respectability that businesses and banks were closed and flags flown at half-mast. Oscar J. Dunn, the Negro Lieutenant-Governor of Reconstruction days, was buried here in 1871 with full Freemason honors.

On the other side of Basin Street from the St. Louis cemeteries is the Church of Our Lady of Guadeloupe, which was opened in 1827 (and dedicated to St. Anthony) as a mortuary chapel after a severe yellow fever epidemic had convinced the city that there was too great a danger of contamination from exposed bodies in burial services in the cathedral. Such a church, so close to the cemetery, would avoid "those funeral porcessions which are but too apt to scatter throughout the city the fatal miasma of fever." Anyone who exposed a corpse in the cathedral was made liable to a fifty-dollar fine.*

The great granite fields of the Metairie cemeteries came into being in the 1840s when more space was again needed and the city authorities preferred sites away from the city as it was commonly held that one possible source of yellow fever was the fumes arising from the tombs. A cemetery was dedicated out by Bayou St. John, connected with the mortuary chapel by a railway built specially for carrying corpses and mourners, but both cemetery and railroad failed for lack of patrons dead or alive. Later another St. Louis cemetery, No. 3, was dedicated on Esplanade Avenue, while other plots of land along Metairie Ridge were filling up. The problems posed by yellow fever and cholera epidemics resulted in the strictest burial regulations, above-ground burial being mandatory except for Jews and indigents and except for emergencies, as in the worst epidemics when there was no time to build tombs. In *Creoles of Louisiana*, George Cable has a particularly macabre description of the burial ceremonies of 1853—the desperate shortage of grave-diggers, shallow graves washed open by the rain, families obliged to bury their own dead.

Up where the freeway crosses Metairie Road is the greatest city of the dead, where Metairie, Cypress Grove, Fireman's, and St. Patrick's cemeteries cluster around slightly higher land. Here the dead are settled and prosperous; there are none of the uncertainty and damp discomfort of those earlier tombs in St. Louis, Nos. 1, 2, and 3. Even the immigrant societies, the United Slavonic Benevolent Society, the Hellenic Orthodox, the Cefalutana, are well established behind impressive mausolea. The most pompous are the tombs of such pillars of American society as the Elks and the Masons; the latter in fact have a cemetery of their own while the hill crowned by the bronze elk can be seen way down Canal Street as one drives up to the cemeteries. The really wealthy families tend to be buried in Metairie Cemtery, the only one to have the occasional

---

*The church was later converted into a parish church for Italians and, later still, rededicated to Our Lady of Guadeloupe.

tree (and avenues between the tombs tastefully named after flowers and trees) in spite of the havoc the roots may cause to such lavish creations—which is why most cemeteries do not have them. It was once a race course; fashionable young men would race each other to the race track along the shell road that ran up the New Basin Canal (the digging of which caused so many deaths in the first place). Cemetery architecture at its best, says one guidebook; true indeed in some degree, for there is nothing quite so soul-destroying as these grim ranks of granite and marble memorials, in summer their hard gray walls radiating a heat as hot as any hell.

There are at least thirty cemeteries in New Orleans, a great waste of space in the opinion of many. As well as the older ones, there are new ones in the suburbs offering a more American, less New Orleanian way of death; sanctuaries such as the Garden of Memories could be found anywhere. A modernized New Orleans burial is advertised by the Hope Mausoleum—"The Modern Way of Burial, Six Thousand Crypts, Perpetual Care, Offers Superior, Above-Ground Interment Facilities," or Lakelawn Park and Mausoleum, which offers "Single, Companion, and Family Arrangements, Private Family Rooms, Private Tombs, Ground Plots." Empty family tombs are erected in Metairie Cemetery with the practical suggestion that you buy ahead of time.

There is at least one shrine in the city originally built against yellow fever, that of St. Roch. The chapel here was first called Campo Santo by its founder, a German priest who modeled it on the Campo Santo dei Tedeschi in Rome. After the loss of so many parishioners in the epidemic of 1868, he invoked the intercession of St. Roch, famous for his miracles among plague sufferers in the Middle Ages, promising to build a shrine to the saint. The chapel, which is now surrounded by the cemetery, is hung with gruesome plaster limbs and other parts of the body (including what looks like a heart) testifying to cures attributed to the saint. Notices in the press thank the saint for his intercession.

In the outlying Negro communities of the city, to the east of New Orleans and over on the West Bank, one can sometimes find small burial grounds half-submerged beneath live oaks and swamp cypresses; perhaps there was once a plantation here and these were the places where the slaves were buried. Memories here are short; space is limited, and no one can afford memorial tablets except, here and there, the dead of two world wars, whose burial expenses were paid by the government. There is one by the small Negro community of Cut-Off just below Algiers and another in a patch of swamp nearby —oases of rural calm in the midst of the bustling development of modern suburbs.

The great cemetery day in New Orleans is All Saints' Day, a remnant of its more Latin heritage. For days beforehand, there are notices in the hardware stores, such as "Paint Your Tomb White, With Bondex Waterproof Paint." Everyone whitewashes their family tombs and decorates them with flowers, taking a fresh pot of chrysanthemums to replace the dessicated stems of last year, or a clean bunch of plastic flowers to replace the faded ones. In front of many tombs are uncomfortable wrought-iron chairs and benches, where it was once the custom for the women of the family to display their winter fashions and receive condolences every November 1st; the custom has disappeared but even modern tombs incorporate a sort of granite seat. Coffee and gumbo used to be sold to nourish the mourners, but now it is ice-cream and hot dogs. In Mark Twain's day, before the advent of plastic flowers, the image of "perpetual care" was supplied by the *immortelle*, "coarse, ugly and indestructible," made in the form of a cross or wreath with rosettes of black linen pinned on, "a kind of sorrowful breastpin." "The immortelle requires no attention; you just hang it up, and there you are; just leave it alone, it will take care of your grief for you, and keep it in mind better than you can; stands weather first-rate, and lasts like boiler-iron." Fresh wreaths appear around new tombs (and plastic ones around older); occasionally one will see the forlorn framework, its flowers blown to the winds exposing the indecent wire and foam-rubber foundations.

With some reason, New Orleans has developed its own sort of quack medicine, and cures for all ills. As one Frenchman wrote, "*La pharmacie ne saurait être inutile dans un pays où l'on est gourmand, où l'on boit avec excès, où l'on passe des fatigues les plus grands et la plus grand oiseveté, où les indolentes femmes ne sont agile que pour se faire obéir de leurs esclaves."* A doctor in Royal Street concocted a bitters for the sick to mix with their therapeutic brandy; this claims, as do many mixed drinks in New Orleans, to be the original cocktail. Another early medicine was Duffy's Pure Malt Whiskey (A Scientific Remedy Not a Beverage): if you drank it, "no disease can *possibly* remain lodged in the body." There was also Dr. J. N. Lee's Portable Hot Air Bath Chamber and Thermal Wrap used as a preventative and a cure in the 1880s. Nowadays faith-healers advertise regularly in the press, and New Orleans' drugstores stock a remarkable number of "elixirs" designed to expel every modern variety of evil humor from the body.

16. Jazz

JAZZ MADE the city's name in the twentieth century. For about twenty years the seamy side of this great Delta port came to life in the music of a people it had chosen to ignore, in the very years when the politicians of New Orleans and of the South in general were working their hardest to deprive them of political and social rights. The music itself was partly the result of segregation from white influence, which retarded acculturation, and kept Africanism alive in Southern slaves. Jazz was almost exclusively a Negro product, and white adaptations, known as Dixieland jazz, never acquired the same harmony with the instrumentation. Jazz first received popular nationwide acclaim, however, with the appearance of the white Original Dixieland Jass Band in New York in 1917. Today jazz lingers in a fading old age beneath the bright lights of tourism, its musicians playing their last poignant but beautiful notes before hundreds of attentive outsiders. But the city has lost interest.

Jazz in New Orleans was created by its most oppressed people, and every moment of the history of jazz reminds one of this. But New Orleans had always taken a pride in its fondness for music. This was the city with the first permanent opera company in the United States, where the opera season was reckoned even by hypercritical

European tourists to be a smart and cultured affair, though the Civil War had doused its splendor. There was an ingrained popular affection for music, and all year round there were parades, complete with bands—militia regiments, national days, lodge celebrations, the firemen's parade, and, of course, Carnival parades. The memorial parade for President Garfield in 1881 had thirteen or more organized Negro bands representing various benevolent organizations. No lakeside picnic was complete without its accompanying serenade. The social season revolving around Mardi Gras, with more and more balls every year, encouraged dance bands galore. The music played on these occasions before the 1890s had little affiliation with the jazz of the turn of the century, but there was a heritage of patronage that enabled jazz to emerge from the back-street slums where it had developed. This background of musical patronage must be largely responsible for the flowering of traditional jazz in New Orleans. The actual musical background of Negro music could be found elsewhere in the slave states, but nowhere else was there such a hungry market for music.

Prior to the 1890s, New Orleans music was principally in the hands of the colored Creole musicians; they led the dance bands, the marching bands, the picnic serenades. They were not interested in allowing into their midst their uncouth country cousins (although willing to teach them music) who were flocking into the uptown sections of what are now the city's colored ghettos, especially around South Rampart Street. Jazz was essentially an expression of lowerclass Negroes. Earlier Congo Square had given an inkling of what was to come, with its conglomeration of African drums and chants, but the Sunday celebrations had gradually petered out in the 1880s, and there was little overt connection between the crude Africanism of such officially sponsored outlets and other aspects of the jazz background—plantation songs, river songs, spirituals, slave blues— sorrow songs as W. E. B. Du Bois called them. From this rural music developed the blues, a music peculiarly suited to individual expression and improvisation.

As such an individual music, jazz in New Orleans has survived through its personalities. But it is worth glancing briefly at its history.

Dance halls and street bands were the main outlets for early jazz, the street bands more promising than the dance halls, which were largely monopolized by the Creole bands. Buddy Bolden's Ragtime Band is generally considered the first jazz band, but it may have had other unknown predecessors. To the Creole musicians downtown, the new music was unorthodox and noisy, played by country Negroes usually with no musical education—though several of the better and later players had studied music with the downtown musicians, and one of the most heated controversies in the early years of jazz was whether a player could or could not read music. The relative lack of musical education on classical European lines explains the reliance of the jazz on such characteristic African elements as rhythm and instrumentation, which are the hallmarks of traditional jazz. The vocal antecedents of jazz were taken up in the jazz band by the wind instruments—cornet, trombone, clarinet, tuba, and others; such instruments had been easy to find and cheap to buy since the disbanding of the Confederacy bands after the Civil War and of the martial paraphernalia of Reconstruction.

It was as marching music that jazz came into the open. Many of the earliest jazz marches are still played today. "The Maple Leaf Rag," and "Bill Bailey, Won't You Please Come Home" are still regular features of any New Orleans parade, and not solely for the benefit of the tourist either. Most of the great jazz musicians learned their trade as small children skipping and dancing behind the band, playing any old homemade instrument—cigar-box guitars, tin cans, pennywhistles. One sees Negro children today on their front porches banging out a hideous cacophony of chords on their mothers' washtubs. The music caught on remarkably fast, though as late as 1918 the *Times-Picayune* could describe jazz (a product for which New Orleans was just becoming famous in many parts of the country) as a manifestation "of a low streak in man's taste, that has not yet come out in civilisation's wash . . . jass [*sic*] music is the indecent story syncopated and counterpointed."

By the early 1900s the great bands and those increasingly in demand for the innumerable musical occasions of New Orleans were the black uptown bands, and Creole musicians found themselves having to study their technique instead. Ten-piece brass bands such as the Onward, Tuxedo, and Eureka bands would be out for Sunday school outings, cornerstone layings, funerals, fund-raising, and Mardi Gras, complete with banners, gorgeously arrayed grand marshals and uniforms for the members, whose strange, noisy, revolutionary music drew crowds wherever they played. Maggie Tappins meeting hall at 1719 Dryades Street in the Negro quarter was popular for lodge meetings and the starting point for many parades; on most Sunday afternoons in the summer, the marchers and the Eureka Band or some other band would gather for a neighborhood parade, regardless of the heat. About the heat jazz musicians are remarkably stoical, as anyone who has seen them playing in the stifling confines of Preservation Hall will appreciate—it is never the musicians who mop their brows. You still see notices in the Negro areas now, pinned up on house windows, advertising a Sunday outing —picnic and brass band an essential ingredient. The bands were also used for advertising, perched on huge drays; the trombone player was relegated to the tailgate so that his plunging arm would not bruise the other players. Louis Armstrong describes playing with a band hired to advertise a prize fight, boxing having been legalized in New Orleans in 1890. Sometimes there were battles of music between two bands meeting accidentally on the same street corner, trying to outplay each other or at least burst each other's eardrums.

Dance music was another source of ready patronage. Dancing was as much a part of the New Orleans scene as music—ranging from the Creole and quadroon balls of the early nineteenth century to the Carnival balls of the later decades, dances at country clubs, taxi dance halls, and on the street at Mardi Gras. Every neighborhood was said to have its own dance steps. There were dance halls all over town, even in the poorest sections, where a tarpaulin would sometimes be rolled out in a vacant lot, the fresh air in summer compensating for the lack of a roof in winter. One of the city's oldest dance halls is still to be seen on the corner of Washington Avenue and Prytania Street, the Crescent City Skating Rink (now the Behrman Gymnasium); the band used to play for half an hour on the balcony above the entrance to attract people inside. Social dancing became all the rage in the last decades of the nineteenth century, but the music was mostly supplied by the well-organized colored Creole dance bands. Only in the late 1890s did the latter begin looking uptown at the new noisy music for their inspiration. Meanwhile the new musicians found employment in the bars and brothels that wanted to provide music for their clients but had no wish to pay the price of the established musicians and bands. These emerged as the sponsors of jazz dance music, and hence the connection between New Orleans jazz and the only licensed brothel area in the United States, Storyville.

Prostitution had been licensed in New Orleans before Storyville, for a brief period from 1857 to 1859; its segregation was revoked after a suit had been brought by the owner of a brothel, Mrs. Emma Pickett, who resented paying the $250 license fee. By the end of the century there were various red-light districts, but the blocks bordered by Canal, Basin, St. Louis, and North Claiborne streets were the most conspicuous.* Brothels had first been attracted to the area toward the end of the eighteenth century, when the Carondelet Canal levee along St. Louis Street contained the usual crowd of boatmen and their entertainments. The district acquired its name after it was represented on the city council by Sidney Story, a righteous gentleman who advocated the segregation of prostitution. In 1897 he won his point; the district was defined and licensed, and it showed its gratitude to Story by adopting his name.

There were reckoned to be about two thousand prostitutes in Storyville at the height of its fame, most of them living in hideously squalid "cribs," narrow single-story houses divided into partitions, which were rented out by the night. But there were also the more glamorous "mansions"—the jazz patrons—from which the district acquired its notoriety. Château Lobrane d'Arlington was run by Josie Arlington, mistress of Tom Anderson, self-styled boss of Storyville, who published an annual Blue Book as a guide to the district. Lulu

---

*Several brothels on Perdido Street had been owned by John McDonogh and H.M. Stanley found one there filled with "giggling wantons . . . in such scant clothing, that I was amazed"—no wonder after such an experience that he should have greeted Dr. Livingstone so phlegmatically.

White (who advertised herself in the Blue Book as "the handsomest octoroon in America and aside from her beauty she has the distinction of possessing the largest collection of diamonds, pearls and other rare gems in this part of the country") also "made a feature of boarding none but the fairest of girls" in her Mahogany Hall; some of its vividly painted windowpanes and stylish Japanese wallpaper in geisha fashion are today preserved in the Jazz Museum. Another octoroon, "Countess" Willie Pazza, was said to have kept a musical box under her mattress. Music was an essential ingredient of these brothels and bars and of the dance halls that opened up along the fringes of the district, such as the Tuxedo Ranch Hall and the 101 Ranch, where many musicians had regular stands. The piano took over from wind instruments as the principal jazz instrument, more suited to the smaller space. The cheaper houses had mechanical pianos (pianolas); the better ones, small orchestras. Even outside on the streets there was music; Louis Armstrong relates how as a boy he used to go down to Storyville with a group of friends and sing on street corners.

Storyville provided the patronage and the classrooms for the great jazz musicians of New Orleans. In its heyday it was reckoned that all but one or two regular dance orchestras were playing in this vast gaudy bawdy house. Several musicians, however, had already graduated to more lucrative fields by the time the district was closed in 1917 (at the insistence of the War Department, anxious for the welfare and health of troops stationed in and around the city awaiting embarkation for Europe, and despite Mayor Behrman's defense of "the God-given right of men to be men"). Jelly Roll Morton and Kid Ory had gone to California; Kid Oliver had gone to Chicago. The departure of jazz from the city was, as much as anything, part of the general migration of Negroes to the North that occurred in the years after the war; many musicians had caught the travel bug earlier, perhaps from playing aboard one of the river steamers—excursion boats and showboats —and were able to find jobs for those who came later.

> I can't keep open, I'm gonna close up my shack,
> The chief of police done tore my playhouse down,
> No use in grievin', I'm gonna leave town.

The development of jazz has been described often elsewhere; one or two jazz experts in particular have captured that strange mixture of exoticism and squalor that makes the study of black New Orleanians and their music so interesting. It is the individuals involved, however, who gave the jazz years in the city such an extraordinarily sympathetic flavor in spite of the poverty and violence and sickening political and social segregation of the background. Buddy Bolden, for instance, who was born the year of Emancipation, was one of the most picturesque of the early jazz leaders and the inspiration of many younger musicians. He was a local barber who was hired to play in the uptown Lincoln Park, and it was he who is credited with inventing the "hot blues" as a breakaway from the conventional dance music of the downtown Creole musicians. Bolden eventually went mad and was committed to an asylum in 1907, where he died in 1931. Then there were the "professors," the most famous of whom perhaps was Professor James Humphreys, begetter of at least two generations of jazz players. He used to go once a week to Magnolia Plantation about thirty miles below New Orleans (now a mournfully dilapidated shell occupied by a family who were probably once field hands on its sugar fields) to teach the children on the estate, many of whom later became professional jazz musicians in New Orleans. His son Willie played clarinet and his daughters Lillian and Jamesetta played bass; of his grandsons, Willie, Jr., plays clarinet; Earl, trombone; and Percy; trumpet. Of all the old musicians around New Orleans Percy Humphreys looks one of the most stalwart, plodding along as leader of the Eureka Brass Band, sitting in the middle of a group in Preservation Hall, playing for the funerals of his contemporaries.

Bunk Johnson's musical career mirrors the ups and downs of New Orleans jazz and of many of its exponents. He was born in 1879 and was taking lessons on the cornet by the time he was seven. He was among the many musicians inspired by Bolden's noisy, infectious blues style and occasionally played for Bolden. He traveled a lot around Texas and Louisiana, had a regular job in Storyville before the war, then again took to the road but never went to the big money spots, such as Chicago or New York, where several of his contemporaries were making their names. In 1932 his horn was damaged in a fight, and soon afterward he lost his teeth; with the Depression affecting jobs, he virtually gave up playing. Several musicians, like Johnson, were only rescued from oblivion by the careful researches of jazz enthusiasts, who created something of a jazz revival in the 1940s. Johnson's resurrectors bought him a new set of false teeth, and he went on playing until his death in 1949.

It would be unfair not to mention Louis Armstrong, however well known his story. He was born in New Orleans in 1900 and picked up his music on the streets, listening to bands; he used to sneak into dance halls and ask the cornet players if he could borrow their instruments when they were resting. He was sent to a reform school in 1915 (the Waifs' Home, formerly the Milne Home for Boys founded by the Scotsman of the lakefront, Alexander Milne), where he had music lessons. In 1918 he was given a tempting glimpse of wider horizons when he played aboard the excursion boat S. S. *Capitol*, which ran between St. Louis and New Orleans during the summer. Later he played at the Tuxedo Ranch Hall and at Tom Anderson's cabaret. In 1923 he left the city for Chicago at the invitation of Kid Oliver. But he returned to New Orleans regularly, joining in a funeral or a parade, and in 1949 he was chosen King of Zulu, king of the principal Negro Carnival club.

The jazz revival of the 1940s—which was due largely to William Russell, a violinist and repairer of musical instruments, who reorganized Bunk Johnson's band during World War II—and its aftermath have been a rather depressing business as far as New Orleans is concerned, the enthusiasm being mostly engendered elsewhere. Jazz has never ceased to be played in New Orleans, but the better exponents left, and New Orleans jazz has never approached the peak of creative inspiration of the early 1900s. The revival has had a few marvelous results: historical jazz recordings, which include a particularly interesting series by Samuel Charters made in the 1950s from all the fragments of jazz he found still in the city—street music, marching bands, dance halls, and reminiscences; and the resurrection of old jazz players—Bunk Johnson, George Lewis, Punch Miller, Billie and Deedee Pierce, and others, most of whom were found to be living in such poverty that in many cases it prevented them from playing. There is also a jazz club, founded in 1948, which sponsored the opening of the Jazz Museum in 1961 and which gives Sunday afternoon concerts in a respectable hotel ballroom. And without the revival there would be no Preservation Hall.

Preservation Hall suffers from a split personality. It was set up in 1961 in a large, dirty room just off Bourbon Street by jazz enthusiasts who wanted to enable the old musicians to earn some money by playing the music that had made the city so famous fifty years earlier. A different group plays every night in unpretentious surroundings much like many of the less glittering dance halls of the early jazz years. The music can be magnificent; but more often the musicians are playing down to their audience, white and middle-aged, drumming their heels in happy memory of their dancing years and willing to pay five dollars to have "The Saints . . ." played during the evening. The worst evenings in Preservation Hall (and none fail at some point to evoke the blues nostalgia essential to traditional jazz) are on the level of the officially sponsored jazzfest. This is organized from two angles: the home product and the progress of jazz, Count Basie, Dave Brubeck, and others. The latter only serve to show how stultified and fossilized traditional jazz playing—a music that succeeded because of its scope for exciting improvisation—has become.

It is easy to sound rather disdainful of the jazz played in New Orleans nowadays, and most of the Negro youth, for instance, will have nothing to do with it, regarding the players as little better than aged Uncle Toms content to play to white audiences in virtually segregated halls. Certainly it lacks the inspiration, the verve, the adventurousness of jazz in its heyday; certainly the traditional jazz now heard is a museum piece, preserved (as the name of its most agreeable patron suggests) like plums in the syrup of tourism. But if the syrup is merely sickly, the plums have a most haunting flavor, and this is how it is with New Orleans jazz today. There is still a sense of music in the streets, as Samuel Charters found with his recordings; one regularly meets a couple of old Negro women in the Quarter at night singing on a street corner, and street musicians are often to be found on South Rampart on Saturdays. During the weeks before Carnival, every porch seems to have a juvenile spasm band practicing on its front steps.

And there are the jazz funerals. There seem to be one or two of these during the winter months, hardly surprising, considering the average age of most traditional jazz musicians in the city. The elaborate music ceremonial of the funeral parade probably originated with the band's being used for funerals of eminent lodge members, Masonic lodges playing a large part in Negro society and Negro funerals known for their elaborateness: "The more lodges you belong to the more music you gits when you goes to meet your maker." Nowadays jazz funerals seem to be reserved for old jazz players whose colleagues turn out to give them magnificent musical farewells. They attract a lot of outsiders seemingly divorced from the bleak sadness of the occasion, but no one, however shallow his curiosity, can withstand the overwhelming pathos. Some famous musicians have drawn thousands to their funerals: four thousand were said to have followed Oscar Celestin's coffin when he died in the 1930s. From the funeral parlor to the church, and from there to the cemetery, the band plays such mournful tunes as "Nearer My God to Thee" and "Flee As a Bird to the Mountain"; after the interment, as the crowd of mourners leaves the cemetery, the band comes alive with "Oh Didn't He Ramble," "Ain't Gonna Study War No More." Sometimes the funerals will take one to small graveyards on the West Bank overshadowed by weeping moss-hung oaks, sometimes to the crowded precincts of the St. Louis cemeteries, where the Grand Marshal has to restrain his baton and the tuba player maneuvers uncomfortably between the tombs.

George Lewis' funeral took place on a most funereal day in January 1968—gray, wet skies; muddy, wet streets; stark, bare, wet trees. The crowd consisted of sight-seers and mourners. Among the mourners were black-clad, respectable old gentlemen who would unexpectedly produce a wind instrument from their mackintoshes and surreptitiously join in the dirges for a few bars before turning to pass the time of day with a companion. Two bands attended—Olympia and Eureka—the musicians, in their black mackintoshes and peaked caps, looking a little like chauffeurs. Then there were the Grand Marshals, blue and white wreaths and badges of office round their necks, and the Grandest Marshal of all, of the Olympia Brass Band, a huge, rather elderly Negro in a black dress suit, top hat under one arm, executing a slow ritual dance in front of the funeral cortège as it reached the church. And all the while this mournful and sad music, made still more mournful by the grieving weather. And in the midst of the flowers on the coffin was a clarinet made of flowers, Lewis' instrument. That's the way to die.

17. Carnival

CARNIVAL IS the crux of New Orleans life. Food and Carnival are the two things New Orleanians seem to enjoy talking about most; both give the city immense pleasure, both attract thousands of tourists. But Carnival is the real money and social spinner of the two. Carnival petrifies and stratifies New Orleans society, providing it with a perennial *raison d'être* (in its own eyes at least). Since the first organized parade was held in 1837, it has claimed to be "the greatest free show on earth"; the show may indeed be free, but it incites people to heights of extravagance. It is regarded with great serious-ness for it is a huge business speculation. One has to live in New Orleans to understand how much Carnival as a festivity and Carnival as a social institution mean to New Orleanians, preoccupying them throughout the year; if a conversation flags, it can always be revived with talk of Carnival. In spite of commercialization, and still more in spite of romanticizing (most books on the subject read like tourist advertisments), it provides New Orleans with light and life and makes such demands on the city's sense of enjoyment that without it New Orleans might die a slow death.

As a Catholic tradition, Carnival has been celebrated in New Orleans since its foundation; the Carnelevamen, the putting away of meat for Lent, has always been marked by Mardi Gras celebrations, a final fling before the rigors of Lent set in—though never all that rigorous in New Orleans. "The French and Spanish subjects of Louisiana are strict Romanists," wrote John Pope at the end of the eighteenth century, "and therefore enthusiastically fond of Pageantry in their religious festivals." "Religion itself is made matter of show and spectacle," reported Buckingham disapprovingly, "and people are invited by the newspapers to the Catholic Cathedral on particular occasions, just as they would go to a play." During the eighteenth century Mardi Gras in New Orleans was the occasion for masked balls and parades, which were confined to the one day of Shrove Tuesday. Masking was forbidden from time to time as too conducive to a breakdown of law and order; the Spanish authorities prohibited it in the 1790s at the height of their American suspicions, and the Americans in 1806 at the height of their Spanish suspicions and the Burr conspiracy. Claiborne wrote apologetically to Madison: "I fear you will suppose that I am wanting in respect in calling your attention to the balls of New Orleans; but . . . they occupy much of the public mind and from them have proceeded the greatest embarrassments, which have hitherto attended my administration." By now there was a thriving carnival season from Twelfth Night to Mardi Gras. Latrobe found hardly an evening without a ball, an opera or the theater, and there were two public balls a week, though neither rated very high socially; ladies were usually allowed in free. Private balls were held by the established Creole families—rather gloomy affairs one gathers, hence the popularity of the gayer quadroon balls.

In 1838, copying a custom that had grown up in Mobile, Alabama, a parade was organized on Mardi Gras, and in 1857 some enthusiastic Americans organized themselves into a society (known for some obscure reason as a *krewe*) to combat Creole exclusiveness. It produced the first Comus parade, so-called from its theme "The Demon Actors of Milton's Paradise Lost," which rather inaccurately borrowed Comus as its leader on the first float, with Satan on the second and last; everyone else came behind on foot. By 1859 the parade was already attracting outsiders (including a conspicuous number of prostitutes); Sir Charles Lyell noted "the ludicrous surprise, mixed with contempt, of several unmasked stiff grave Anglo-Americans from the north, who were witnessing for the first time what seemed to them so much mummery and tom-foolery." Other visitors recorded their impressions of the "well organised and tasteful representations . . . intended to educate and please." Steamboats coming downriver were crowded with revelers, and the St. Charles Hotel was packed with planters and their families beginning the day at breakfast in full evening regalia. There were no celebrations during the Civil War, and during Reconstruction the authorities were always rather nervous as to how they would turn out: in 1869 *De Bow's Review* gleefully pointed out that "there was not a Negro, nor scallawag present, at this assemblage of the elite of foreign and domestic society in the city," and in 1873 the Comus parade chose as its theme "The Missing Link to Darwin's Origin of Species" with the President and his Administration unmistakably represented as monkeys and reptiles. The previous year the krewe of Rex, King of Carnival, had been inaugurated, and Mardi Gras was declared a public holiday—"one of the results of an imperial mandate on Rex on his first visit." In the last two decades of the century, Carnival clubs began proliferating and the city began its commercialization of the celebrations, which has now developed into such a vast and profitable enterprise.

There are several fascinating aspects of Carnival in New Orleans, only slightly less so to the outsider than to the New Orleanian. There is the social aspect, one that demands an extraordinary amount of money and devotion from the well-to-do New Orleanians, centering more around the balls and the selection of kings and queens than around the parades. There is the commercial aspect—the proliferation of carnival paraphernalia, especially since the last war. And there is Mardi Gras itself; a lot of people still enjoy Mardi Gras for its own sake, for the excuse to dress up and behave like fools for one day in the year.

On the social aspect, the Carnival organizations quickly became as exclusive as the Creole society they had rebelled against. What Mrs. Trollope wrote of Creole society—that "they meet together, eat together and are very grand and aristocratic; each of their balls is a little Almacks and every portly dame of the set is as exclusive in her principles as a lady patroness"—was true of Carnival society by the end of the century and is still true of certain segments today. Even William Faulkner observed of New Orleans that "those who are not of the elect must stand forever without her portals." Membership in the older Carnival krewes is exclusively male and demands pedigrees; in a city with such a reputation for political corruption, it is interesting that so exclusive a krewe as Comus is not known ever to have succumbed to political blandishments. It is also interesting that an organization that seems, on the face of it, so out of touch with reality should inspire ambitions in politicians; and every New Orleans politician would dearly love to be a member. The secrecy that surrounds the deliberations of the krewes is responsible for the mystique of Carnival; those involved in the Carnival world can speculate for hours who the queens of the various elite krewes will be. There are hundreds of krewes now, representing every echelon of New Orleans life, and between Twelfth Night and Mardi Gras there are balls every night. But few of these count for anything socially.

Membership in the krewes is supposed to be as secret as freemasonry in every other country but America, and in a way the krewes play a part very similar to that of freemasonry elsewhere in providing a framework for New Orleans society, which is as much concerned with self-preservation as any aristocracy, and more successfully than many. The krewes are ruled by their captains, with ducal assistants, the kings being chosen as gaudy centerpieces for Carnival. Comus is the most select krewe, as befits the oldest, and its members constitute the hierarchy of New Orleans society. Other high-ranking krewes have such picturesque names as Proteus, Atlanteans, and Momus. These all have parades before their balls, which fall in the last week of Carnival, and no money is stinted to make both parade and ball as lavish and extravagant as pageantry should be—such flamboyance could never get away with being halfhearted.

The focal point of every parade is the king and that of the ball is the presentation of the queen and her court to the king and his court. The king is chosen from among the krewe members, the captain having the final voice; seniority, heavily influenced by genealogy and also bank account (many will deny this latter influence but it is comparatively rare for anyone to be chosen who is not comfortably off, at the very least), is the guiding principle for selection. The king's expenses, though considerable, are nothing compared with what a queen's parents will pay for the honor. The queen is a debutante, usually the daughter of a member, her selection again dependent upon genealogy and income, and her court consists of other debutantes. No debutante is likely to be queen more than once in the season, but the longer the family tree the more courts she is likely to attend among the older krewes, a financially daunting prospect for all but the most conservative or ambitious parents.

All the best balls—and many others—are held in the Municipal Auditorium, a hideous hulk of a building facing on what used to be Congo Square, which has two auditoriums and can therefore accommodate two balls in one night—quite convenient in a short pre-Lenten season when all the balls have to be crammed into a few weeks. The use of a theater for the balls, even such an uncongenial one as this, stems from the earlier carnival celebrations when balls were usually held in the Théatre d'Orleans. The balls are extraordinary affairs, the apparent lack of conviviality quite incomprehensible to the outsider. They begin with a masque, usually enjoyed hilariously by the members taking part and to a lesser extent by the audience trying to guess the identities of the masked performers. At the end of the masque the queen and her court of debutantes are presented by the dukes of the krewe to the king, and the whole court to the audience. Each krewe member is allotted a certain number of invitations. Some of these will be merely to attend the ball and those invited thus are expected to dress up as if for the ball but to sit upstairs in the dress circle and watch. Other invitations—to women—are for "call outs"; the women occupy the stalls and will be "called out" for their dance (one of a dozen or so—no more—of which every ball consists) by their host, who will present them with a favor at the end. Yet a third kind of invitation may be sent to men to be "on the committee" for the ball; this means attending one's host on the ballroom floor after the masque and finding his "call outs" for him. Few women have more than one call-out invitation—great care is taken by the krewe organization to eliminate duplications—but many spend their year getting acquainted with as many members as possible to ensure as many dances as possible; the more naive spend the evening amusing themselves in their stalls, gossiping about the queen, their clothes, and other guests.

The krewe members are as gay as can be, being allowed to bring alcohol into the dressing rooms offstage, but the women have in theory to abide by the dry laws of the auditorium. Prohibition gave people enough practice in avoiding such petty restrictions, and in the spacious ladies' cloakroom you will find elegant ladies of every age producing delightful little hip-flasks, specially designed for evening bags, to help the evening sparkle. The management is sufficiently understanding to provide paper cups and ice for those who prefer not to drink it straight. One krewe has the kindness to lay on champagne in the ladies' cloakroom.

Above all else, the balls provide material for gossip—gossip that can be prolonged throughout the year, centering on the kings and queens of the elite krewes and reaching a climax in the search for the identity of the king and queen of Comus, the peak of social prestige. Second, perhaps, to Comus is the krewe of Rex—important for its size rather than its aristocracy. Rex is the least exclusive of the major krewes, membership being limited mainly by ability to pay the high cost. Men are often members on account of their business, and fees are put down to expense accounts; call outs for the huge Rex ball, which takes place the evening of Mardi Gras (the other side of the Municipal Auditorium from the Comus ball), have become a businessman's way of entertaining clients and their wives. The organization of the krewe is in the hands of a group of about four hundred and fifty members known as the School of Design; they elect the king and decide the theme for the parade. This is the krewe that is supposed to spend most lavishly. Whereas ball guests on the lists of Comus members are minutely scrutinized—neither Jews nor outsiders are invited without a lengthy debate—and members are warned that anyone caught exchanging invitations will be eternally blackballed, tickets for the Rex ball, on the other hand, can sometimes be "acquired" through the Chamber of Commerce. As one observer wrote, "The tableaux and ball which terminate the evening's festivities have ever been a subject of the deepest anxieties in the circles of the best society of our city."

The krewes themselves are said to spend between $2 and $3 million each Carnival season. Parades average as much as fifty thousand dollars and balls twenty-five thousand. This does not include what the members spend on their costumes (having no idea what they are paying for until the moment of dressing up before a parade), their favors for the ball, and their carnival throws. In return, thousands of tourists are attracted to the city for Mardi Gras, and New Orleans' economy is given an annual fillip. Many New Orleanians, however, complain that those people who by reason of their social position and affluence would elsewhere be relied upon to patronize the city's cultural activities and charitable causes in New Orleans spend their last penny on Mardi Gras. Unlike similar organizations of social prestige elsewhere, New Orleans men are likely to belong to more than one krewe, and there is no such thing as cheapness in numbers. On one occasion in the 1890s, it is said, the same man was approached to be king of Proteus, Comus, Atlanteans, and Momus —and accepted; one's imagination boggles at the thought of how much money he must have spent on being so honored.

Year-round preparations spread out the Carnival benefits to the economy—floats to be ordered and built, costumes to be made, and debutante dresses to be attended to. The queens used to order their dresses from France but they are now made, at a cost of about five thousand dollars each, by one of two shops in New Orleans; there is a nice understanding that neither shop will undertake the dresses of both queens of Comus and Rex. The Queen of Comus in 1924 had so lavish a mantle for her gown that it was used as an altar cloth in the church where she was later married; her gloves, a mere accessory, were dipped in fourteen-carat gold.

The carnival throws are a fairly recent extravagance, giving rise to such concerns as the Cutprice Novelty Company, and Pressner's Carnival Mart advertising "beautiful and distinctive throws" from

Japan and Hong Kong." It is difficult to see the distinctiveness in the mountains of beads accumulated for Carnival (though people will debate the relative merits of a string from Hong Kong versus a string from Czechoslovakia) but grabbing for throws is reckoned by many to be half the fun of Mardi Gras. Usually it is taken so seriously as to threaten the carnival spirit. Maskers on board the floats sometimes spend two hundred dollars or more on their sacks of throws. The most sought after throws are the doubloons, their popularity arising from one of the most successful advertising campaigns ever mounted. The first doubloons were thrown by the Rex krewe in 1960; that doubloon is now worth as much as sixty-five dollars. The other krewes hastened to cash in on the idea—doubloons can be sold to raise money for the parades—and now all krewes mint doubloons stamped with their emblems. Those thrown during parades are rather nasty aluminum ones, but bronze ones are handed out at the balls and silver and gold ones are occasionally minted for special occasions. Nowadays doubloons are also minted, outside the carnival organizations, to raise money for charitable and other projects, but the carnival doubloons remain the most highly prized. "Swaporamas" are held for addicts, there is a Carnival Coin Collectors' Club, and checklists are published to advise collectors. Woolworth's sells special plastic folders for displaying the coins, over a million of which are thrown each Mardi Gras.

Another flourishing side of the Carnival economy is the costumes. On Mardi Gras itself the whole of New Orleans dresses up, and the poorer you are the less makeshift your disguise, the more inclined you are to splurge on your appearance. An amazing number of costume shops are on Dryades and South Rampart Streets in the Negro area of Central City, for some of the most exotic and expensive costumes worn outside the parades are those worn by the Negroes, in particular the "Indians," organized Negro clubs that wander around the city on Mardi Gras. Sad and tattered-looking for most of the year, the shops radiate affluent self-confidence between Christmas and Lent: "King and Queen Crowns and Scepters," cries one; "Jul's sequin glue," another; "Complete balls designed and executed," says the most ambitious. Inside are row upon row of finery, exceedingly unimpressive until occupied by a drunken reveler.

It is all very well going on about the social and financial aspects of Carnival; after all, it is those aspects that most obsess New Orleanians. But, in spite of social pretensions and commercialization, Mardi Gras is a fantastic and almost enjoyable saturnalia. It could occur only in a Southern city; it embodies all the romanticizing of the South, more real to a New Orleanian than twentieth-century economics. Mark Twain called it the Sir Walter disease, clinging to outdated enthusiasms inspired by Scott's novels. Only on Mardi Gras is this inflated romanticism bearable.

Sir Charles Lyell commented in the middle of the last century on the pleasure of finding people in the United States who were prepared to take a holiday—most Americans seemed to spend all their time working. Nowadays a good many Americans find their way to New Orleans to enjoy themselves, and there is a rare spontaneity about Mardi Gras, which still survives annual assaults of hooliganism and overcrowding. Hotels are booked out months in advance; residents of the French Quarter rent out their flats and rooms for exorbitant sums; tourists begin arriving in their thousands about a week before Mardi Gras as they have since the business began, railway guides soon after the Civil War advertising "A Round of Pleasure Never Equaled in America, Outside the Limits of New Orleans, the Gayest, Most Attractive and Most Healthy Winter Resort in the World." The city is draped in the carnival colors of purple, green, and gold, and Bourbon Street bars play—continuously, it seems—the gushing theme song of Carnival, "If Ever I Cease to Love."

Parades begin in the week before Lent, several around the town every night and more on Saturday and Sunday before Lent. New Orleans parade fever seems to stem from a combination of enthusiasm for Latin religious pageantry and American martial display. Most of the parades start from Calliope Street near Jackson Avenue, where the floats are assembled; they move slowly up St. Charles Avenue and back downtown to Canal, heading for the Municipal Auditorium for the ball. Only one krewe parades by torchlight now; all the others have their floats lit by a thousand dazzling bulbs though they all have their quota of Negroes draped in white sheets hired to leap around between the floats with kerosene flambeaux. There are perhaps twenty floats in most parades, each one a master-piece of papier-mâché art, towering far above the crowd, and the most important truck in the parade is the Public Services truck, which goes at the head with a rod sticking out of the roof to note the low hanging branches along the avenue. Preparation for the parades goes on perpetually; most krewes have chosen their next year's theme by April and the workshops of Blaise Kern, who builds most of the floats, are busy the year round. The floats are made from clay models—plaster molds covered with incredibly fanciful papier mâché, supported by metal braces. They are usually shell-shaped, with the krewe members standing in the middle, and are pulled by tractors. In the old days they were pulled by mules, and no one knew how long the parade would take; spare mules were taken along to replace those that sat down and refused to move.

The floats are like candy floss, they look fragile enough to be engulfed by the crowds, and one trembles for the safety of the krewe members hurling their throws into the screaming faces—"Hey mis-ter, hey mister, give us a doubloon."

The floats give point to the parade, but each parade is an excuse for countless hangers on to join in—high school bands (some of them from way beyond Louisiana), marching jazz bands such as the Eureka or Olympia, police squads, motorbike riders (the most con-spicuous are the Farhad Grotto motor scooters, a Masonic chapter of middle-aged men dressed in purple and white satin, on purple and white scooters), drum majorettes shivering in their miniskirts, and, most magnificent of all, a Budweiser dray pulled by Clydesdale horses.

There are a number of parades on Mardi Gras itself, the most popular being the Rex parade and its affiliates, who tag on behind; the Zulu parade, which is exclusively Negro; and, of course, Comus in the evening. The parade of the Mighty King of Zulu is by far the most spontaneous. It was first presented in 1901, starting from a shed behind a Perdido Street saloon, and in 1916 the Zulu Social Aid and Pleasure Club was founded as a burlesque of the white organizations.* Rex was supposed to arrive from a faraway country, so the Zulu King came from Africa. The first king wore a lard tin for a crown and had a banana stalk for scepter and, instead of doubloons, gilded and silvered coconuts were thrown into the crowd. The King of Zulu is blatantly full of the pomp and conceit of Carnival and is accompanied by the still more conceited Big Shot of Africa, a part played for many years by a particularly small Negro with a float all to himself, in the middle of which he sat smoking an outsize cigar. The participants dress up as Zulus and blacken their faces still blacker. They used to parade by water, on the New Basin Canal, and on the river for a while after the canal had been filled in, but nowadays they usually set off from beside Congo Square. The parade tends to turn its back on white areas, wending its unpredictable course from one familiar bar to another, ending up in a rather disintegrated state. Its only deadline is for the King of Zulu to meet his queen in front of the Gertrude Geddes funeral home in Central City. Black Power now threatens Zulu, not very effectively, following the parade to distribute leaflets rebuking the participants for behaving like fools when taking the name of one of Africa's most illustrious tribes. It would take more than politics to dampen the liquorish spirit of Zulu.

In classical Greece, Rex, son of Old King Cole and Terpsichore, used to arrive by water the day before Mardi Gras from his home on Mount Olympus ("blown by soft zephyrs, his bark had ascended the yellow Mississippi and dropped anchor at the quay"), but nowadays he is more down to earth. Except, that is, in the style of his proclamation, which sets the tone for the day's celebrations, announcing one year that his "Royal Soothsayers consulted Ancient Tomes of Secrets Celestial, Concocted Incantations Incredible and Pursued Divers Divinations" to fix the day during which "Sour Melancholy be banished to Outer Space and the Dreary and Dull be tossed into Permanent Orbit." The long journey he is supposed to have made may account for the Oriental theme of many parades;

*Negro marching clubs are mostly known as social aid and pleasure clubs, the pleasure rather more apparent than the social aid.

once he was accompanied by the Shah of Persia, another time by the 389th Egyptian Lancers.

Rex parade is by far the largest and most ostentatious. It curls up and down St. Charles, down to Canal Street, where Rex is toasted at the various clubs along the route—the Pickwick Club and the Louisiana, both almost as vital socially to the ambitious New Orleanian as the Boston Club, where Rex (who has to be a member of the Boston Club to be chosen) eventually meets his queen. It is followed straight on by the Elks Krewe of Orleanians and the Krewe of Crescent City parades—over two hundred decorated trucks, mostly put together the night before. Prizes are awarded for the best float, many of which are decorated by streets or families, or, as the name suggests by Masonic chapters (a nice combination of Latin and American religions). Sometimes truck floats advertise for extra couples to fill the scenario, charging so many dollars for the ride, with soft drinks provided and lavatories—rather an essential because the huge lumbering parade (described with American aplomb as the World's Largest) can take many hours to complete the course. Passengers are usually unmasked but heavily made up and elaborately costumed.

From dawn on Mardi Gras, the city has been aroused by marching clubs. Some of these are named after districts—such as the oldest, the Jefferson City Buzzards formed in 1892, and the Garden District Marching Club—others are named after streets and others formed by bars, such as Charlie Parasol's Corner Club. These parade through their neighborhoods, complete with brass bands, stopping at all the bars on the way, waking up all and sundry to the fact that this is Mardi Gras.

The crowds are thickest in Canal Street, and there is a pleasanter, rather less crushed atmosphere along St. Charles Avenue, though the habit of private individuals' putting up scaffolding platforms to get a better view has rather spoiled it. People also bring along stepladders for their children to sit on, which impede the steady *va-et-vient* of the crowd moving up and down the parade route, visiting along the way. Down along Canal Street one can hardly move, but there is space to breathe in the French Quarter, and that is where the much-vaunted Carnival spirit reaches its most hysterical pitch. The costumes are superb. The most spectacular are the Indians, the Negro clubs. Anyone who can afford the costume can join a tribe though most members are in their twenties. The Golden Blades is the oldest tribe; others are Yellow Pocahontas, the Golden Eagles, the Creole Wild Wests. Each tribe has a chief, a chief's wife, and a witch doctor. Members of the tribe wander around the French Quarter in groups of three or four looking for each other, doing exaggerated dances and singing songs, which can be prolonged for hours and which mostly originate in the West Indies and date from the nineteenth century, when there was a lot of travel between there and New Orleans. There are also groups of Negro women, such as the Baby Dolls, the Gold Diggers and the Zigaboos; the Baby Dolls with their exaggerated hip swagger are mostly Perdido Street tarts.

Then there are the entrants for the great He-She parade and competition for the most effective transvestite; you can be fairly sure that any luscious female with next to nothing on in the way of costume is in fact a male competitor. There are apes draped in Spanish moss, Frankenstein monsters, and a whole zoo of animals —"the most authentic gorilla costumes in town," advertised one costume shop, "the suits have six-inch hair." And devils, skeletons, and King Kongs. There is an unbelievable amount of litter; the advent of the no-return bottle (not that anyone would bother to collect their bottle deposit on such a day) has had a disastrous effect on Mardi Gras when one seems to walk through a horrifying carpet of broken bottles and rattling beer cans (occasionally salvaged by a spasm band, a group of small boys who produce a strange medley of chords from them). Everyone seems to wander around drink in hand; tourists can be picked out by their clasping the distinctive high ball or hurricane glasses, the latter a particularly disgusting pink drink, which visitors to the city feel compelled to sample. Everyone radiates drunken bonhomie; doubloons and plastic necklaces are tossed in every direction; music blares from every corner; the din is sometimes overwhelming and the enjoyment remarkably infectious.

It calms down by the evening, when Comus parades, a rather decorous affair conditioned by a feeling of surfeit that no one would dream of admitting. Comus is a delightful parade, its theme perhaps slightly more intellectual than some. It follows the usual route, and at the Boston Club, where a tier of seats has been built out over the street, the King of Comus pauses to be toasted by Rex and his queen from the stand. The Comus ball is the highlight of the social season, and its masque is the most resplendent; the climax comes at midnight when Rex and his queen come through from the other half of the Municipal Auditorium to join Comus and his queen.

And so there is a final blaze of color and music just as "the Lenten morn is gently thrust upon the earth, and as the sad-hued tones of the penitential song rise to the early dawn, the bedraggled skirts of Mardi Gras fade from view and the feast is over." As one returns home from the ball, the garbage trucks are already out, and on Ash Wednesday every beer can, carnival throw, and plastic cup has vanished from the street, and Carnival has once again vanished into the secret conclaves of the krewes.

18. To The Sea

New Orleans is diminished from the river. From the height of a vessel on the Mississippi, you may stare disdainfully on once-familiar sights rendered remote by the great powerful river, an interlude in the dark-green swamp of the Delta. You move slowly past wharves, warehouses, and breweries, and beneath the gigantic frame of the Mississippi Bridge. The narrow frontage of the wharves is covered with merchandise, ropes, and preoccupied stevedores, and the names of the wharves are a riddle to the stranger—Poydras Street Wharf, Erato and Julia Street wharves, and above them, more American and reassuring—First, Second, and Third Street wharves, before Napoleon Avenue Wharf reveals more francophilia. The only glimpse of the old city you have from the river is Jackson Square, the rest of it lying hidden behind dingy warehouses. The square itself is dwarfed by the modern city with its skyscrapers crowned by huge oil-company signs, and the diminutive cathedral looks like another ship tied up to discharge its load, in this case, a cargo of sight-seers.

From New Orleans to the sea is about a hundred miles. It used to take from twenty-four hours to two weeks to sail the distance, depending on the wind and the current; now it can be done in five or six hours. One can also drive the first eighty miles along the River

Road as far as Venice and go from there to the Gulf in a super-powered motorboat designed to carry oil crews to and from and around about their operations in the Delta and the Gulf. It is a battered windswept land, at the mercy of the waters that surround it and upon which it floats, devastated all too regularly by hurricanes that lift the frail frame cottages a mile or more, by floods that come in the wake of hurricanes, and more rarely by vicious tornadoes.

This land is, or rather was, the kingdom of Leander Perez. Judge Perez, who died in 1960, was for over thirty years President of the Parish Council of Plaquemines Parish, which includes most of the west bank from Belle Chasse to the river mouth and the lower part of the east bank; when he retired two years before his death, he handed on the job to his son. Oil was discovered in the parish in 1928.* Perez took good advantage of the difficulty of establishing property boundaries and lease rights in this low, waterlogged land, and oil companies allegedly had to pay out vast sums to have their leases confirmed and their operations permitted. Perez built up his political power under Huey P. Long and used it during the 1960s to "protect" Plaquemines from desegregation orders, vowing to oppose racial integration to the death—which he did. He was excommunicated in 1962 for refusing to desegregate the parish schools and churches and fought an antidiscrimination order to the armed forces by forbidding navy personnel from the naval base in the parish to visit local bars. He lost both battles—there was token desegregation in the schools, and the navy went to bars in New Orleans—but he lost none of his prestige. When he died in 1969, he was buried with all the elaborate honors of a New Orleans funeral, to the cynical amazement of the press, who were unaware that his excommunication had ever been rescinded.

On either side of the river, the cultivated land is only a narrow strip between levee and swamp. The west bank is more densely populated than the east, for the best fishing and trapping grounds

*"The swamp buggies of the seismographic crews crosshatch its lonely marsh-lands, hunting the oil on which a good part of the parish seems to float like a green scum," according to an article in *Fortune* magazine.

are to the west of the river, round Barataria Bay and Grand Isle, and fishing and trapping were the bases of river-road economy until oil came into the area in a big way just after World War II. The Jesuits were probably among the first successfully to exploit the rich alluvial soil of this stretch of river "coast"; at Jesuit Bend, just below Belle Chasse, they had their first plantation. In the nineteenth century, plantations continued for forty miles below New Orleans. Most of them grew sugar, but nowadays the water table of the Delta is said to have risen, making it impossible for local farmers to compete on their smaller plots with the vast green acres further west round Bayou Lafourche and Bayou Teche. Now mostly vegetables and citrus fruits are grown; orange wine was one of the delicacies of the area until the great frost of 1962 wiped out most of the citrus orchards. Oil has changed the scene tremendously in the last twenty years; industry has followed, and oil depots and gigantic trailers carrying pipeline and drilling equipment to Venice have transformed much of the road into a succession of dumps, gas stations, and truck stops. But from the river, with its loftier viewpoint, it is easier to appreciate how much of the old life remains; one can see the fishing vessels moored beyond a second levee, the nets hung out to dry, the piles of oyster shells waiting to be planted, shrimps drying on vast trays in season, sheds sheltering skiffs and flatboats and pirogues for trapping and catching the turtles that make New Orleans' turtle soup such a delight.

Occasionally one glimpses relics of more prosperous farming days, a grove or avenue of stately live oaks planted perhaps by a farsighted landowner to shade his house long after his death, or a line of wooden shanties occupied by the plantation's fieldhands. Sometimes the houses themselves remain, most of them wholly or half ruined, their owners impoverished by a succession of blights beginning, but by no means ending (as many would like to make out), with the Civil War. There is the Stella Plantation House just below Phoenix on the east bank, now a prosaic post office, though customers are directed to the rear of the house for postal business so as not to disgrace the front graciously shaded by its mossy oaks. Hideously dilapidated is Magnolia, once occupied by Governor Warmoth—rows of bedrag gled washing hang on the gallery and piles of wrecked cars block the doorways. The grandest of these riverside houses, Belle Chasse, belonged to Judah P. Benjamin, the brilliant Jewish lawyer who became Confederate Secretary of State and whose sugar plantation was run with the help of a hundred and forty slaves. Once Belle Chasse displayed all the grandiloquence of New Orleans' golden age when every Southern gentleman claimed to be part of a civilization as great as the Greek and built palatial pseudo-Greek temples, dedicated, according to moralizing Northerners, to Mammon. Benjamin himself fled from the United States after the Civil War and went to Britain, where he had another notable legal career. Belle Chasse lay abandoned and half in ruins for many years until it was pulled down not so long ago to make way for a municipal swimming pool.

Between Belle Chasse and New Orleans are the landmarks of two embarrassing humiliations for the British. English Bend, the last great meander in the river, which flows almost straight from there to the Gulf, is where Bienville, out exploring from his brother Iberville's expedition, rounded the bend to find himself face to face with an English expedition that had set out from Carolina also to explore the Mississippi, with a view to settling there and thwarting French designs. Bienville coolly informed the English captain that he had made an unfortunate mistake, this was not the Mississippi which lay away to the west, that an entire French fleet was coming down any moment, and that the area had anyway already been claimed and fortified by the French. Somewhat daunted, the English turned around and went back the way they had come, the only sign that they had ever been there the derisive name given to the bend.

Just upriver of English Bend, the pink plantation house of Beauregard marks the site of the far greater humiliation of the Battle of New Orleans. This is Chalmette. In December or January it is easy to appreciate the miseries of the British soldiers making their way across the marshes in the damp cold of a Delta winter; a chill miasma lurks over the sodden ground, badly drained and feverish to this day.

The road on the east bank ends at Bohemia about forty miles short of the west bank road, but there are several riverside communities on the east bank below the road inhabited predominantly by Dalmatians who earn their living by oyster fishing in the brackish beds on the edge of the Gulf. New Orleans' oysters are huge and delicious; most New Orleanians prefer to eat them cooked in a number of exotic ways or well disguised beneath tomato ketchup and hot sauce and horseradish, but a treat not to be forgotten is to buy one's bushel, laboriously open them by a bayou, and swallow them without a frill. The Dalmatians are only the most recent wave of immigration among many earlier such as French, Spanish, Isleños from the Canary Islands, and even Philippinos and Malays, the latter allegedly responsible for introducing the shrimp-drying industry. Place names give little clue as to the origins of their inhabitants except for Ostria and Olga, isolated Dalmatian communities on the east bank. Most have grandiose pretensions—Triumph, Empire, Diamond—little in keeping with their appearance. Others are more descriptive—Port Sulphur dyeing its environs a sickly yellow, Patash, Pointe â la Hache (said to be where steamboat crews were sent ashore to chop wood for the eternally hungry furnaces). Some are possessive, named after an early pioneer—Boothville, Buras, Bertrandville, Naomi. And some are extremely imaginative—Bohemia, Happy Jack, Phoenix, and Venice.

As to the inhabitants, the best way to understand their mixture is to drive past their houses and look at the names on the letter boxes perched like periscopes by the side of the road. Many still earn their livings by trapping in winter, turtling in spring, and shrimping in summer. Buras is the most Dalmatian of the accessible river settlements; here you find Pivash Life Insurance, Miljak's Motel, Cognevitch Drive, Pobrica's Trailer Park. From a white wooden church, Our Lady of Good Harbor, with two diminutive onion domes, emerges a heavily moustachioed Serbian fisherman, crossing himself as he strides from its gloom to his oyster boat. A Yugoslav once wrote of Plaquemines Parish that "it was barren of all growth save marsh grasses, wild indigo that rattled in its dry pods on winter nights and stunted mangroves . . . it is here that we planted our oysters, sowing the seed shells in the low water and cultivating the beds with curses and songs."

Delta dwellers make a skillful use of their environment, but trapping is the great money-spinner (apart from the oil industry). Nutria and muskrat fill the traps (an average of 10 million muskrat pelts were sold in a year in the 1960s), large rodents whose pelts make Louisiana the richest fur-producing state in the United States; they burrow into the river banks, and their tunnels used to be a major cause of the levees collapsing under flood pressure. The nutria were imported from South America between the wars and escaped from their cages in a hurricane, multiplying thereafter in the fertile Delta in such profusion as to threaten the muskrat with extinction. Campaigns were mounted against the nutria; twenty-five cents was offered for each animal shot, and nutria meat used to be sold to feed ranch minks. Hurricanes regularly reestablish the delicate balance of nature, drowning or starving thousands of nutria in the invasion of salt water. Trapping is a precarious way of life.

Shrimping is becoming a major industry in the Delta. Several of the Delta towns have large shrimping fleets, which set out for the Gulf after being blessed at the onset of the main shrimping season in July. The fleets often stay out a fortnight or more, off-loading their catch on to larger vessels equipped with freezing apparatus. One of the largest fleets is at Empire, moored in lines beyond the second levee.

From Empire water visibly takes over from land. The river channel widens; stretches of water beyond the levees come closer; houses are fewer. Wax myrtle trees grow here in profusion, and in the early days of the colony their wax was made into candles and exported to the West Indies. Here is Fort Jackson, whose guns and massive star-shaped battlements were reckoned to be an impassable barrier to the Union fleet that assembled for the capture in 1862. The fort did indeed withstand a terrifying five-day bombardment but was powerless in the end to prevent Farragut from cutting the chain barrier across the river and thence sailing unimpeded up to New Orleans. The fort surrendered a few days after the city did. Faded damp-stained engravings of the engagement now line the oozing walls of the mosquito-infested shelters, guarded by aged caretakers who look like veterans of the campaign. Outside the fortifications was once virgin swamp, only recently tamed by an engineering company. Part of the moat is filled with water hyacinth, on which nutria can be seen gorging themselves and green and blue herons wait patiently for dragonflies in the shade of a mournful cypress.

Beside the fort is a tall needle of a monument dedicated to Robert Cavelier de la Salle, who first sailed down the Mississippi from Canada. The monument was erected under the auspices of Leander Perez, whose name and legend on the shaft are rather more prominent than La Salle's; every July Fourth, loyal parishioners and ambitious local politicians assembled at the monument to honor the Judge in the presence of various lesser Perezes, who now rule the parish.

It was probably somewhere about this point that Iberville met his first Indians, part of the Houma tribe, at whose village he found a letter and a blue serge coat left there by the Chevalier de Tonti. Tonti had sailed down the Mississippi with La Salle in 1682, returned to Canada when La Salle went to France, and a few years later set off again down the river to meet his friend. La Salle never appeared and Tonti left his letter and coat at the Indian village in hopes that someone would find them. Finding them—the coat scattered in several parts among the chiefs of the village—proved to Iberville that he was on the right river. Tonti was also largely responsible for the happy relations between the local Indians and the first French settlers. They exchanged presents and smoked peace pipes, known as calumets, though before long the French were involved in spite of themselves in the internecine quarrels of the various tribes.

Indians hardly figure in the story of New Orleans except to contribute some street names, the most unpronounceable of which is Tchoupitoulas. The Indian villages of the Delta were wretched places, dirty and squalid, decimated regularly by chronic fighting and disease. Indians seem to have fallen easily into the role of exhibits; it became the custom for them to gather outside New Orleans once a year at Carnival time to collect a gift from the governor in return for their friendship. Picturesque groups of Choctaw squaws were to be seen squatting in the French Market and a smaller market in Gentilly, Le Breton Market, bartering sassafras (which is sold in a powdered form—*filé*—as the most important ingredient of the New

Orleans gumbo) and bay leaves, blankets and baskets for guns, knives or trinkets. Other Indians lived on the fringes of the city, hunting in the swamps and selling their produce to the inhabitants. Their numbers were thinned by disease and gradually reduced to nothing before a vanguard of more enterprising farmers. There are none left in the Delta now, the only signs of their villages the burial mounds that can occasionally be seen rising above the swamp.

The Delta remains a strange and exotic area; one might think it untouched by human hand as one paddles with difficulty up a dark overgrown bayou, only to find suddenly a contorted "Christmas tree" sticking out from the knobbled knees—breathing roots—of the cypresses, marking the head of an oil well. Longfellow, who never in fact visited Louisiana, described Evangeline's wanderings through "a maze of sluggish and devious waters, which, like a network of steel, extended in every direction." Sometimes in the cypress swamps the water between the trees and roots is so covered with green weed as to appear the smoothest of lawns. Sometimes the trees meet over a narrow bayou, tendrils of Spanish moss sweeping the water, water snakes sleeping on dead branches, wakeful turtles watching, heads raised on fallen trunks for the slightest movement, occasionally, in dryer parts, an armadillo scuffling through dead leaves. The water is slimy and shallow, and a pirogue is the only boat able to penetrate right into the swamp. Pirogues used to be dug-out cypress logs, but now the aluminum variety is commoner. Even a pirogue is thwarted, however, by the menacing water hyacinth. Water hyacinth was exhibited at the Centennial Exhibition in New Orleans in 1884, where it was bought by gardeners as a decorative plant; it now covers vast acres of the Delta. In spring its orchidlike flowers spread a violet carpet over the bayous, but in winter it almost vanishes. Sometimes the blockage of a bayou is only temporary, the carpet subject to the whims of wind and current, which will waft it from place to place, but elsewhere it takes on additional density where other plants have taken root and added to the impenetrability.

The smell of the swamp in midsummer is unmistakable, a rancid sweaty smell. There is a hot background murmur, of subdued crickets, of egrets or herons flapping overhead, of wind whispering through the Spanish moss or scraping the spiked palmetto leaves. A grackle may raucously perform his aerial acrobatics or the red-winged blackbird, balancing on a reed, deride the heat with his curious sing-song note like a boy's voice breaking. Or the clear beautiful song of the exquisite cardinal may pierce and lighten the humid heaviness of a Delta noon. Or the ever louder hum of mosquitoes may remind the lotus-eater of the need to return home at the end of the day, or gray mullets tempt him to stay as they somersault in and out of the water.

Venice stands at the end of the road from New Orleans, an ugly settlement of trailers, oil tanks, and powerful red and white tugs in farcical contrast to its namesake and its gracious gondolas. Beside them are fishing boats off-loading shrimp, and patriotically colored red, white, and blue crabs, their claws waving sadly through the baskets. The area is torn and disfigured by oil paraphernalia—barges, pipeline, drills being assembled, overhauled, shifted, heavy equipment so cumbersome on land, apparently so maneuverable on water. The settlement is at the head of Grand Pass, once known as the Jump because the river jumped through to the Gulf at this point.

Below Venice the land either side of the river becomes little more than the levee and the batture covered with dense vegetation—cottonwoods, mostly, which send clouds of white fluff over the water in a summer breeze, canebrakes, and stubby oaks. Past the old quarantine station there is Pilottown, which looks like the end of the world. Its predecessor, the Balise, was even nearer the end, described —as Pilottown itself might be—as a half-drowned village standing in a "wild hopeless-looking, impassable sort of marsh," the nearest firm land ten or twenty miles away. In Pilottown the nearest thing to firm land is the banks of shells, blinding in the sun, straddled by precarious wooden walkways. Here the river and bar pilots live with their families, and here the river pilot hands over to the bar pilot. The only sign of life is the river traffic: great freighters that can travel as much as two hundred miles upriver to Baton Rouge; tugs pushing or pulling a queue of oil barges barely visible above the surface of the water, oil machinery, piles of shell dregged from Lake Pontchartrain, tankers, grain carriers, and fishing vessels from the large professional to the small and amateur.

Pilottown is a little above the Head of Passes, the four principal

mouths into which the true delta of the Mississippi splits at the end
of a long thin peninsula of land which the river has built up over the
centuries. The passes are known as Southwest, South, Southeast and
Passe à l'Outre, each of which has a bar at the entrance. Southwest
Pass is the deepest and therefore most used by oceangoing vessels.
"A most unpoetic mouth," wrote Oakey Hall, its distorted shape
reminiscent of "dental wrenches and forceps." Hall's river pilot
likened it to brandy: the more you know it the better you like it. But
the mouth of so famous a river is disappointing "considering the
number of watery relations who avail themselves of his good nature
to escape from forests, swamps and dreary solitudes thousands of
miles in the heart of the North American continent." The river in
flood is reckoned to pour several streams of silt twelve miles into the
sea; the mud lies on the surface so that when ships plow through it,
they clear a path of deep blue water. When the river is low, the sea
takes its revenge and sweeps up the mouths, scouring out the channels.

Now the banks become more fragile; in the early summer, when
the river is at its highest, one wonders why they bother to have a
bank at all. Grackles somersault in the air, fly from one bulrush to
another squawking at each other. By the water's edge the fan-shaped
spiked fronds of the palmetto just stand above the surface, once used
to thatch fishermen's shacks in the Delta. In winter one can see
through the trees as the undergrowth dies down instantly after the
first cold. But in summer it is an intricate green tapestry. Standing
sentinel, slightly out from the bank in a few feet of water are the
cypresses—sad, emaciated trees except in the first flush of their new
spring finery, draped in the eternal mourning of Spanish moss.

The marshes at the river mouth teem with wild life, very little of
which is evident from midstream. At night, almost drowning the
noise of the engines is the insistent chorus of frogs (some of the
noisiest frogs are aptly known as pig frogs) and crickets, the latter
soaring to superb crescendos of sound. There are alligators too,
though never seen on the river now and seldom seen though often
heard in the remoter bayous—you can hear them barking on a windy
day. In the old days, ships' passengers used to see them basking on

the banks, and nervous ladies were reassured of their harmlessness
—"the savages used to play with them while bathing without suffering any harm," wrote one early missionary who claimed that he and
his companions were protected from them by God. According to a
rather unreliable source, some of the alligators were so old that
vegetation could be seen growing on them; the same source, convinced of the creatures' aggressiveness, advocated escaping from
them by zigzagging because their vertebrae were too stiff for them
to follow anything but the straightest course. Newcomers swore they
ate humans; slave-owners, hoping to discourage slaves from escaping,
would argue that they preferred Negroes "because of a certain exha-
lation."

The river now is channeled into the Southwest Pass, which is
deepened by the force of its current as well as by Eads's system of
jetties artificially confining the river, but from a ship all that can be
seen is the top of a seemingly narrow levee from which the jetties
jut out into the river. "I never beheld a scene so utterly desolate as
this entrance of the Mississippi," wrote Mrs. Trollope. Its remote-
ness and monotony have been compared with the Sahara; even the
modern tourist with his insatiable greed for the unfamiliar is hard-
pushed to rhapsodize about the Delta. Mrs. Trollope's desolation has
to some extent been turned inside out by oil companies, the immense offshore oilfields supplying millions of tons of oil and gas daily.
Weirdly shaped platforms—for drilling, production, servicing wells,
and so on—stand in the shallow water of the Gulf and Delta like
clumsy triffids. Sometimes one sees them towed to new sites by
diminutive tugs, "hipping" them through the muddy water by tying
them alongside. At intervals along the Southwest Pass are gleaming
white storage tanks built on shell foundations, aluminum pipes of
every size and shape, radio aerials among the bulrushes, and hefty
workboats, seemingly as full of brawn as the men aboard, hurtle
through the bayous, taking the amphibious oil men from work to
their "boatels." Here they live disciplined lives for one week and the
opposite for the alternate week when they go to their homes in the
grizzly little riverside oil shanty towns of Venice and Buras, Triumph, and Boothville.

Once the last waterlogged stretch of land was inhabited by flocks of brown pelicans, so many of them that it was adopted as the state bird of Louisiana. Of the pelican, Zadok Cramer wrote in his 1817 *Navigator:* "The Pelican is said to have a melancholy countenance, is very torpid, and to a great degree inactive, so much so, that nothing can exceed its indolence but its gluttony, and that hunger is the only inducement it has to rouse it from its stupid sleep. It is asserted that they seem to be fond of music." But now there are no brown pelicans left in Louisiana, and only an occasional gull flies overhead in search of scraps tossed from the ship's wake as it cuts through the turgid brown waters of the "lordly but gloomy tempered" river to the clear waters of the Gulf.

Bibliography

Account of Louisiana, Being an Abstract of Documents in the Offices of Departments of State and of the Treasury. (1803).

Alexander, J. A. *Louisiana under the Rule of Spain, France and the United States* (1911).

Alexander, J. E. *Transatlantic Sketches.* London: Richard Bentley, 1833.

Allen, W. H. "Last Trip by a Steamboat Clerk." *Knickerbocker,* XLVI (December 1855).

Armstrong, Louis. *Satchmo. My Life in New Orleans.* New York: Prentice Hall, 1954.

Arthur, S. C. *Old New Orleans.* New Orleans: Arthur Publications, 1944.

Ashe, Thomas. *Travels in America.* London: Richard Phillips, 1808.

Audubon, J. J. "Improvements in the Navigation of the Mississippi," in *Delineations of American Scenery and Character.* London: Simpkin, Marshall & Co., 1826.

Bancroft, Frederic. *Slave Trading in the Old South.* Baltimore: J. H. Furst Co., 1931.

Baudier, R. *The Catholic Church in Louisiana.* New Orleans, 1939.

Berquin-Duvallon. *Vue de la colonie espagnole du Mississipi.* Paris, 1803.

Bossu, N. *Travels Through That Part of North America, Formerly Called Louisiana.* London: T. Davies, 1771.

Brackenridge, H. M. *Views of Louisiana.* Pittsburgh, Pa.: Cramer, Spear & Eichbaum, 1814.

Buckingham, J. S. *The Slave States of America.* London: Fisher, Son & Co., 1842.

Bureau of Government Research. *Vieux Carré, New Orleans: Its Plan, Its Growth Its Architecture.* New Orleans, 1968.

Burson, C. M. *The Stewardship of Don Estéban Miró.* New Orleans: American Printing Co., 1940.

Butler, Benjamin. *Private and Official Correspondence* (1917).

Cable, George Washington. *The Creoles of Louisiana.* London: J. C. Nimmo, 1885.

———. *Dr. Sevier.* Edinburgh: David Douglas, 1883.

———. "Pirates of Barataria." *Century Magazine,* 1883.

———. *The Silent South.* New York: Charles Scribner's Sons, 1885.

Carrigan, J. A. "The Yellow Fever Epidemic, 1853." *Journal of Southern History,* August 1959.

Caskey, Willie M. *Secession and Restoration of Louisiana.* Baton Rouge: Louisiana State University Press, 1938.

Charters, Samuel B. *The Music of New Orleans.* 4 vols. New York: Folkways Records.

Chase, John. *Frenchmen Desire Good Children.* New Orleans, 1960.

Clapp, Rev. Theodore. *Autobiographical Sketches and Recollections.* Boston: Phillips, Sampson & Co., 1857.

Clark, John G. "New Orleans and the River." *Louisiana History,* VIII, 2.

Clark, T. D., ed. *Travels in the Old South. A Bibliography.* Norman: University of Oklahoma Press, 1956–59.

Cochut, André. *Law, son système et son époque.* Paris, 1853.

Coleman, W. H. *Historical Sketchbook and Guidebook to New Orleans.* New York, 1885.

Coulter, E. M. *The South During Reconstruction, 1865–77.* Baton Rouge: Louisiana State University Press, 1947.

Crain, Robert L. *Politics of School Desegregation.* Chicago, 1968.

Cumings, S. *Western Pilot.* Cincinnati: N. & G. Guildford & Co, 1832.

Dabney, T. E. *The Industrial Canal and Inner Harbor of New Orleans.* New Orleans Board of Commissioners of the Port, 1921.

Darby, William. *A Geographical Description of Louisiana.* Philadelphia, 1816.

Devol, G. H. *Forty Years a Gambler on the Mississippi* (1887).

Didimus, Henry. *New Orleans As I Found It.* New York: Harper & Bros., 1845.

Dodd, W. E. B. *Cotton Kingdom.* New Haven, 1921.

Dollard, John, and Allison Davis. *Children of Bondage* New York: Harper & Row., (1964).

Dorsey, F. L. *Henry Shreve, Master of the Mississippi.* Boston: Houghton Mifflin Co., 1941.

Dufour, Charles. *The Night the War Was Lost.* New Orleans.

Faulkner, William. *New Orleans Sketches*. New York: Random House, 1968.

Fearon, H. B. *Sketches of America*. London, 1818.

Featherstonhaugh, G. *Excursions Through the Slave States*. New York, 1844.

Fenner, E. D. *History of the Epidemic Yellow Fever at New Orleans in 1853*. New York, 1854.

Ficklen, J. R. *History of Reconstruction in Louisiana*. Baltimore: Johns Hopkins University Press, 1910.

Fineran, J. K. *Career of a Tinpot Napoleon: The Political Biography of Huey P. Long* (1932).

Flint, Rev. Timothy. *Recollections of the Last Ten Years*. Johnson Reprint Association, 1968.

Fortier, Alcée. *A History of Louisiana*. 4 vols. New York: Manzi, Joyant & Co., 1904.

Fossier, A. E. *Charity Hospital*.

Fremantle, A. J. *The Fremantle Diary*, ed. Walter Lord. Boston: Little, Brown & Co., 1954.

French, B. F., comp. *Historical Collections of Louisiana*. New York and Philadelphia, 1846–53.

Gallier, James. *Autobiography* (1864).

Gayarre, Charles. *History of Louisiana*. 4 vols. New York, 1854–66.

Hall, A. O. *The Manhattaner in New Orleans*. New York and New Orleans, 1851.

Hall, Basil. *Travels in North America in the Years 1827 and 1828*. 3 vols. Edinburgh, 1829.

Hanotaux, G. *L'Union des Etats-Unis et de la France à l'occasion du deuxième centenaire de la fondation de la Nouvelle-Orléans*. Paris, 1918.

Hamlin, Talbot. *Greek Revival Architecture in America*. New York, 1944.

Hentoff, Nat, and A. J. MacCarthy, eds. *New Perspectives on the History of Jazz*. New York: Rinehart & Co., 1959.

Howard, Perry H. *Political Tendencies in New Orleans 1812–1952*. Baton Rouge: Louisiana State University Press, 1957.

———, et al. *The Louisiana Elections of 1960*. Baton Rouge: Louisiana State University Press, 1963.

Huber, L. V. *Impressions of Girod Street Cemetery*. New Orleans, 1951.

———, and Samuel Wilson, Jr. *Baroness Pontalba's Buildings*. New Orleans, 1964.

———, *The Basilica on Jackson Square*. New Orleans, 1966.

Ingraham, Joseph. *The Quadroon* (1840).

———. *The Southwest, by a Yankee* (1835).

Jaffee, Al. *Jazz at Preservation Hall*.

Jones, Howard Mumford. *American and French Culture.* Chapel Hill: University of North Carolina Press, 1927.

King, Grace. *Creole Families of New Orleans.* New York: The Macmillan Co., 1921.

————. *New Orleans, the Place and the People.* New York: The Macmillan Co., 1895.

Klein, Selma L. *Creoles and Anglo-Americans 1803–60.*

Landry, Stuart O. *The Battle of Liberty Place.* New Orleans, 1955.

————. *The Boston Club.* New Orleans.

————. *Duelling in Old New Orleans.* New Orleans.

Latrobe, Benjamin. *Impressions Respecting New Orleans,* ed. Samuel Wilson, Jr. New York: Columbia University Press, 1951.

Laussat, Pierre Clement de. *Memoirs and Correspondence* (1940).

Le Page du Pratz. *The History of Louisiana.* London, 1763.

Les Cenelles. New Orleans, 1845.

Long, Huey P. *Every Man a King.* Chicago: Quadrangle Books.

Longfellow, Henry W. *Evangeline, A Tale of Arcadia.* Boston: William D. Ticknor & Co., 1848.

Lonn, Ella. *Reconstruction in Louisiana after 1868.* New York: G. P. Putnam's Sons, 1918.

Louisiana Historical Quarterly. New Orleans.

Louisiana Native American Association. "Address to Citizens of Louisiana and Inhabitants of the U.S.A." New Orleans, 1839.

Lyell, Sir Charles. *A Second Visit to the United States of North America.* 2 vols. London, 1849.

Lyon, Elijah W. *Louisiana in French Diplomacy 1759–1804.* Norman: University of Oklahoma Press, 1934.

Marryat, Frederick. *A Diary in America.* 3 vols. London: Longman & Co., 1839.

Martineau, Harriet. *Retrospect of Western Travel.* 3 vols. London, 1838.

Mississippi River Commission. *The Atchafalaya Outlet.* New Orleans, 1964.

————. *Channel Improvement and Stabilization.* Vicksburg, Miss., 1968.

————. *Flood Control in the Lower Mississippi Valley,* Vicksburg, Miss., 1968.

Murray, Amelia Matilda. *Letters from the United States, Cuba and Canada.* 2 vols. London, 1856.

Murray, Charles Augustus. *Travels in North America 1834–36.* 2 vols. London, 1839.

Myrdal, Gunnar. *An American Dilemma.* New York: Harper & Bros., 1944.

Nau, J. F. *The German People of New Orleans.* Leiden: E. J. Brill, 1958.

Nettels, Curtis. *The Roots of American Civilization.* New York, 1938.

Newton, Francis. *The Jazz Scene.* London: MacGibbon & Kee, 1959.

Niehaus, E. F. *The Irish in New Orleans.*

Nolte, Vincent. *Fifty Years in Both Hemispheres.* London, 1854.

Nordhoff, Charles. *The Cotton States in the Spring and Summer of 1875.* New York, 1876.

Olmsted, Frederick. *The Cotton Kingdom,* ed. Arthur M. Schlesinger. New York: Alfred A. Knopf, 1953.

Opotowsky, Stan. *The Longs of Louisiana.*

Orleans Levee Board. "Shore Protection in Orleans Parish." New Orleans, 1956.

Percy, Walker. *The Moviegoer.* New York, Knopf, 1961.

Phillips, T. B. *Life and Labour in the Old South.* Boston, Little Brown & Co, 1929.

Pittman, Philip. *The Present State of the European Settlements on the Mississippi.* London, 1770.

Power, Tyrone. *Impressions of America 1833–35.* 2 vols. Philadelphia, 1836.

Prévost, A. F. *Histoire de Manon Lescaut et du Chevalier Des Grieux.* Paris, 1781.

Quick, J. H., and E. Quick. *Mississippi Steamboatin'.* New York: Henry Holt & Co., 1926.

Reinders, R. C. *End of an Era: New Orleans 1850–60* Gretna, La. (1964).

Reynolds, George H. *Machine Politics in New Orleans 1897–1926* (1936).

Rightor, Henry. *The Standard History of New Orleans.*

Robin, C. C. *Voyage dans l'interieur de la Louisiane.* Paris, 1807.

Rohrer, J. H., and M. S. Edmonson. *The Eighth Generation: Cultures and Personalities of New Orleans Negroes.* New York: Harper & Bros., 1960.

Roush, J. F. *Chalmette.* Washington, D.C.: U.S. National Park Service, 1958.

Rousseve, C. B. *The Negro in Louisiana* (1937).

Rowland, D. *Letterbooks of W. C. C. Claiborne.* Madison, Wisc., 1917.

Russell William H. *My Diary North and South.* 3 vols. London, 1863–65.

Saxon, Lyle. *Father Mississippi.* New York: Century Co., 1927.

———. *Lafitte the Pirate.* New York: Century Co., 1930.

Schultz, Christian. *Travels on an Inland Voyage.* 2 vols. New York, 1810.

"Select Committee on New Orleans Riots—Report." 39th Cong., 2d sess., H. Doc. 16.

Shugg, R. W. *Origins of the Class Struggle in Louisiana.* Baton Rouge: Louisiana State University Press, 1939.

Sinclair, Harold. *Port of New Orleans.* Garden City, N.Y.: Doubleday, Doran & Co., 1942.

Smith, R. A. "Oil, Brimstone and Judge Perez." *Fortune,* No. 57 (1958).

Soule, L. O. *The Know Nothing Party of New Orleans: A Reappraisal* Louisiana State University Press (1961).

Stanley, H. M. *Autobiography,* ed. Dorothy Stanley. London: Sampson, Low & Co., 1909.

Stoddard, Amos. *Sketches Historical and Descriptive of Louisiana.* Philadelphia, 1812.

Surrey, N. M. M. *The Commerce of Louisiana During the French Regime 1699–1765.* New York: Columbia College, 1891.

Tallant, Robert. *Mardi Gras.* Garden City, N.Y.: Doubleday & Co., 1948.

Thackeray, William M. "Roundabout Papers." *Cornhill* magazine, IV (December 1861).

Tregle, J. C. "Early New Orleans Society." *Journal of Southern History,* XVIII (1952).

Trollope, Frances. *Domestic Manners of the Americans.* 2 vols. London: Whittaker, Treacher & Co., 1832.

Twain, Mark. *Life on the Mississippi.* Boston: J. R. Osgood & Co., 1883.

Ursuline nuns. *Rélation du voyage des dames Religièuses Ursulines de Rouen à la Nouvelle-Orléans.* Paris, 1872.

Vogel, C. L. *The Capuchins in Louisiana 1722–66* (1928).

Waitz, J. E., ed. *Journal of Julia le Grand 1862–6.* Richmond, Va., 1911.

Warmoth, Henry. *War, Politics and Reconstruction: Stormy Days in Louisiana.* New York: The Macmillan Co., 1930.

Whipple, Benjamin Henry. *Southern Diary 1843–44,* ed. L. B. Shippee. Minneapolis, 1937.

Whitaker, A. P. *The Mississippi Question 1795–1803.* American Historical Association, 1934.

Whitman, Walt. "Daggerdraw Bowieknife Esq." New Orleans *Daily Crescent,* 1848.

Wilson, Samuel, Jr. *Guide to New Orleans Architecture.* New Orleans, 1959.

Winston J. E. *Notes on the Economic History of New Orleans 1803–34* (1928).

Wood, Minter. *Life in New Orleans in the Spanish Period.* Unpublished thesis, 1938.

Woodward, C. Vann. *Origins of the New South 1877–1913.* Baton Rouge: Louisiana State University Press, 1951.

Works Project Administration. *New Orleans City Guide.* Boston, 1938.

Index